Roe v. Wade

HISTORY
IN THE HEADLINES

Roe v. Wade Fifty Years After

EDITED BY
Rhae Lynn Barnes & Catherine Clinton

The University of Georgia Press *Athens*

Athens, Georgia 30602
www.ugapress.org

Set in Garamond Premier Pro and ITC Franklin Gothic
by Rebecca A. Norton

Most University of Georgia Press titles are
available from popular e-book vendors.

Printed digitally

Library of Congress Cataloging-in-Publication Data
Names: Clinton, Catherine, 1952– editor. | Barnes, Rhae Lynn, editor.
Title: Roe v. Wade : fifty years after / edited by Catherine Clinton
and Rhae Lynn Barnes.
Other titles: Roe vs. Wade
Description: Athens : University of Georgia Press, 2024. | Series: History
in the headlines series | Includes bibliographical references.
Identifiers: LCCN 2024008353 (print) | LCCN 2024008354 (ebook) |
ISBN 9780820365688 (hardback) | ISBN 9780820365671 (paperback) |
ISBN 9780820365695 (epub) | ISBN 9780820365701 (pdf)
Subjects: LCSH: Abortion—Law and legislation—United States—History. |
Birth control—Law and legislation—United States—History. |
Roe, Jane, 1947–2017—Trials, litigation, etc. | Wade, Henry—
Trials, litigation, etc. | Trials (Abortion)—Washington (D.C.)
Classification: LCC KF3771 .R67 2024 (print) | LCC KF3771 (ebook) |
DDC 342.7308/78—dc23/eng/20240224
LC record available at https://lccn.loc.gov/2024008353
LC ebook record available at https://lccn.loc.gov/2024008354

To all the everyday women—in this country and abroad—who fought for the right to have control over their own bodies and continue the struggle for reproductive freedom, for this generation and those who follow.

Contents

A Note from the Volume Editors

On December 13, 2023, the United States Supreme Court confirmed that it would consider the appeal of the controversial court case *Food and Drug Administration v. Alliance for Hippocratic Medicine*. The decision will come down before this book is released, highlighting the constantly shifting reproductive landscape in the United States after the reversal of *Roe v. Wade* in 2022.

The Alliance for Hippocratic Medicine (AHM) describes itself as "uphold[ing] and promot[ing] the fundamental principles of Hippocratic medicine," including "protecting the vulnerable at the beginning and end of life." The Alliance was incorporated in August 2022 and is headquartered in Amarillo, Texas.

The Alliance has claimed that the U.S. Food and Drug Administration (FDA) should not have approved mifepristone (also known as "the abortion pill") in 2000 for early pregnancy termination. Mifepristone is currently approved by the FDA to be taken up to ten weeks during pregnancy. It is also routinely prescribed to assist and alleviate naturally occurring miscarriages. The AHM sought an injunction to remove the drug from the market nearly a quarter-century after its introduction and widespread use. As of the publication of this book, over half of all abortions in the United States are medicinal, using mifepristone. It has over a 99 percent safety rate.

On February 16, 2024, the Alabama Supreme Court issued a ruling declaring that embryos created through in vitro fertilization (IVF) should legally be considered as children. Many of the state's IVF clinics have since paused services, and further court cases are likely to follow.

Acknowledgments

Bringing this book to fruition has been a collaborative endeavor. We are grateful to the extraordinary network of scholars who generously contributed to its realization.

First and foremost, we extend our heartfelt appreciation to Jim Downs, our series editor. Jim's vision, guidance, and dedication has been instrumental in shaping this project from its inception. Jim, thank you for being a cherished colleague.

We are deeply grateful to Jane Kamensky, Annette Gordon-Reed, Gillian Frank, and Sinead McEneaney for their invaluable input on speakers during early planning stages. Their insights enriched the historical narratives we explored.

We extend our appreciation to the Hutchins Center for African and African American Research at Harvard University, particularly Henry Louis Gates, Jr., Abby Wolf, Velma DuPont, Krishna Lewis, and the 2022–2023 Cohort of Fellows, for their logistical support, facility donations, and encouragement. Their dedication to fostering creative intellectual engagement and promoting historical scholarship for the masses has been a source of inspiration throughout our journey. The Charles Warren Center for Studies in American History at Harvard University also materially supported this project. We particularly thank Walter Johnson and Tiya Miles for their on-campus contributions.

At University of Georgia Press, we are indebted to our editor, Mick Gusinde-Duffy, whose steadfast support and editorial acumen have been invaluable. We also extend our gratitude to Press Director, Lisa Bayer, for her exceptional assistance in bringing this volume to life. We are deeply appreciative of the contributions of Jarden Kazik Asser, Lea Johnson, and Jason Bennett at University of Georgia Press who worked tirelessly behind the scenes to ensure the smooth production of this work.

We express our heartfelt gratitude to our anonymous peer reviewers, whose insightful feedback and enthusiasm significantly enhanced our contextualization of this intricate history. We also acknowledge the invaluable contributions of the History in the Headlines board members, who have consistently demonstrated their commitment to scholarly excellence through their meticulous review assignments.

The work of Liz Reichman (J.D., M.A.), lecturer at the University of Texas in San Antonio, who meticulously prepared the state-by-state appendix and Joseph Malcomson (M.A.), who methodically shaped the bibliography, have been instrumental in refining this work and its accessibility.

Fiona de Londras gratefully acknowledges the support of the Leverhulme Trust through the Philip Leverhulme Prize.

Rhae Lynn Barnes extends her appreciation to the History Departments at Princeton University and Harvard University and the University's Committee on Research in the Humanities and Social Sciences for their support. Marissa Nicosia, Jenni Ostwinkle Silva, Elizabeth A. Steele, and the Barnes Family have been steadfast sources of encouragement, joy, and care of all kinds throughout this endeavor. Their faith in the meaningfulness of our work have been a driving force.

Catherine Clinton expresses her profound gratitude to her husband, George Ward Byers, and her sons, Ned Colbert and Drew Colbert (who called to support and console when *Dobbs v. Jackson* was announced). She also extends her appreciation to the University of Texas in San Antonio: Nicole Poole, Administration Services Officer, and Professor and Chair Wing Chung Ng of the Department of History. Her heartfelt thanks go to the Denman Chair for its generous funding, and she is especially grateful for the supplemental support provided by Professor Jason Yeager, Associate Graduate Dean, and Professor Glenn Martinez, Dean of the College of Liberal and Fine Arts. Finally, Catherine appreciates the junior colleagues in her patria chica: Ali Atabey, Cindy Ermus, Abraham Gibson, and especially Jorge Felipe Gonzalez, whose enthusiasm and dedication to historical scholarship inspire confidence in the future and the next generations of historians making headlines.

Roe v. Wade

Introduction

On January 22, 1973, the United States Supreme Court, in a landmark decision that reverberated through American society, affirmed a woman's constitutional right to abortion. Jane Roe, a pseudonym, v. Henry Wade, District Attorney of Dallas County was a historic victory secured amidst the burgeoning Women's Rights Movement. *Roe* promised a future where women could control their own bodies. It seemed to herald a new era of gender equality, granting women autonomy based on the post-Civil War Fourteenth Amendment (1868) to the United States Constitution born of American slavery and emancipation.

This landmark decision made over half a century ago, enshrined women's reproductive rights. It introduced a woman's legal right to privacy and established suitable periods for when the planned termination of pregnancies might be permissible—within the first trimester. Although much of the actual language in the decision revolved around technical and legal jargon, women's rights activists—nationally and globally—believed *Roe* was a significant victory and beacon of progress in the "women's liberation campaigns," as an essential step forward for reproductive freedom, gender equality, and bodily autonomy.

With the ruling of *Dobbs, State Health Officer of Mississippi v. Jackson Women's Health Organization* on June 24, 2022 (see Appendix B), legal, feminist, and reproductive rights experts experienced a terrible boomerang. The results of this decision, reversing the *Roe v. Wade* ruling and setting precedents for nearly half a century, threw U.S. legislators and women's rights activists into newly contested terrain. The war over rights (women's versus fetal) has gained enormous significance in the 2020s and has contributed to an escalation of the culture wars within the United States, which is evident in an increasingly polarized political landscape. Tracing the meaning and impact of the *Roe* ruling and subsequent developments will put some legal, medical, and moral issues into sharper relief.

In this groundbreaking volume, a team of renowned scholars, historians, and public intellectuals explores the centuries-long struggle for reproductive freedom in the United States. Together, they delve into the tumultuous and intricate history of abortion in the United States, tracing its evolution from an open and common practice in colonial and nineteenth-century America to a hushed and often illegal taboo in the mid-twentieth century to a central battleground in the culture wars and in the fight for gender equity. Probing the legal, social, cultural, and political landscapes that shaped the abortion debate, the authors study the factors that fueled the decades-long struggle for reproductive freedom and the seismic shift that followed the *Dobbs* decision.

The volume unravels the complex interplay of race, class, geography, sexuality, and intersecting identities, revealing how these factors have shaped access to reproductive healthcare and the power to determine one's own bodily autonomy. It also delves into the far-reaching international implications of the struggles for reproductive justice, highlighting the global impact of American policies on women's rights abroad. *Roe v. Wade: Fifty Years After* offers a profound understanding of the forces that have shaped reproductive rights in the United States, illuminating the path ahead in the pursuit of reproductive justice for all.

"History in the Headlines" had this volume already in the planning stages when the *Dobbs* decision was handed down. Reflecting on the historical circumstances that have developed over the past half-century since the landmark *Roe* ruling, confronting the issues surrounding these challenging times has preoccupied millions of Americans, most notably young people, who are dramatically affected by these issues. The flurry of attention on abortion and its history has been staggering. Disinformation from the media, combined with the incomplete or inaccurate education of most Americans on reproductive matters, has led to a search for balance amid seismic shifts, a struggle with myths and misogyny going full tilt within our current political climate, the new post-Dobbs.[1]

Our goal in this book was to bring together a round table of historical, legal, and cultural experts. We sent invitations to a diverse group, including those who identify as men and women, with a focus on their diversity of thought, the institutions where they work and serve, their age, race, sexual orientation, their country of origin, whether they are mothers, and the socioeconomic conditions in which they grew up. While many experts could not participate because they were called up to serve, among other capacities, as expert witnesses and key scholar-activists in the aftermath of *Dobbs*, we were fortunate to have a vibrant and engaging panel in September 2022 and are joined in writing by authors whose robust articles may be found in this book.

We invited scholars cognizant of the transition from a reproductive rights movement to the reproductive justice campaigns of the 1990s and onward.[2] This shift had become a significant critique of the women's rights movements of an earlier generation, particularly among those who regarded the *Roe* ruling as a penultimate victory. For instance, the perception of Margaret Sanger, who was heralded as a foremother of reproductive rights activism, has been drastically reevaluated by examining her views on race and eugenics during her long career.[3] Thus contextualization has modified a single focus on issues of birth control and abortion. The innovative work of scholars on sterilization in twentieth-century America has altered and expanded our appreciation of the complexities of the term "control" in any birth control debate.[4]

Black reproductive justice advocate and scholar Loretta Ross suggests: "Neglecting to make the link between race, rights, and reproduction, the pro-choice movement has always insufficiently analyzed how political activism by communities of color particularly alarms opponents of civil rights, Indigenous rights, women's rights, gay rights, etc."[5] As the mainstream reproductive rights movement often neglected issues of central concern for BIPOC (Black, Indigenous, and People of Color) women, reproductive justice advocates emphasized a more comprehensive range of legal reform and social justice. Subsequently, a more inclusive agenda was devised as the movement expanded.[6]

This book was created for an inclusive audience of all readers interested in understanding the recent history of sex, reproduction, and abortion in the United States in the decades since *Roe*. We want to emphasize that this book is for a broad audience, not limited to individuals who identify as women or those who were already aligned with the "pro-choice" stance before the *Dobbs* decision. While the freedom and access to abortion hold cataclysmic importance to those who do not want to or cannot carry a pregnancy to term, studies have shown that abortion affects the entire family, especially whether children will face the consequences of poverty.

In the immediate wake of *Roe*, maternal mortality during abortions declined. Thirty-nine women are known to have died from unsafe abortions in 1972. This was almost certainly a drastic undercount.[7] Yet, using the same measure, there were only 3 such deaths in 1975, and over 40 years later, just 0.5 percent of women who undergo abortions require hospitalization for complications.[8]

A cadre of feminists and a significant portion of the American public welcomed the *Roe* decision, believing it would usher in a new era of civil rights and equality for U.S. women. The anti-abortionists launched an immediate call to arms. This movement reinvigorated its dramatic opposition to a woman's right to terminate her pregnancy, labeling their efforts as "Right to Life" or "Pro Life." Feminists countered with a "Right to Choose" or a "Pro Choice" stance. The stage was set for a battle royal between advocates of a woman's right to control her body, particularly in terms of reproduction, and the forces that wanted to limit, if not eliminate, a woman's access to abortion (rebranding their position as "fetal rights"). Political alliances were forged, and belligerent rhetoric followed. Saving the lives of the unborn became the focus of the pro-life movement, outweighing concerns for pregnant women.[9]

During the late 1970s and early 1980s, Protestant evangelicals and the religious right began to unite with Catholic pro-life campaigners to form a unified front against secularization within American culture, particularly concerning the acceptability of abortion as a woman's right. The pro-life crusaders had been somewhat separated along a North versus South divide, which shifted dramatically in the decade after *Roe.* As Daniel K Williams argues, ". . . many of the southern states that liberalized their abortion laws in the 1960s and early 1970s are now at the forefront of movements to restrict abortion."[10]

In some cases, pro-life extremists resorted to murder to advance their cause. When zealots took up arms, the battle became a nightmarish scenario.[11] The year 1993 ushered in horrific episodes of domestic terror related to abortion in the United States. On March 10, 1993, Dr. David Gunn was murdered in Florida by three gunshots to his back outside of the Pensacola Women's Medical Center. Five months later, on August 19, 1993, Rachelle Shannon shot Dr. George Tiller, a physician who headed the Wichita Women's Health Care Services. (He survived but was assassinated in 2009, dying after being shot in a church.)[12] In December 1994, a rifleman attacked abortion clinics in Brookline, Massachusetts.

Harassment and violence continue down to the present. In a recent study, 60 percent of abortion doctors who experienced doxxing[13] had their medical board files posted to anti-abortion websites, nearly 90 percent had their photographs posted, and 41 percent had their private contact information and residence posted. In some cases, doctors had their social security numbers made public.[14]

Pregnancy has long been associated with women's primary roles and patriotic duty. Birth rates varied according to class, region, and race throughout American history, but there was a steady decline from the American Revolution onward. Scholars suggest that white American women reduced family size, with more significant decreases in the northern colonies compared to the southern regions, during the eighteenth and nineteenth centuries. This decline was startling because women were expected to be fruitful and multiply, and the new nation was eager to expand westward and repoplulate. Indeed, the Founding Fathers prescribed that republican mothers in the early national era must be committed to rearing "liberty-loving" sons.[15]

At the same time, the forced reproductive labor of enslaved Black women meant steadily increasing populations of Black children, often through violent sexual encounters beyond their control as Black enslaved women were legally unable to consent when an enslaver "owned" their bodies. In 1662, Virginia passed Act XII or the Enactment of Hereditary Slavery Law that read "that all children borne in this country shall be held bond or free only according to the condition of the mother." Not only would any child born to an enslaved Black woman be born enslaved, they would be enslaved for life. This forced reproduction was seen as a necessary part of American slavery which resulted in a Black-majority population in South Carolina. By 1720, enslaved Black Americans had become a self-repopulating captive labor force in the colonies that would become the United States. This was in stark contrast with other slave societies like Jamaica where sexual violence was rampant, but their staple crops like sugarcane which were dangerous to cultivate meant the enslaved were worked to death (rarely living beyond seven years on a plantation) where the labor force was constantly replenished by newly kidnapped and trafficked West Africans. Due to this mass forced reproduction, Black women sought private means—especially through healer knowledge of herbal remedies—to control their fertility and reproduction.

Within the young republic, marriage was becoming more affective and, in some instances, less transactional. Mortality rates were also declining, and thus fewer children meant the possibility of improved quality of life. Contraception during this era could depend upon both partners. Studies of Quaker couples in early America show that women relied on cooperation and mutual benefits to improve their relationships and reduce pregnancies. This pattern would emerge for white middle-class Americans in the nineteenth century.

One of the significant transformations of the century can be attributed to women exercising greater control over reproduction. The average birth rate of 7.04 per married female in 1800 was cut in half by 1900 to 3.56.[16] This was achieved amid enormous obstacles to females' ability to exercise birth control. Women had very little knowledge about the process of sexual reproduction, and their understanding of conception was even more limited. Physicians offered advice based on little more than pragmatic guesswork. A leading medical figure of the postbellum era, Dr. J. Marion Sims, like many of his peers, believed that menses was an indication of "an aptitude for impregnation."[17] Yet, the "rhythm method," as it came to be known, offered hope rather than effectiveness, considering the rudimentary state of medical knowledge. Therefore, Sims and most of the medical profession advocated a "safe period," which today we calculate through scientific evidence as the time when conception is most likely. Some doctors provided the opposite advice.[18]

Contraceptive knowledge in late nineteenth-century America was limited. By the 1850s, rubber condoms were advertised and sold in eastern cities. Although the diaphragm was invented, this device was not widely available in the United States until the 1920s. Yet, Dr. Edward B. Foote's *Medical Common Sense* (1864) referred to a "womb veil" and endorsed the use of a pessary (a device designed for insertion into the vagina) as a contraceptive method.[19]

Evidence indicates that middle- and upper-class women tried numerous methods to prevent conception, especially in the late nineteenth century. The crusade for "voluntary motherhood" sprang from women's concerns over health and family.[20] To increase a woman's capacity to rear and nurture her children, many mothers wished to limit the number of their offspring. Many middle-class husbands supported their wives on this sensitive issue. Some women suggested that limiting the birth rate could harm women's future status. But feminists argued that limiting family size might eventually strengthen women's societal position. Women's hopes for "planned parenthood" reflected a collective bid for female self-control rather than any movement for sexual freedom. Since most women depended on their families for emotional and financial support, many were unwilling to undermine their maternal prestige. Feminist advocates of family limitation hoped fewer children would improve women's status within the household and the larger society. Many advocated abstinence instead of contraceptives, fearing the hostility "free love" crusaders attracted might taint them.

Victoria Woodhull, a suffragist who ran for President of the United States in 1872, championed birth control as the means to freedom from social restrictions. Woodhull and a handful of feminists were sexual radicals, attempting to divorce issues of sexual relations from reproduction.[21] They believed separating sexuality and procreation was necessary for women's autonomy. Most feminists feared the repercussions of such radicalism and steered the birth control movement along more conservative lines. The very language used reflects the fears of its advocates: "voluntary motherhood" appealed more to the general public than any calls for "freedom" or "control." The voluntary motherhood movement focused on questions of reproduction but sought to reform rather than demolish institutions that kept women confined. They hoped to advance their cause with campaigns that anchored women to the home.

Opposition to birth control persisted. Many religious leaders opposed any movement which divorced the sex act from reproductive purposes. Traditional church views condemned any attempt to interfere with procreation. The male establishment perceived that a crusade to restrict family size would free women to leave their designated spheres, enabling them to pioneer new roles.

The elite establishment joined ranks against birth control because they felt threatened by the waves of immigrants flooding the country at the end of the century. Theodore Roosevelt was outspoken on the question of "race suicide." In 1901, he warned: "All the other problems before us in this country, important though they may be, are as nothing compared with the problem of the diminishing birth rate and all that it implies."[22] He preached that native born white women must maintain high birth rates to prevent the country from being overrun by "hunger-bitten hordes." This ideology was equally popular in the U.S. South among upper-class whites, who feared the booming Black birth rate.

Physicians, as well as women, were caught up in the politics of family limitations. The legal movement to prohibit abortion was first directed at doctors and others who performed operations. New York was the first state to enact an anti-doctor statute in 1829.[23] Most northern states followed suit within twenty years. By the time the American Civil War broke out, physicians had decried the falling birth rate, and many blamed the decline on the prevalence of abortion.

Abortion had been somewhat clandestine before the Civil War but not so rare as one might suppose. Experts estimate one abortion for every 30 live births from 1800 to 1830. By the mid-century, this figure had escalated to one abortion for every six live births, showing an upsurge despite statutes against the practice. Periodicals were filled with advertisements for abortifacients, substances that induce abortions. The manufacture and sale of "female pills" flourished. If medicines failed, women might resort to surgical means.[24]

During the 1850s, abortion parlors began to flourish in eastern cities. Madame Restell was a notorious practitioner in New York City who did hundreds of abortions a year following the opening of her office in 1838.[25] She was often the target of print media and caricatures in popular culture, most notably by comedian and newspaper publisher George Washington Dixon known for inventing the blackface character Zip Coon. Dixon helped secure Restell's prison sentence, but after being released from prison in 1841, she resumed her practice, now using veiled language to advertise her services through New York City's thriving newspaper culture. She ran ads for "A Certain Cure for Married Ladies, With or Without Medicine."[26]

After the Civil War, because of mounting public protest and concern about repopulating after the devastation of war, states began to enact stricter legislation. After 1868, contraception was banned in New York (the first of many states), prohibiting free access to birth control information and devices.

In 1872, the New York YMCA launched a program to enforce this prohibition. They hired Anthony Comstock as a special investigator dedicated to "prosecute, in all legal forms, the traffic in bad books, prints and instruments."[27] Comstock began his crusading career when he destroyed his family's store of liquor in a fit of prohibitionist zeal. After his return from the battlefront, having joined the federal army after Gettysburg, he honed his style by attacking the distribution of pornographic material: "On March 2, 1872, he and a police captain raided booksellers along Manhattan's Nassau Street, the heart of America's smut industry. In one shop, he purchased *The Confessions of a Voluptuous Young Lady of High Rank*. In others, he bought *Women's Rights Convention* and *La Rose d'Amour*."[28] Once in court, Comstock and the police captain were able to convince a judge of the material's obscenity.

In March 1873, Congress passed a measure "for suppression of trade in and circulation of obscene literature and articles of immoral use." The legislative doctrine known as "the Comstock law" became notorious. Although the law may have been conceived as a measure to "protect children against erotica . . . it was possible to construe this law as banning printed advocacy of free love."[29] Both advertisements and information were subject to prosecution, and Comstock was hired as a special agent of the U.S. Postal Service.[30] Therefore, what began as a means of "protection" transformed into an era of prosecution. The transmission of knowledge for contraception or termination of a pregnancy was regulated, with any decision taken out of the hands of individual women and placed within the realm of the medical and legal professions.

Scholars suggest that the nineteenth-century birth rate was reduced primarily by abortion. Feminists engaged in fierce debates. Many were concerned mainly with those circumstances which made abortion necessary. Many attempted to shift the discussion to safe and effective contraception. In addition, women emphasized that most abortions were performed on married women, primarily mothers. We know that despite all sorts of obstacles and prohibitions, women continued to seek out abortions as the state and society conspired to crack down on the termination of pregnancies.

The American Medical Association and religious leadership combined efforts, and by the twentieth century, abortion was effectively outlawed. It was permitted only in rare cases, which were determined by physicians, 95 percent of whom were male. By 1930, an underground network of abortion providers had sprung up across the country, mainly but not exclusively in urban centers. Botched or self-induced abortions accounted for nearly 20 percent of maternal deaths in the United States by the mid-twentieth century. This was a growing problem that physicians and the public recognized as endangering the birth rate *and* women's health.[31]

By 1955, Planned Parenthood (a group founded in 1916 by crusader Margaret Sanger) held a national conference where doctors in attendance called for a reform to abortion laws.[32] A series of cases in the 1950s and 1960s culminated in a push for a woman's access to legalized abortion based on women's rights. Along with the Equal Rights Amendment and equal pay for equal work, the right to an abortion was a fundamental demand of the women's movement in the 1960s. With the advent of *Roe* in 1973, women believed they had the right to determine their reproductive futures with the guarantee of access to safe and legal abortion. However, it should be noted that the fact that the ruling effectively left this decision "to the medical judgment of the pregnant woman's attending physician" rather than the woman herself was significantly downplayed by the feminists celebrating this legislative victory.

Congress continued to limit low-income women's access to abortion by including provisions in annual appropriation bills that prohibited federal funds from being used for such purposes. In 1976, Illinois Congressman Henry J. Hyde raised his objections to *Roe* by proposing a bill to ban the use of federal funds to pay for pregnancy termination through Medicaid. In 1980, the U.S. Supreme Court in *Harris v. McRae* (1980) upheld the constitutionality of the Hyde

Amendment.[33] Once again, the predominately white male legislative establishment controlled millions of poor women in the United States.

Technology and ideological conservatism intersected in the 1970s. Advances in science challenged *Roe*'s reliance on the rule of the "first trimester" as the period during which the fetus might not survive outside the womb. With the sophistication of ultrasound imaging, physicians could more accurately observe fetal growth and predict fetal viability. By the 1990s, the pro-life movement aggressively began to advertise this feature.

Pro- and anti-abortion protests in the decades after *Roe* relied on a spectacular visual culture to evoke sympathy from possible voters for respective causes, as well as to garner the attention of journalists covering their sensational tactics. Using social movement organizing tools that reached back to as early as abolition in the nineteenth century, women's fights for the vote in the early twentieth century, and, more recently, the Civil Rights and Anti-Vietnam War Movements, both sides used *graphic* and *symbolic* imagery to personify the dead—mothers from botched and illegal abortions and the fetal "unborn." Further, both groups increasingly brought young children to demonstrations.

The pro-choice advocates featured women who died due to pregnancy complications, childbirth, or illegal, so-called "back alley" or "hanger" abortions in the pre-*Roe* era. In these protests, famous slogans included "Women's Lives Matter" and "Keep Abortion Legal." Protestors would feature imagery of bloody wire coat hangers, emphasizing the toll on women. The battle of images was played out in political campaigns and aggressive advertising.

On the anti-abortion side, advocates attempted to emphasize the humanity of the results of any pregnancy: the "unborn." They conflated pregnancy termination with the end of human life or *murder*: an abortion denied a person the ability to live a whole life. A group in Minnesota launched an active billboard campaign in 1989, emphasizing the notion of "life" beginning with the fertilization of an egg. A popular slogan in these early advertisements was "A baby is a baby—heartbeat 24 days from conception!" The movement featured a series of interlocking campaigns highlighting the Right to Life's vigilant effort to paint abortion as murder.[34]

In the 1980s, anti-abortion protests, frequently affiliated with white evangelical groups, turned out in substantial numbers to protest outside both government buildings and medical clinics. Sometimes demonstrations were so large and chaotic, like the protest outside of an Orange County, California clinic in March 24, 1989, that police had to lift clinic patients above the screaming crowds to allow them to enter or exit the clinic.[35] Women seeking the right to terminate their pregnancies were subjected to danger as well as intimidation.

In January 1981, anti-abortion rally participants at the California State Capitol held signs reading "If you liked Hitler, you'll love abortion," equating the genocide of six million European Jews during World War II with abortion in the United States.[36] Small children at the rally held up signs reading, "pick on someone your own size."[37] Anti-abortionists affiliated with the Traditional Values Coalition erected a "Cemetery of Innocents." They held a 12-hour vigil to memorialize the 4,400 abortions the group estimated were occurring daily during the George H. W. Bush administration. (In March of 2023, Governor Sarah Huckabee Sanders signed into law a bill for a privately-funded "monument to the unborn" to be installed at the Arkansas capitol grounds in Little Rock.)[38]

Much like the pallbearers that carried "Jim Crow" caskets during anti-segregation protests during Civil Rights, anti-abortionists in 1981 gathered white men in suits to carry coffins "of aborted fetuses to gravesites," with gory banners portraying disembodied fetus parts blown up to billboard size. Three years later, in 1984, anti-abortion protesters turned up at a public meeting held by Representative Jerry Patterson with a garbage can filled with doll parts. As plastic legs and arms overflowed with crumpled newspapers, they placed a sign reading "HUMAN GARBAGE." In June 1985, pastors Norman Stone and Jerry Horn held up a miniature casket they propped open, showing what they claimed was a bloody and fully-formed aborted baby of seven weeks (with a full head of hair) at the rally of Americans Against Abortion outside of the Wilshire Federal Building in Los Angeles. It is unknown what they held up—at seven weeks, a fetus would only be 10 millimeters, or the size of a blueberry. But these visual stunts became a standard operating procedure for aggressive pro-life protestors.[39]

The *Los Angeles Herald Examiner* ran photos in August 1989 of "Operation Rescue," an anti-abortion white evangelical group that preached politics from the pulpit by holding prayer services and calls to action during worship. A white male pastor can be seen with his arms outstretched to the heavens, singing with his eyes closed before a congregation sitting and standing in aisles of folding chairs under fluorescent lights. Beside him, a teenager ironically wearing a "lifeguard" T-shirt is on bent knees with hands clasped firmly in prayer as older congregants wearing veterans' hats look on.[40]

Church youth groups like teenagers from an Assemblies of God Church in November 1987 began bussing minors to state capitols and Washington D.C. to protest abortion, pornography, and drugs.[41] In

June 1990, abortion opponent Tom Hogue was photographed by the *Sacramento Bee,* a newspaper published in California's capital. The photo depicted him walking through 440 small white crosses and stars of David on the California State Capitol lawn. Reverend Louis P. Sheldon put it plainly: "The cemetery's message is that 'abortion kills babies.'"[42]

When "Operation Rescue" focused on the Georgia capital of Atlanta during the Democratic National Convention in July 1988, the prolonged harassment of those seeking termination of pregnancies and those providing guidance and medical care escalated. This group called for a "Day of Rescue," aimed at dissuading women who sought to terminate their pregnancies, targeting 100 cities nationwide. They urged followers to swarm and create human barricades around abortion clinics. In early October, protestors blocked abortion clinics for five days in what became known as the "Siege of Atlanta." More than a thousand were arrested for their civil disobedience. Although civil disobedience was acceptable to both sides, by the 1990s, pro-life advocates had crossed over into violent tactics. They were targeting abortion clinics with death threats, bombings, and vandalism. Governments tracked these escalations, and from 1977 to 1988, an epidemic of anti-abortion violence took place in the United States, involving 110 cases of arson, firebombing, or bombing.[43]

The Freedom of Access to Clinic Entrances Act (or the FACE Act) was introduced by Democratic Senator Ted Kennedy and signed into law by President Bill Clinton on May 26, 1994. The bill intended to outlaw the use of 1) force, intimidation, or injury that would prevent a woman from seeking or obtaining "reproductive health services" or an abortion; 2) prohibit assault or intimidation against protestors exercising their First Amendment right to religious freedom; and 3) prohibit and prosecute anyone who intentionally damages a reproductive health facility. The act defined "reproductive health services" widely to include women's access to hospitals, clinics, physician offices, surgeons, counseling, and referral services.[44] The law was distinctive for protecting the rights of anti-abortion protestors as well.

FACE was a new tool for investigating and taking legal action against abortion-related violence. A 1999 report on the frequency of "incidents" before and after FACE at abortion clinics found decreased violence two years after its passing. The violence they tracked included "blockades, vandalism, invasions, bomb threats, death threats, assaults, and stalking."[45]

First-time non-violent offenders received a maximum sentence of 6 months of jail time and a $10,000 fine. Those who inflicted bodily harm on another could face a maximum of a decade-long imprisonment. If death resulted, they faced life in prison.

Pro-choice protestors during this same era launched their own elaborate spectacles. In 1989, students at the University of California at Davis laid flowers in front of a wall with the name "Jane Doe" inscribed thousands of times to honor women who died during illegal abortions before 1973. At the Memorial Union Patio on campus where students held around-the-clock vigils, this visual protest was organized by the National Organization of Women student members.[46] A San Jose resident held up a pro-rights sign reading "Our bodies, our lives, our right to decide. Abortion without apology. We won't go back!"[47] She wore a T-shirt that read: "Walk for Choice/ Walk for Women/ Walk for Children/ Walk for Families/ Walk for Freedom."

In 1994, an estimated 300,000 protestors descended on Washington, D.C. to march from the Washington Monument to the U.S.

Capitol. They were rallying against a pushback on abortion rights and came armed with signs and T-shirts, buttons, and banners: "My body, my baby, my business." "Keep your laws off my body." "Mother of two by choice."[48]

Americans have wrestled with abortion rights across political platforms from high to low culture, from mainstream to social media. Cultural and intellectual history is catching up to the pop culture trends that have long been at the forefront of public discourse on reproduction. Music, films, television shows, and literature throughout the twentieth and twenty-first centuries have increasingly been active sites for engagement over pre-marital pregnancy, miscarriages, postpartum depression, access to birth control, sexual assault, and abortion.

During the past half-century, popular culture has been one of the most common ways young Americans have learned about abortion and discourses surrounding it in modern-day life. In the American silent film era, at least ten films focused on abortion between 1913 and 1932, like the feature-length drama *Where Are My Children*? (1916) inspired by obscenity charges brought against Margaret Sanger. Over 300 film and television episodes filmed and released in the United States featured abortion as one of its significant plot points between the silent film era in 1916 and 2012 when Barack Obama won his second presidential term in the era of online streaming.[49]

Storylines on the subject of a woman's decision over an abortion increased over time. Of these films, like the 1980s cult classics *Fast Times at Ridgemont High* (1982) and *Dirty Dancing* (1987), 55 percent resulted in protagonists having an abortion, including the film adaptation *For Colored Girls* (2010). A quarter of the film and television plots involving an unexpected or unwanted pregnancy resulted in a subsequent birth and parenting, including the titular character in the popular broadcast series *Jane the Virgin* (2014–19). In the influential show *Sex and the City* (1996–2004), fans followed with interest as single corporate lawyer Miranda Hobbes' decided (in the episode "Coulda, Woulda, Shoulda" in 2001) not to get her scheduled abortion and choosing instead to carry her child to term, giving birth to her son Brady. In popular films like *Knocked Up,* a 2007 romantic comedy starring Katherine Heigl and Seth Rogan and *Blue Valentine,* a 2010 romantic drama starring Michelle Williams and Ryan Gosling, less than five percent of women opted for adoption. However, this was the case in the Oscar-winning 2007 indie film *Juno*, starring Elliot Page (formerly Ellen Page) in the title role. In other films, the characters' pregnancies resulted in pregnancy loss, no resolution, or the protagonist dying due to abortion complications. This was the tragic fate of Kate Winslet's character in the 2008 film, *Revolutionary Road.* She portrayed a 1950s suburban middle-class wife, opposite Leonardo DiCaprio as her husband. When she attempts to perform a vacuum abortion by herself, it leads to mass hemorrhaging, ultimately resulting in her bleeding to death in her own bathroom.

Throughout American film history, abortion has predominately been portrayed as a plight for white, attractive, middle-class young women, especially teenagers or young mothers. In the twenty-first century, this trend has persisted on screen, as exemplified by recent films like *Unpregnant* (2020) and *The Handmaid's Tale* (2017–23, see the episode "Milk" in 2021).

From 1963 to 1972, the decade preceding *Roe* and coinciding with the Civil Rights movement, Anti-Vietnam movement, and Women's Liberation, 29 films or T.V. shows focused on women's abortions.

Cabaret, the 1972 American musical directed by Bob Fosse and starring Liza Minnelli set in Weimar Germany, was based on the hit Broadway production first staged in 1966, and Sally Bowles, the female lead, chooses termination of her pregnancy without consulting the father.

After *Roe*, the number of productions highlighting terminating a pregnancy quickly jumped every subsequent decade. There were 44 productions between 1983 and 1992, and 58 between 1993 and 2002, such as the fictional HBO T.V. movie *If These Walls Could Talk* (1996)). The film depicts three women inhabiting the same house 22 years apart (in 1952, 1974, and 1996) and grappling with unwanted pregnancies. This dramatic epic featured Demi Moore, Sissy Spacek, Shirley Knight, CCH Pounder, Anne Heche, Jada Pinkett, Rita Wilson, and Cher. Between 2003 and 2015, there were 116 releases related to abortion, including feature films like *Grandma* (2015), starring Lily Tomlin and Julia Garner.

A noticeable shift can be observed in many scripts from the turn of the twenty-first century, as lead characters demonstrate a higher level of education about their decision to undergo an abortion. Often times, the central plot revolves around understanding the local and state regulations and navigating through obstacles. Regardless of impediments, most fictional women of twenty-first-century projects are determined to end their pregnancies, which may involve fundraising, traveling out of state, or subjecting themselves to degrading psychological or non-essential medical interventions. Also, most of these plots portray abortion seekers as having supportive communities—a family figure or best friend who helps them in their quest.

Further, the barrier that suggested only white people were impacted by abortion broke when Shonda Rhimes, a prolific and influential screenwriter and producer, arrived on the scene.[50] She wrote episodes for broadcast networks in which both lead characters, *Scandal*'s African-American Olivia Pope (played by Kerry Washington) and *Grey's Anatomy*'s Asian-American Cristina Yang (played by Emmy Award-winning Sandra Oh), elected to resolve their pregnancies independently while in the context of a relationship. Outside the United States, European film communities, like those in Germany, France, and Sweden, have a substantial cinematic catalog that explores the topic of abortion.

American popular music is another venue where women's reproduction, infanticide, stillbirths, and abortions have often been the subject of storytelling. The earliest iterations were primarily in American country music and folk and blues music—genres that, from the outset, provided a platform for women musicians to be singer-songwriters, as opposed to the studio songwriting system and other music genres that were decidedly male-dominated.[51]

Desertion by lovers may have been an equal opportunity musical theme, but women performers were able to broaden and deepen this famous lament. Being shunned by religious parents while pregnant and unmarried was common in Dolly Parton's early songwriting career. In 1968, Parton released a song called "The Bridge." She wrote the song years earlier while a teenager living in a one-room cabin in the Great Smoky Mountains of Tennessee. The song's narrator, a pregnant teenage girl in the pre-*Roe* era, reveals heartbreak and shame: "Tonight while standing on the bridge/ My heart is beating wild/ To think that you could leave me here/ With our unborn child." Ultimately, she ends her own life by jumping off the bridge where she had shared her first kiss with the lover who impregnated her.[52]

Two years later, in 1970, Parton released the melancholic ballad

"Down from Dover," which begins with the opening line, "I know this dress I'm wearing doesn't hide the secret." In the song, the narrator pines for her lover, who left her pregnant. After her parents voice their shame, she hides until she gives birth to a stillborn baby girl. She reasons this was "her way of telling me/ He wasn't coming down from Dover." In real life, Parton's mother, Avie, had twelve children before the age of thirty-five. Parton never gave birth to a child due to undiagnosed endometriosis and a subsequent hysterectomy. Still, her ballads were filled with overburdened mothers, pregnant teenage girls, women abandoned by their lovers, and the hardships faced by women in the culture from which she sprang.

A year before *Roe*, country western star Loretta Lynn released her album and title track "One's on the Way." The 1972 song is a satirical take on living in Topeka, Kansas as a stay-at-home mother with more children than the narrator could handle while expecting another. In the final verse, she reflects on the shifting historical context for women's reproduction she is witnessing in mass media: "The girls in New York City, they all march for women's lib/ And better homes and garden shows the modern way to live/ And the pill may change the world tomorrow, but meanwhile, today . . ." while she waits for women's rights "Lord, one's on the way." In 1975, she openly sang praises of oral contraception in her song "The Pill," which detailed the life of a tired wife and mother who had endured years of back-to-back pregnancies in an unfaithful marriage. Finally, with access to the ability to regulate her reproduction and uncouple sex from procreation, she declares, "This old maternity dress I've got/ Is goin' in the garbage/ The clothes I'm wearin' from now on/ Won't take up so much yardage." She declares: "I'm makin' up for all those years/ Since I've got the pill."

In Madonna's 1986 music video "Papa Don't Preach," the chart-topping song (co-written by Brian Elliot and Madonna) is sung from the perspective of a young teenage girl who begs her "papa" to treat her like an adult because she is pregnant and wants to *keep* her child. She refuses to undergo an abortion or put the child up for adoption. The verses reveal that her family and friends "keep telling me to give it up / Saying I'm too young I ought to live it up," suggesting she feels peer pressure not to become a teenage mother.

In the chorus, she boldly proclaims, "But I've made up my mind," underscoring that ultimately, she gets to decide matters for her body and life. She intends to "keep my baby." After her mother died of breast cancer in 1963, Madonna was raised by her Italian Catholic father. "Papa don't preach" could symbolically represent the traditional "father knows best" patriarchy of families, with the singer pleading with her biological father to let her choose what to do for herself—regarding her reproductive body and her own future. It could also represent Catholic "fathers" or priests representative of the Catholic Church, in a moment when debates over abortion raged. Equally compelling were the forced removals and secret rehoming of children born to unwed mothers by Catholic convents. During the 1980s, systematic child molestation at the hands of the Church was only starting to emerge.

These cultural conversations would continue to enflame, as when Irish pop star Sinéad O'Connor provoked significant controversy over how to protest the Catholic Church: O'Connor tore a picture of Pope John Paul II on live television during her 1992 performance on NBC's *Saturday Night Live*. O'Connor shouted, "fight the real enemy," as she shredded the papal image. Although Madonna, among other celebrities, condemned her attack on the Pope, she also garnered anti-Catholic acolytes. Within weeks, a group called themselves the "Sinead Brigade" stood outside St. Patrick's Cathedral in New York, ripping up papal portraits supporting "her efforts to expose the Catholic hierarchy as agents of oppression."[53]

While the airwaves and other media reflected shifting popular attitudes, conservative forces fought back at what they argued was a normalization—or celebration even—of "murder by abortion." The Christian Broadcast Network (CBN), founded in 1960 by evangelist and fundraiser Pat Robertson (rebranded as The Family Channel in 1998 and eventually sold to the Fox Network), wholeheartedly embraced and promoted the pro-life, anti-abortion cause. By 2017, it was estimated that the popular CBN program *The 700 Club* attracted a million viewers daily or through syndication. By 2023, over 150 religious television stations were broadcasting, and over 1,600 Christian radio stations flooded the airwaves. The proliferation of radio and broadcast media reflect a national pushback on "liberal media bias."[54] Naturally, this has led to direct-mail and direct-action campaigns, such as the "Peace in the Womb Christmas Caroling," and other programs by groups such as the Pro-Life Action League.[55] These crusades continue with internet outreach.[56] These efforts aim to garner media attention and shift the political agenda towards a more conservative path.

From *Roe* onward, anti-abortion forces wanted to challenge women's right to choose by appealing to sympathetic state legislatures. Pro-life advocates hoped to overturn access to abortion and began by chipping away through legal limitations on a state-by-state basis. Simultaneously, polls demonstrated that the sentiment to limit or erase a woman's right to reproductive freedom was waning. Nevertheless, court clashes showed mounting obstacles to compromise or reconciliation. Cases began to make their way to the Supreme Court regularly.[57]

The same year the Hyde Amendment was passed, Missouri pushed a case to the Court with *Planned Parenthood v. Danforth* (1976). The Court ruled to strike down a state law that banned saline injections for pregnancy termination and required consent from a husband (for a wife) and a parent's signature for minor daughters to terminate a pregnancy. In *Colautti v. Franklin* (1979), the Court rejected a Pennsylvania statute requiring doctors to protect a fetus's life that "may be viable" during and after an abortion. In *Harris v. McRae* (1980), the Court upheld the federal Hyde Amendment, stating that a woman has no constitutional right to have an abortion at public expense. (However, since 1994, the Hyde Amendment has permitted public funding for abortions where the pregnancy resulted from rape or incest.) In *H. L. v. Matheson* (1981), the Court upheld a statute requiring the doctor performing the abortion to notify *one parent* of a minor girl living at home with her parents. In *Webster v. Reproductive Health Services* (1989), a Missouri statute declared "[t]he life of each human being begins at conception," and that "unborn children have protectable interests in life, health, and well-being." The Court sidestepped several issues but upheld a statute that denied state funding and required state employee participation in performing or counseling for abortion. In *Planned Parenthood of Southeastern Pa. v. Casey* (1992), the Court held states *could* require parental consent for a minor's abortion, could require a waiting period between seeking and obtaining an abortion, and might require detailed "informed consent," including medical information about the abortion. The *Casey* case abandoned the trimester framework, replacing it with pre- and post-viability tests. Four justices dissented from *Casey*'s "reaffirmation" of *Roe*.

During the two decades following *Roe*, lawmakers and activists battled in the courts and state and national legislatures to guarantee women's reproductive rights or to secure personhood and protective rights for the fetus. By 1992, all fifty states had passed laws against marital rape. In 1994, Congress passed the Violence Against Women Act to provide support and comprehensive, cost-effective responses to domestic violence, sexual assault, dating violence, and stalking. In this year, no bills were introduced in Congress to outlaw abortion. Because the *Planned Parenthood v. Casey* decision in 1992 had reaffirmed a woman's constitutional right to an abortion, pro-life activists concentrated their activities on local and state legislation. In 1994, there were 304 abortion-related bills introduced in 38 state legislatures.[58]

In 1994, Norma McCorvey, the "Jane Roe" of *Roe*, published her autobiography, *I Am Roe*. At the center of a landmark legislative case, she was being courted by evangelicals to try to revise the narrative of *Roe* as something to celebrate. She finally did repudiate her pro-abortion stance in 1995 and publicly expressed her regret for the role she played as a "pawn" of pro-abortion activists. She converted to Catholicism and condemned the *Roe* decision because abortion "hurt" women. Yet she also upset pro-life colleagues when she insisted that women still had a right to terminate pregnancies during the first trimester. As her 2017 *New York Times* obituary suggested: "McCorvey fully shed her courtroom pseudonym in the 1980s, lending her name first to supporters of abortion rights and then, in a stunning reversal, to the cause's fiercest critics as a born-again Christian. But even after two memoirs, she remained an enigma, as difficult to know as when she shielded her identity behind the name Jane Roe."[59]

With the heating up of the "abortion wars," states attempted to regulate anti-abortion activism. In *Hill v. Colorado* (2000), a Colorado statute was upheld prohibiting sidewalk counseling within 100 feet of a "health care facility," including an abortion clinic, by making it illegal to approach within 8 feet of a person, whether to counsel, educate, show a sign, or pass out a leaflet.

During the turn of the twenty-first century, battles over "partial birth abortions" arose. It is essential to understand that this term is not a medical one but a political one. In 2003, after eight long years of Congressional infighting, the Partial-Birth Abortion Ban Act was signed by President George W. Bush. This law prohibited doctors from knowingly performing a "partial-birth abortion." Defined by this law as "deliberately and intentionally vaginally deliver[ing] a living fetus until, in the case of a head-first presentation, the entire fetal head is outside the body of the mother, or, in the case of breech presentation, any part of the fetal trunk past the navel is outside the body of the mother."[60] Pro-life forces have been particularly adept at making claims about this issue and using sensational data to promote their cause.[61]

Most pro-life advocates have focused on a judicial strategy since the turn of the twenty-first century. In 2000, with the case of *Stenberg v. Carhart*, the Supreme Court struck down Nebraska's ban on the dilation and extraction procedure—a surgical term for removing an intact fetus from the uterus. This procedure is used both after miscarriages and for abortions in the second and third trimesters of pregnancy. But in 2007, following a change in the makeup of the Supreme Court, the Court upheld a ban on the dilation and extraction procedure in *Gonzales v. Carhart*. This strategy has resulted in dramatic political developments, such as the 2016 Republican presidential nominee's pledge ("I'll appoint Supreme Court Justices to overturn *Roe v. Wade*") to secure pro-life votes.[62]

Even as polls demonstrated a growing majority of Americans—both men and women—supported a woman's right to choose, the politics of reproductive rights continued to foster dramatic extremes, leading to sensational headlines, such as the case of an Oklahoma woman being convicted of "manslaughter" in 2021 following her miscarriage.[63] Pro-life activists seized the opportunity to close off options for women to access abortions by instituting rigid regulations on women's bodies within local and state jurisdictions.

In 2013, the Texas state legislature introduced a series of draconian proposals, from banning abortions after 20 weeks to requiring clinics performing abortions to upgrade their facilities to "surgical centers," with doctors required to obtain hospital admit privileges within 30 miles. With these regulations in place, 37 of the state's 42 clinics would be forced to close. When Republicans attempted to call a vote for these laws to pass by midnight (the mandated close of business) on June 25, the Democratic state senator Wendy Davis rose and began speaking at 11:18 a.m. She was determined to defeat the proposals through delay with her filibuster. Davis held the floor for over 12 hours, drawing hundreds to the Austin capitol building and another 150,000 live via a YouTube channel. Millions more witnessed the protest when the hashtag #StandWithWendy went viral following President Barack Obama's salute on Twitter (now renamed X). Images of Davis in her pink running shoes were beamed around the globe as she followed rigid protocol: no food or water, no leaning on a desk, no bathroom breaks, and no sitting. Davis failed in her quest to prevent these proposals from becoming law but became a media star and later ran for governor on the Democratic ticket (unsuccessfully) in 2014, pledging to uphold women's rights.

The Texas legislature became emboldened on this issue of curbing abortion rights and has passed a series of laws that were meant to limit, if not eliminate, women's reproductive rights:

- A 2016 state mandate that clinics be required to bury or cremate tissue resulting from an abortion. Overturned.
- A 2017 ban on second-trimester abortion methods. Overturned.
- A 2017 ban on insurers including abortion as part of any comprehensive health insurance plan, requiring people to purchase separate coverage for abortion care.
- A 2019 bill criminalized abortion providers who do not provide medical treatment to a fetus if born after an abortion. (Technically impossible in Texas because abortions are banned after 20 weeks, and a fetus is not viable until 24 weeks, according to state law.)
- A 2019 bill which bans government affiliation with abortion providers and their affiliates.

In 2021, the Texas state legislature passed its most extreme anti-abortion measure, with provisions that attracted national attention and outrage. Its *Senate Bill 8* specified that abortions were banned as early as six weeks, *well before* many women knew they were pregnant. Further, this law authorized "private individuals" to file lawsuits to enforce the abortion ban. Any healthcare provider could be sued by *anyone*—from a relative to a stranger—for performing an abortion past the sixth-week mark. An even more fanatical scheme was introduced when the lawmakers attempted to institute incentives by offering to pay "damages" of at least $10,000 to anyone who successfully sues an abortion provider or anyone who "aids and abets" someone seeking an abortion after approximately six weeks in pregnancy—in essence, encouraging "bounty hunting."

Perhaps it is not surprising that on April 7, 2023, Judge Matthew J. Kacsmaryk of Amarillo, Texas ordered a hold on the federal approval of mifepristone, a drug the FDA approved in 2000. Kacsmaryk, former deputy counsel of the conservative First Liberty Institute and nominated by Donald Trump when he was president, wrote in his opinion that mifepristone "is a synthetic steroid that blocks the hormone progesterone, halts nutrition, and ultimately starves the unborn human until death." A few hours later, Judge Thomas O. Rice of Spokane, Washington, issued an order which said the opposite and directed authorities to keep mifepristone available. The pill to dissolve a pregnancy is becoming as controversial as the pill to prevent pregnancy.

Medication remains at the center of the current controversy over women's rights to control their own bodies and medical care. The *New York Times* explained that this was "a preliminary ruling invalidating the Food and Drug Administration's 23-year-old approval of the abortion pill mifepristone, an unprecedented order that—if it stands through court challenges—could make it harder for patients to get abortions in states where abortion is legal, not just in those trying to restrict it."[64] Dozens of strategies have arisen to create continuing access for women who seek mifepristone.[65]

While the Nixon-era court would establish abortion as a fundamental human right under the Due Process Clause of the Fourteenth Amendment, decades of judicial maneuvering would eventually pay off for the pro-life activists with the *Dobbs v. Jackson* (2022) decision (see Appendix B). *Dobbs* has overturned a woman's right to safe and accessible abortion. Appointments to the Supreme Court became part of a political chess game to advance an anti-abortion agenda—not unlike the nineteenth-century machinations concerning rulings on the status of slavery and enslaved persons.

In March 2016, Senator Mitch McConnell blocked a hearing for Merrick Garland, Barack Obama's nominee to the Supreme Court, to succeed Justice Antonin Scalia, who died the previous month. The 293-day standoff was unprecedented. Court politics escalated. Trump-nominated Justices Neil Gorsuch (April 2017), Brett Kavanaugh (October 2018), and Amy Coney Barrett (October 2020) all proclaimed in public testimony during their confirmation hearings that they would *follow the rules of precedent* on issues tied to *Roe*. However, these three joined the majority ruling on *Dobbs*, overturning nearly half a century of established precedent.

Justices Beyer, Sotomayor, and Kagan wrote "with sorrow" in their scathing dissent that *Dobbs* is the "first time in history" when the highest Court in the land is "rescinding an individual right in its entirety." Just as the *Dobbs* decision was leaked to the press in May 2022, polling of the American people shows that *Roe* has had a powerful effect on public opinion.

Over 70 percent of Americans said they favored access to legal abortions. Among those Americans who say abortions should be illegal, nearly half believe it should be legal if the pregnancy "threatens the life of the woman." A quarter suggests "it depends" on the situation. By far, the largest group who continue to oppose abortion unconditionally remains white evangelical Protestants, as 86 percent argue that human life begins at conception, and abortion—as murder—must be banned.[66]

Globally, around 73 million abortions take place each year. Six of 10 unintended pregnancies (61 percent) end with an induced abortion. The World Health Organization (WHO) designated abortion as a "common health intervention" that is very safe when "carried out using a method recommended by WHO, appropriate to the pregnancy duration and by someone with the necessary skills." They argue that lack of access to safe, timely, and affordable abortions carried out with respect for the patient is "a critical public health and human rights issue."[67]

In 2019, slightly over half a million abortions in the United States were reported to the CDC: an abortion rate of 11.4 abortions per 1,000 women aged between 14 and 44 years and 195 abortions per 1,000 live births.[68] Overall, abortions have been trending downward in the United States, with its reported peak at 1.6 million in 1990.[69] Unlike popular culture, which depicts teenagers as most likely to seek abortions, women in their 20s accounted for most abortions (or nearly 60 percent of reported abortions). Among teenagers who received an abortion, women aged 18–19 accounted for 70 percent of all adolescent abortions, indicating that these procedures were often sought immediately after high school or during their first year of college. Only 0.2 percent of abortions were performed on girls under 15.[70] These statistics represent legal abortions conducted by physicians in clinics, hospitals, or doctor's offices and do not account for other means like obtaining abortion pills via a friend or family member.

While two-thirds of American women say that either a close friend, family member, or they themselves have had an abortion, only half of the men surveyed claim to know someone who terminated a pregnancy.[71] One in four American women will have an abortion before the age of 45.[72]

There are two main categories of abortion practices: surgical and medication. In 2000, the Food and Drug Administration (FDA) approved the use of pills for medication abortion, involving a two-pill combination of 200 mg of mifepristone (which first blocks pregnancy-supporting hormones) and 800 mg of misoprostol administered 24–48 hours later (which causes the uterus to clear). They can be taken up to 10 weeks of gestation and dispensed via mail, pharmacy, or in offices for states that ban telehealth for medical abortions, like Texas and Louisiana. Medication abortion successfully ends 99 percent of pregnancies for patients at 7 weeks gestation and 97 percent successful at 10 weeks or less.[73] The use of medication abortion has increased substantially in the twenty years it has been available. As of 2020, 54 percent of all abortions in the United States—the majority—were conducted through medication abortion. Additional studies have shown that this method remains safe after 10 weeks.[74]

Surgical abortions in the first trimester are conducted via suctioning or D&C. In this process, the medical team will use a speculum to view the inside of the vagina, just like in gynecological exams. They then clean the vagina and cervix with gauze, apply numbing medication, and then dilate (or open) the cervix with the FDA medicine Dilapan-S which softens and dilates the cervix to both induce labor and expand the cervix for gynecological medical techniques. Finally, they insert a narrow, flexible tube inside the vagina up to the uterus. Suction is applied to one end of the tube while the end inside the woman collects pregnancy tissue.[75] Surgical abortions can occur while a woman is awake and conscious of light cramping, or while asleep (though opting for anesthesia requires the procedure to be conducted in two stages).

Women are allowed to eat and snack before a surgical abortion. Many clinics encourage women to bring headphones to listen to relaxing music, or to be accompanied by a supportive companion. Ninety-five percent of legal abortions in the United States occur at a clinic specializing in abortion, while only 5 percent of private medical physicians perform them in their offices or hospitals.[76] Six states—California, Illinois, Maine, New York, Oregon, and

Washington—require all state-regulated health plans offered by private companies to include abortion coverage.[77]

Unsafe abortions are costly on multiple levels. Michigan Governor Gretchen Whitmer suggests an abortion ban "would rob women of their reproductive freedom and the ability to decide whether and when to have a child. It also would rob women of their economic freedom and their right to decide whether to become a parent: the biggest economic decision a woman will make in her lifetime."[78] Legalized abortion gives women control over their economic decision-making. The inability to access safe abortions can shape the mother and child's ability to access education and radically reduce their lifetime earnings, which can have intergenerational economic repercussions.

In 2006, the WHO found that households where a woman survived an *unsafe* abortion experienced a staggering loss of $922 million (in U.S. dollars) due to long-term disability needs and income loss.[79] In 2020, women self-paid a medical average of $560 for an abortion at a time when 36 percent of all American adults, according to the Federal Reserve Board, could not afford to pay $400 for an emergency.[80]

Diana Greene Foster, a professor in the Department of Obstetrics, Gynecology, and Reproductive Sciences at the University of California, San Francisco (McArthur Awardee, 2023), studied 1,000 women who had abortions at the end of their state's gestation limitations (six weeks, etc.) and those who were denied an abortion and turned away. The goal of this "Turnaway Study" was to look at both their emotional health and socioeconomic status. Did abortion access help, hurt, or remain neutral in these women's lives? Did women who had abortions see a plummet in their emotional and psychological well-being?[81]

Many have suggested that women can lapse into severe depression and should be protected from the prolonged impact of choosing to have an abortion. Even Supreme Court Justice Anthony Kennedy suggested depression might be a side effect of abortion during his majority opinion for *Gonzalez* (2007).[82] Was childrearing as detrimental to a woman's financial life as was believed? And what happened to a woman's other children?

The study *did not* engage with when the product of conception or an embryo becomes a person. The study only focused on women and what happened to them. The study found the opposite of what popular culture preaches: 95 percent of women who receive an abortion report later in life that they still believe it was the right decision. Women who had been denied abortions had higher levels of anxiety, depression, and self-worth issues. Other findings in the study include those listed below:

- Women who were denied abortions were worse off financially.
- Women who were denied abortions were less likely to have additional children later in life.
- Women denied abortions were likelier to experience domestic violence and domestic partner abuse.

First, the study found that low-income women are disproportionately more likely to seek an abortion. The major reason women sought abortions was financial. Women who sought abortions felt they could *not afford a child or an additional child.* A close second reason was that women felt their relationship with the man with whom they conceived a child could not support a child. These abortion seekers were also more likely to be women who lived alone—meaning that they did not have a family support network to help raise a child.

Women denied an abortion struggled to maintain a job while pregnant and immediately after birth. They could not afford full-time childcare. As a result, women who were denied abortions are more likely to be financially dependent on a partner. The study found that "incidents of domestic violence skyrockets 'cause you're financially dependent on your partner because you have to be home with the kid . . . being denied an abortion increases the chances that you're tethered to a violent partner."[83]

Race and ethnicity had a profound impact on abortion rates and attitudes. In 2008, the abortion rate for non-Hispanic white women was 12 abortions per 1000 reproductive-age women, compared with 29 per 1000 for Hispanic women and 40 per 1000 for non-Hispanic Black women. Disparities in abortion rates reflect socioeconomic status (SES), with women with incomes less than 100 percent of the federal poverty level (FPL) having an abortion rate of 52 abortions per 1000 reproductive-age women, compared with a rate of 9 per 1000 among those with incomes greater than 200 percent FPL.[84] White women and Black women are the largest demographics to pursue abortions, with 33.4 percent and 38 percent in 2019, respectively.[85]

Abortion is safer in the United States than giving birth. When women do not have access to safe abortions, there are dangerous health complications, including an incomplete removal of pregnancy tissue, heavy bleeding, infection, uterine perforation, or irreversible damage to the genitals, the anus, and internal organs. In 2017 and 2018, only two women died of reported legal abortions to the CDC in the United States.[86]

The Pregnancy Mortality Surveillance System (PMSS) has tracked a disturbing upward trend of pregnancy-related deaths in the United States. Women dying from pregnancy complications have spiked. In 1987, 7.2 women died per every 100,000 live births.

By 2018, that rate jumped to 17.3 deaths per 100,000 live births. These deaths also expose deep racial inequality in American healthcare ranging from systemic racism to unequal access to quality care. Forty-one point four Black women die per 100,000 live births, and 26.5 American Indian women die per 100,000 live births.[87]

The ongoing debates and legislative twists within governments at the state and national levels suggest that the issue of reproductive justice and safe access to termination of pregnancies will continue to embroil activists in a ferocious struggle. The more than fifty years since the *Roe* decision has demonstrated that scholars can barely keep pace with the rapid and escalating challenges to developments in this critical area of study.

• • •

On September 8, 2022, we welcomed a range of scholars to debate and discuss the critical impact of *Roe* and the standoff where prochoice and pro-life activists remain today. The round table was held at the Hutchins Center for African and African American Research Library and the Charles Warren Center for Studies in American History at Harvard University in Cambridge, Massachusetts.

In addition to including a transcription of our round table, this volume contains vital topical articles about the history of abortion and reproduction rights and an extensive bibliography. These appendices include selections from the *Roe* and *Dobbs* rulings and a state-by-state guide to abortion's legal status as of 2023.

We do not intend for this to be a volume that comprehensively captures all that has happened, nor to in any way calculate what *may* happen—but we seek to share our informed views and continue to listen and learn from one another. We are committed to the ongoing sharing of ideas and information *without restrictions*, and we seek a social fabric that includes women's reproductive rights as paramount to the welfare of the republic and the preservation of our democracy.

Rhae Lynn Barnes
Hutchins Institute for African &
African American Research at Harvard University,
Assistant Professor of American Cultural History
at Princeton University

Catherine Clinton
Denman Chair of American History
at The University of Texas in San Antonio,
Professor Emerita at Queen's University Belfast

Notes

1. Historical evidence supports the fact that the Catholic church only opposed terminating pregnancies within the nineteenth century: "In the 1869 document *Apostolicae Sedis*, Pope Pius IX declared the penalty of excommunication for abortions at any stage of pregnancy. Up to then Catholic teaching was that no homicide was involved if abortion took place before the foetus was infused with a soul, known as 'ensoulment.'" The recognition of "ensoulement" was also referred to as "quickening" when the pregnant woman might feel the baby move within her—usually at three months, or the end of the first trimester. See Patsy McGarry, "Catholic Church Teaching on Abortion Dates from 1869," *Irish Times*, July 1, 2013.

2. Silliman, Fried, and Ross, "Undivided Rights."

3. Ruth C. Engs, "Margaret Sanger, Birth Control, and the Eugenics Movements: Changes in Historiographical Interpretations" (paper presented at "A New Look at the New Era: Reassessing the 1920s," Williams College, November 14–15, 2014), http://hdl.handle.net/2022/19058.

4. See Schoen, *Choice and Coercion*; Lisa Ko, "Unwanted Sterilization and Eugenics Programs in the United States," PBS, January 29, 2016, https://www.pbs.org/independentlens/blog/unwanted-sterilization-and-eugenics-programs-in-the-united-states/; and Alexandra Stern, "Forced Sterilization Policies in the U.S. Targeted Minorities and Those with Disabilities—and Lasted into the 21st Century," University of Michigan Institute for Healthcare Policy & Innovation, September 23, 2020, https://ihpi.umich.edu/news/forced-sterilization-policies-us-targeted-minorities-and-those-disabilities-and-lasted-21st.

5. Danielle M. Pacia, "Reproductive Rights v. Reproductive Justice," Bill of Health, November 3, 2020, https://blog.petrieflom.law.harvard.edu/2020/11/03/reproductive-rights-justice-bioethics/.

6. See Roberts, *Killing the Black Body*; Solinger, *Beggars and Choosers*; Rosalind Petchesky, *Abortion and Woman's Choice: The State, Sexuality and Reproductive Freedom* (Boston: Northeastern University Press, 1990); Solinger, *Wake Up Little Susie*; and Evelyn C. White, *Black Women's Health Book: Speaking for Ourselves*, rev. ed. (Seattle: Seal, 1994).

7. Willard Cates Jr. and Roger Rochat, "Illegal Abortions in the United States: 1972–1974,"

Family Planning Perspectives 8, no. 2 (Mar.–Apr. 1976): 86–88 and 91–92.

8. Ushma D. Upadhyay, Ph.D., MPH et al., "Incidence of Emergency Department Visits and Complications after Abortion," *Obstetrics & Gynecology* 125, no. 1 (January 2015): 175–183.

9. Holland, *Tiny You*.

10. Daniel K. Williams, "This Really is a Different Pro-Life Movement, *The Atlantic*, May 9, 2022. See also Williams's *Defenders of the Faith: The Pro-Life Movement Before Roe v. Wade* (New York: Oxford University Press, 2016).

11. "Violence to Abortion Providers," Feminist Majority Foundation, https://feminist.org/our-work/national-clinic-access-project/violent-attacks-on-abortion-providers-murders-attempted-murders-kidnapping/.

12. Karen Tumulty, "George Tiller Murdered," *Time*, May 31, 2009, https://swampland.time.com/2009/05/31/george-tiller-murdered/.

13. Doxxing is the act of searching for and publishing private or identifying information about a particular individual on the internet, typically with malicious intent.

14. Joanne D. Rosen and Joel J. Ramirez, "When Doctors Are 'Doxxed': An Analysis of Information Posted on an Anti-Abortion Website," *Contraception* 115 (2022): 1–5.

15. For further reading, see Linda K. Kerber, *Women of the Republic:*

Intellect and Ideology in Revolutionary America (Chapel Hill: University of North Carolina, 1980); and Mary Beth Norton, *Liberty's Daughters: the Revolutionary Experience of American Women, 1750–1800* (Boston: Little Brown, 1980).

16. J. David Hacker and Evan Roberts, "Fertility Decline in the United States, 1850–1930: New Evidence from Complete-Count Datasets," *Annales De Demographie Historique* (Paris) 2, no. 138 (June 2019): 143–177, doi: 10.3917/adh.138.0143.9.

17. Jeffrey S. Sartin, "J. Marion Sims, the Father of Gynecology: Hero or Villain?" *Southern Medical Journal* 97, no. 5 (2004). See also Owens, *Medical Bondage*.

18. See Reed, *The Birth Control.*

19. Janice Ruth Wood, *The Struggle for Free Speech in the United States, 1872–1915: Edward Bliss Foote, Edward Bond Foote, and Anti-Comstock Operations*, vol. 6 (New York: Routledge, 2012).

20. Linda Gordon, "Voluntary Motherhood; The Beginnings of Feminist Birth Control Ideas in the United States," *Feminist Studies* 1, no. 3/4 (1973): 5–22, http://www.jstor.org/stable/1566477.

21. Amanda Frisken, *Victoria Woodhull's Sexual Revolution: Political Theater and the Popular Press in Nineteenth-Century America* (Philadelphia: University of Pennsylvania Press, 2011).

22. Roosevelt, Theodore, "Theodore Roosevelt on Motherhood and the Welfare of the State," *Population and Development Review* 13, no. 1 (1987): 141–147, https://doi.org/10.2307/1972126.

23. J. N. Lahey, "The Effect of Anti-Abortion Legislation on Nineteenth-Century Fertility," *Demography* 51, no. 3 (June 2014): 939–948, doi: 10.1007/s13524-014-0293-x.

24. Andrea Tone, *Controlling Reproduction: An American History* (Wilmington, Delaware: S. R. Books, 1997).

25. Syrett, *The Trials of Madame Restell*; and Jennifer Wright, *Madame: The Life, Death, and Resurrection of Old New York's Most Fabulous, Fearless, and Infamous Abortionist* (New York: Hachette, 2023).

26. Dale Cockrell, *Everybody's Doin' It: Sex, Music, and Dance in New York, 1840–1917* (New York: Norton, 2019), 73.

27. Judith Giesberg, *Sex, and the Civil War: Soldiers, Pornography, and the Making of American Morality* (Chapel Hill: the University of North Carolina Press, 2019). For how the Comstock Law has resurfaced in contemporary debates, see the interview with Terry Gross on NPR, "Fresh Air," https://www.npr.org/sections/health-shots/2023/01/17/1149509246/the-u-s-faces-unprecedented-uncertainty-regarding-abortion-law-legal-scholar-say.

28. Bill Greer, "Texas Judge Revives Anthony Comstock's Crusade against Reproductive Freedom," *History News Network*, May 21, 2023, https://historynewsnetwork.org/article/185707.

29. Helen Lefkowitz Horowitz, *Battles Over Sexual Knowledge and Suppression in Nineteenth-Century America* (New York: Knopf, 2002), 385.

30. Nicola Kay Beisel, *Imperiled Innocents: Anthony Comstock and Family Reproduction in Victorian America* (Princeton: Princeton University Press, 1998).

31. Ellen Chesler, *Woman of Valor: Margaret Sanger and the Birth Control Movement in America* (New York: Simon & Schuster, 2007).

32. See "Planned Parenthood & Birth Control History," Gale, https://www.gale.com/primary-sources/womens-studies/collections/planned-parenthood-and-birth-control-history, accessed December 15, 2022.

33. Jessica Arons and Jill E. Adams, "Abortion Law: Roe Was Right, But McRae Was Wrong," *Ms. Magazine*, January 22, 2015, https://msmagazine.com/2015/01/22/abortion-law-roe-was-right-but-mcrae-was-wrong/.

34. Cynthia Greenlee, "The Largely Forgotten History of Abortion Billboard Advertising," *Rewire News Group*, July 30, 2015.

35. Jay Mather, "Anti-abortion protestor," March 23, 1989, Calisphere, https://calisphere.org/item/fe502d41bff84d0eb946a6a01a3a3d98/.

36. Michael Williamson, "A pro-life, anti-abortion rally at the California State Capitol, January 22, 1981, *Sacramento Bee*, http://sacramento.

pastperfectonline.com/photo/5D15AF07-DCC0-429E-8D7A-353669062792.

37. Michael Williamson, "A pro-life, anti-abortion rally at the California State Capitol," January 22, 1981, Calisphere, https://calisphere.org/item/7b57ee3abbca624f6435a156d538fcaf/.

38. "New Law Allows Anti-Abortion Monument at Arkansas Capitol," *Politico*, March 19, 2023, https://www.politico.com/news/2023/03/19/anti-abortion-monument-arkansas-capitol-00087773.

39. Gary Friedman, "Two men with anti-abortion banner watch as bearers carry casket of aborted fetuses to gravesite in Los Angeles, Calif., 1985," October 7, 1985, UCLA Digital Collections https://digital.library.ucla.edu/catalog/ark:/21198/zz0002vk13.

40. https://tessa2.lapl.org/digital/collection/photos/id/28911.

41. Owen Brewer, "Youth group members from Assemblies of God churches gather on the west steps of the California State Capitol to protest abortion, pornography, and drugs," November 28, 1987, Center for Sacramento History, http://sacramento.pastperfectonline.com/photo/B4B9E030-D8F7-499B-9B98-284609642130.

42. Genaro Molina, "Anti-abortion statement," June 12, 1990, Calisphere, https://calisphere.org/item/84b79919a3d6653ac1ac473d7fcaab79/

43. D. A. Grimes, J. D. Forrest, A. L. Kirkman et al., "An Epidemic of Anti-Abortion Violence in the United States," *Obstet Gynecol* 165 (1991): 1263–1268, https://pubmed.ncbi.nlm.nih.gov/1957842/.

44. "Protecting Patients and HealthCare Providers," Department of Justice, https://www.justice.gov/crt/protecting-patients-and-health-care-providers#:~:text=In%201994%2C%20in%20response%20to,obstructive%20conduct%20intended%20to%20injure%2C.

45. Eli L. Rezmovic, "Abortion Clinics: Information on the Effectiveness of the Freedom of Access to Clinic Entrances Act" (United States: Diane, 1999), 2.

46. Owen Brewer, "UC Davis Campus NOW," February 16, 1989, Center for Sacromento History, https://calisphere.org/item/b1cd3c40bd8421d1e6be57ab7815f648/.

47. Ted Sahl, "Protestor for abortion rights," n.d., https://digitalcollections.sjsu.edu/islandora/object/islandora%3A80_630.

48. Robin Toner, "Right to Abortion Draws Thousands to Capital Rally," *New York Times*, April 10, 1989, https://www.nytimes.com/1989/04/10/us/right-to-abortion-draws-thousands-to-capital-rally.html.

49. Comprehensive online search for statistics published by Gretchen Sisson and Katrina Kimport, "Telling Stories about Abortion: Abortion Related Plots in American Film and Television, 1916–2013," *Contraception* 89, no. 5 (May 2014): 413–418.

50. Alessandra Stanley, "Wrought in Rhimes's Image," *New York Times*, September 18, 2014, https://www.nytimes.com/2014/09/21/arts/television/viola-davis-plays-shonda-rhimess-latest-tough-heroine.html?_r=0.

51. For more on the intersection of American music, feminism, songwriting, and women's rights, see Rhae Lynn Barnes, *No Doubt's Tragic Kingdom* (New York: Bloomsbury), forthcoming.

52. Her 1968 album, *Just Because I'm a Woman*, explored this and other themes of premarital sexuality.

53. Music History Calendar, https://calendar.songfacts.com/october/3/6547

54. David Shaw, "Abortion Bias Seeps into News," *Los Angeles Times*, July 1, 1990 (first in a four-part series).

55. Pro-life Action League, https://prolifeaction.org. See also "Marketing Services for Pro-Life Organizations," Choose Life Marketing, https://www.chooselifemarketing.com/who-we-serve/pro-life-marketing/. And "U.S.A. ProLife Donors and Supporters Email/Postal/Phone Mailing list," Mailing List Finder, https://lists.nextmark.com/market;jsessionid=CF9AEAE3437BA72C9F571850298C97F7?page=order/online/datacard&id=325845.

56. See National Right to Life, https://www.nrlc.org/, Prolife Across America, https://prolifeacrossamerica.org/, 40 Days for Life, https://www.40daysforlife.com/en/ among scores of others.

57. See "*Roe v. Wade* and Supreme Court Abortion Cases," Brennan Center for Justice, September 28, 2022, https://www.brennancenter.org/our-work/research-reports/roe-v-wade-and-supreme-court-abortion-cases.

58. *State Reproductive Health Monitor: Legislative Proposals and Actions* 5, no. 4, (December 1994).

59. Robert D. McFadden, Norma McCorvey, "'Roe' in *Roe v. Wade*, is Dead at 69," *New York Times*, February 18, 2017, https://www.nytimes.com/2017/02/18/obituaries/norma-mccorvey-dead-roe-v-wade.html.

60. "Because 'partial-birth' abortion is a nonmedical term coined by opponents of reproductive rights, the crux of the confusion has to do with what the measures aim to out-law, and *when*." See Susan A. Cohen and Rebekah Saul, "The Campaign against 'Partial Birth" Abortion," Guttmacher Institute, https://www.guttmacher.org/sites/default/files/pdfs/pubs/tgr/01/6/gr010606.pdf.

See also Julie Rovner, "'Partial Birth Abortion:' Separating Fact from Spin." NPR, February 21, 2006, https://www.npr.org/2006/02/21/5168163/partial-birth-abortion-separating-fact-from-spin.

61. Susan, Wills, "Partial Birth Abortion: The Writing on the Wall," *United States Conference of Catholic Bishops*, https://www.usccb.org/issues-and-action/human-life-and-dignity/abortion/partial-birth-abortion-the-writing-on-the-wall.

62. Dan Mangus, "Trump: I'll appoint Supreme Court Justices to Overturn *Roe v. Wade* Abortion Case," CNBC, October 19, 2016, https://www.cnbc.com/2016/10/19/trump-ill-appoint-supreme-court-justices-to-overturn-roe-v-wade-abortion-case.html. See also Sarah Bailey, "White Evangelicals Voted Overwhelmingly for Donald Trump, Exit Polls Show," *Washington Post,* November 9, 2016.

63. Asha C. Gilbert, "After Miscarriage, Woman is Convicted of

Manslaughter," *USA Today*, October 21, 2021, https://www.usatoday.com/story/news/nation/2021/10/21/oklahoma-woman-convicted-of-manslaughter-miscarriage/6104281001/.

64. Pam Belluck, "Judge Invalidates F.D.A. Approval of the Abortion Pill Mifepristone," April 18, 2023, https://www.nytimes.com/2023/04/07/health/abortion-pills-ruling-texas.html.

65. See Decca Muldowney, "Inside the Secretive Network of Abortion Pill Vigilantes," *The Daily Beast*, May 23, 2023, https://www.thedailybeast.com/abortion-pill-vigilantes-are-operating-a-covert-network-from-mexico-to-republican-states; and Stephanie Taladrid, "The Post-Roe Abortion Underground," *New Yorker*, October 10, 2022.

66. "America's Abortion Quandary, "Pew Research Center, May 6, 2022, https://www.pewresearch.org/religion/2022/05/06/americas-abortion-quandary/.

67. Ninety-seven percent of all unsafe abortions occur outside of the United States in developing nations, with over one-half taking place in Asia.

68. The latest totals do not include figures from California, Maryland, or New Hampshire, which did not report data to the CDC, https://www.cdc.gov/mmwr/volumes/70/ss/ss7009a1.htm.

69. Jeff Diamant and Besheer Mohamed, "What the Data Says About Abortion in the U.S.," January 11, 2023, https://www.pewresearch.org/fact-tank/2022/06/24/what-the-data-says-about-abortion-in-the-u-s-2/.

70. Katherine Kortsmit, PhD, Michele G. Mandel, Jennifer A. Reeves et al., "Morbididity and Mortality weekly Report," CDC, https://www.cdc.gov/mmwr/volumes/70/ss/ss7009a1.htm.

71. "How the Issue of Abortion Touches Americans Personally," Pew Research Center, May 6, 2022, https://www.pewresearch.org/religion/2022/05/06/how-the-issue-of-abortion-touches-americans-personally/.

72. R. K. Jones and J. Jerman, "Population Group Abortion Rates and Lifetime Incidence of Abortion: United States, 2008–2014," AJPH,

November 8, 2017, https://ajph.aphapublications.org/doi/10.2105/AJPH.2017.304042

73. Rebecca H. Cohen and Stephanie B. Teal, "Medication Abortion," *JAMA Français* 328, no. 17 (2022): 1779–1779.

74. Rachel K. Jones, Elizabeth Nash, Lauren Cross et al., "Medication Abortion Now Accounts for More Than Half of All U.S. Abortions," Guttmacher Institute, February 24, 2022, https://www.guttmacher.org/article/2022/02/medication-abortion-now-accounts-more-half-all-us-abortions.

75. "Surgical Abortion (First Trimester)," UCLA Health, https://www.uclahealth.org/medical-services/obgyn/family-planning/patient-resources/surgical-abortion-first-trimester.

76. Rachel K. Jones, Elizabeh Witwer, and Jenna Jerman, "Abortion Incidence and Service Availability in the United States, Guttmacher Institute, September 2019, https://www.guttmacher.org/report/abortion-incidence-service-availability-us-2017.

77. "The Availability and Use of Medication Abortion," KFF, June 1, 2023, https://www.kff.org/womens-health-policy/fact-sheet/the-availability-and-use-of-medication-abortion/.

78. "Whitmer Files Lawsuit and Uses Executive Authority to Protect Legal Abortion in Michigan," April 7, 2022, https://www.michigan.gov/whitmer/news/press-releases/2022/04/07/whitmer-files-lawsuit-and-uses-executive-authority-to-protect-legal-abortion-in-michigan.

79. "Abortion," World Health Organization, November 25, 2021, https://www.who.int/news-room/fact-sheets/detail/abortion

80. https://www.healthaffairs.org/doi/10.1377/hlthaff.2021.01528 and https://www.federalreserve.gov/publications/2021-economic-well-being-of-us-households-in-2020-dealing-with-unexpected-expenses.htm

81. Foster, *The Turnaway Study*.

82. Linda Greenhouse, "Adjudging a Moral Harm to Women from Abortions," *New York Times*, April 20, 2007. https://www.nytimes.com/2007/04/20/us/20assess.html

83. Terry Gross, "Study Examines the Lasting Effects of Having—Or Being Denied—An Abortion," *NPR*, June 16, 2020, https://www.npr.org/2020/06/16/877846258/study-examines-the-lasting-effects-of-having-or-being-denied-an-abortion.

84. C. Dehlendorf, L. H. Harris, and T. A. Weitz, "Disparities in Abortion Rates: A Public Health Approach," *Am J Public Health* 103, no. 10 (October 2013): 1772–1779, doi: 10.2105/AJPH.2013.301339.

85. Katherine Kortsmith, Michele G. Mandel, and Jennifer A. Reeves et al., Morbidity and Mortality Weekly Report," CDC, November 26, 2021, https://www.cdc.gov/mmwr/volumes/70/ss/ss7009a1.htm.

86. Katherine Kortsmith, Michele G. Mandel, and Jennifer A. Reeves et al., "Abortion Surveillance—United States, 2019," PMSS *Surveillance Summaries* 70, no. 9 (2021): 1–20, doi: http//dx.doi.org/10.15585/mmwr.ss7009a.

87. "Pregnancy Mortality," CDC, https://www.cdc.gov/reproductive-health/maternal-mortality/pregnancy-mortality-surveillance-system.htm?CDC_AA_refVal=https%3A%2F%2Fwww.cdc.gov%2Freproductivehealth%2Fmaternalinfanthealth%2Fpregnancy-mortality-surveillance-system.htm.

Round Table on *Roe v. Wade*
Fifty Years After

September 8, 2022 — *Cambridge, Massachusetts*

MODERATORS

Rhae Lynn Barnes is an assistant professor at Princeton University and the Sheila Biddle Ford Foundation Fellow at the Hutchins Center for African and African American Research at Harvard University (2022–23). Her research centers on the relationship between state power, popular culture, material culture, and the construction of public discourses about race, gender, and sexuality. She was the 2020 President of the Andrew W. Mellon Society of Fellows in Critical Bibliography. She is co-editor of *After Life: A Collective History of Loss and Redemption in Pandemic America* (2022) and author, most recently, of *Darkology: When the American Dream Wore Blackface* (forthcoming). She served as executive advisor to Henry Louis Gates Jr. for the award-winning PBS documentary series *Reconstruction: America After the Civil War.*

Catherine Clinton holds the Denman Chair of American History at the University of Texas in San Antonio and is a professor emerita of Queen's University Belfast. She is the author or editor of more than thirty books, including *Harriet Tubman: The Road to Freedom*

(2004), *Mrs. Lincoln: A Life* (2008), and *Stepdaughters of History* (2016). She is a founding co-editor of the University of Georgia Series *History in the Headlines* and edited its first volume *Confederate Statues and Memorialization* (2019). Clinton served as a consultant for Steven Spielberg's *Lincoln* (2012) and was awarded a Guggenheim Fellowship in 2016. She has served as president of the Southern Historical Association and the Southern Association for Women Historians. She is an elected member of the Society of America Historians and the Texas Institute of Letters.

PANELISTS

Fiona de Londras, who grew up in Ireland, is a professor of Global Legal Studies at Birmingham Law School. Her research concerns constitutionalism, human rights, and transnationalism. She is an editor of the *Human Rights Law Review* and former editor of the *Irish Yearbook of International Law* and *Legal Studies*. She is an Honorary Professor at the Australian National University, a member of the Executive Committee of the Society of Legal Scholars, an affiliate of the Oxford Human Rights Hub, and a senior associate of the Global Justice Lab at the Munk School of Global Affairs and Public Policy in the University of Toronto. In 2017, she was awarded the Philip Leverhulme Prize in Law. De Londras is the author of "Constitutionalizing Fetal Rights: A Salutary Tale from Ireland." (2016) and the co-author of *Repealing the 8th: Reforming Irish Abortion Law* (2018).

Alicia Gutierrez-Romine, at the time of the round table, was an assistant professor of U.S. history at La Sierra University in Riverside, California. She is now an associate professor of history at California

State University, San Bernadino. Her research focuses on California, the American West, the U.S.-Mexico border, and the history of medicine. Dr. Gutierrez-Romine's current research explores the life and activism of Dr. Edna L. Griffin, the first Black woman physician in Pasadena, and her role in the Civil Rights movement in Southern California in the 1930s and 1940s. Her manuscript, *From Back Alley to the Border: Criminal Abortion in California, 1920–1969* (2020) traces the history of a medical procedure from the proverbial "back alley" to the U.S.-Mexico border. This innovative work describes in detail what happened in California when medicine became subject to atypical legislation.

Deirdre Cooper Owens was formerly the Charles and Linda Wilson Professor in the History of Medicine and Director of the Humanities in Medicine program at the University of Nebraska-Lincoln. Since the round table, she has joined the Department of History at the University of Connecticut. A popular public speaker, she has published essays, book chapters, and blog pieces on issues that concern the African American experiences. Her first book, *Medical Bondage: Race, Gender and the Origins of American Gynecology* (2017), won the 2018 Darlene Clark Hine Award from the OAH as the best book written in African American women's and gender history. Professor Cooper Owens is also the director of the Program in African American History at the Library Company of Philadelphia, one of the country's oldest cultural institutions.

Johanna Schoen, who grew up in Germany, is a professor of history at Rutgers University-New Brunswick with an affiliation at the Institute for Health, Health Care Policy, and Aging Research. She is the author of two books: *Choice and Coercion: Birth Control,*

Sterilization, and Abortion in Public Health and Welfare in the Twentieth Century (2005) and *Abortion after Roe* (2015), which won the William H. Welch Medal of the American Association for the History of Medicine. In addition, she has edited an anthology on *Abortion Care as Moral Work: Ethical Considerations of Maternal and Fetal Bodies* (2022). For the past decades, she has worked with abortion providers to preserve the history of legal abortion in the United States and to use historical analysis and insights to help preserve access to abortion care. Her current work explores the history of neonatology. In her spare time, Schoen volunteers at Memorial Sloan Kettering Cancer Center where she is a co-chair of the Patient and Family Advisory Council, the Ethics Committee, and the LGBTQ Committee and works on improving end-of-life conversations between clinicians, patients, and caregivers.

Salamishah Tillet is the Henry Rutgers Professor of African American Studies and Creative Writing and the director of Express Newark, a center for socially engaged art and design at Rutgers University-Newark. She is the co-founder of the nonprofit organization A Long Walk Home. She is the author of *Sites of Slavery: Citizenship and Racial Democracy in the Post-Civil Rights Imagination* (2012) and *In Search of 'The Color Purple': A Story of an American Masterpiece* (2021). A much sought-after commentator, Tillet won the Pulitzer Prize for Criticism in 2022 for her writing in the *New York Times* for "learned and stylish writing about Black stories in art and popular culture—work that successfully bridges academic and nonacademic critical discourse."

Karin Wulf is the Beatrice and Julio Mario Santo Domingo Director and Librarian of the John Carter Brown Library (JCB) and a professor of history at Brown University. Wulf is an historian of gender, family, and politics in eighteenth-century British America, Wulf earned her PhD at Johns Hopkins University. Her current book *Lineage: Genealogy and the Power of Connection in Early America* is forthcoming from Oxford University Press. Before coming to the JCB and Brown in 2021, she was the executive director of the Omohundro Institute of Early American History and Culture (2013–21) and a professor of history at William and Mary.

BARNES: Good morning! Thank you so much for joining us at "History in the Headlines" with the University of Georgia Press. My name is Rhae Lynn Barnes. I am a professor of American Cultural History at Princeton University and a research fellow at the Hutchins Center at Harvard University.

The impetus for this project came from a need to create a document that instructors could use in classrooms to explain—not just the history of *Roe v. Wade* (1973) and abortion in America in light of *Dobbs v. Jackson Women's Health Organization* (2022)—but to help Americans understand a more extended history of reproduction and the fight for reproduction rights. From our teaching, we know that students arrive in the classroom with a range of knowledge, not just incorrect information about this history, but also, perhaps, no knowledge or introduction to the history of abortion at all. The history of abortion or reproduction might have been a taboo subject they never encountered in an American history class. And so, we are trying to create something accessible and stimulating to help Americans begin to understand this complex story.

We hope that this will be an organic conversation. Feel free to jump in if someone says something exciting or relevant to you.

Let's go around the room and introduce ourselves.

CLINTON: Before we move along, I'd like to say a word as co-editor.

BARNES: Yes. Of course. Sorry, I thought you'd hop in as we go around.

CLINTON: This series was founded on the principle of getting diverse points of view and lively engagement on a topic that comes out in the headlines into the hands of the general reader because we increasingly see a turn toward public-facing scholarship in our role as professional historians. So that is a very important thing.

I have edited other series, and I worked widely in public history, film consults, et cetera. Yet, I'm really proudest of the books in this series. During controversy, we did [the round table on] Confederate statues and memorialization (2017, published in 2019). Then we got out another volume during an election year (2020)—a book on voter suppression in the United States with Stacey Abrams as one of our round table participants.

We thank all of you for taking the time to come here. It's a busy time for everyone. It is a demanding time on this topic. And thank you so much.

BARNES: Yes. Especially at the beginning of the school year. Thank you.

DE LONDRAS: Should I go first?

BARNES: Sure.

DE LONDRAS: I'm Fiona de Londras. I am the professor of Global Legal Studies at the University of Birmingham in the United Kingdom. I work, among other things, on legal regulation of abortion, and particularly on the transnational movement of national arguments around legal regulation, in respect of which post-*Roe* arguments in the U.S. have been extremely influential in developing law in other jurisdictions and in limiting the development of international law. So that's why I'm here.

BARNES: Excellent. Welcome!

SCHOEN: I'm Johanna Schoen. I'm a Professor of History at Rutgers University. I have written two books on the history of birth control, sterilization and abortion, and abortion since legalization.[1] I recently edited a reader about abortion care as moral work that includes essays from abortion providers and other people discussing the moral and ethical issues surrounding abortion care.[2] I'm now working on the history of neonatal intensive care units, which actually has much more overlap than people think.

COOPER OWENS: Hello! I'm Deirdre Cooper Owens. I'm the Charles and Linda Wilson Professor in the History of Medicine. I also direct the medical humanities program at the University of Nebraska, Lincoln. If that's not enough, I have *another* job directing the African American history program at the Library Company of Philadelphia.

I write about the history of reproductive medicine—mainly the history of gynecology in the modern United States—solely focusing on the nineteenth century. I do a lot of public interfacing work around reproductive justice issues. And so, although I'm constantly advocating for Black women and people to have quality healthcare and for their lives to be saved, at the center of this is about medical access and bodily autonomy. One of my newest book projects will be looking at the history of the C-section in the United States, specifically focusing on Louisiana's role. It's surprisingly unchanging. Thank you very much.

BARNES: Welcome.

---

1 Schoen, *Choice and Coercion*; and Johanna Schoen, *Abortion After Roe* (Chapel Hill: University of North Carolina Press, 2015).

2 Johanna Schoen, ed., *Abortion Care as Moral Work: Ethical Considerations of Maternal and Fetal Bodies* (New Brunswick, N.J.: Rutgers University Press, 2022).

WULF: I'm Karin Wulf, and I'm the director and librarian at the John Carter Brown Library and a professor of history at Brown University. I'm an early Americanist, broadly speaking, but my research focus is on British America. And particularly—from my very first projects through the one I am finishing right now—on family, sexuality, and gender and the state regulation thereof.

TILLET: Impressive group here! My name is Salamishah Tillet. I am the Henry Rutgers Professor of Creative Writing and Africana Studies at Rutgers University. I am also a contributing critic-at-large at the *New York Times*. I write about race, gender, politics, and culture, and am an activist. In 2003, my sister Scheherazade and I started A Long Walk Home, a nonprofit that uses art to empower young people to end violence against girls and women. I'm working on a project called *In Lieu of the Law: #MeToo and the Politics of Justice* that examines Me Too as the world's largest social media movement and its cultural and legal impact on the United States.

BARNES: Amazing. Professor Alicia Gutierrez-Romine will be joining us when her delayed plane gets here. We'll have her introduce herself. She is doing innovative work on the history of abortion in the American West, especially in California, and also the history of women who would travel to Mexico in the mid-twentieth century to receive reproductive medical care and abortions when it was illegal in the United States.

CLINTON: And she works on the racial and class aspects of access to abortion. We decided to begin by asking everyone a question that *didn't* appear on the prompts that we sent out. And we find that—

SCHOEN: Well, that seems a little unfair!

WULF: Oh, no.

BARNES: Surprise!

CLINTON: I will throw my answer out; so you can think about it. So, the question is: when did you *first* learn about *Roe v. Wade*, and what was your response to it?

I was not very far from this particular room at the Hutchins Center. I was at Harvard as an undergraduate and graduated the year of *Roe v. Wade* in 1973.[3] During my college years, there was no birth control allowed. There was no abortion allowed. So, the *Roe v. Wade* decision made headlines. It made us all stand up and think about how wonderful it was to have this kind of brave new move forward. So, my response was ecstatic.

Then, of course, as a scholar, and moving on in my career and working in women's history, race history, et cetera, the politics of sexuality, it was to my great chagrin that within eighteen months . . . I was raped and might have needed this particular policy. But it made me much more aware of the connections between control of the body, the law, and what shaped women's lives.

So since that period, I've been writing about it, thinking about it, and over forty years later, when I became president of a history organization [the Southern Historical Association], I called attention to this issue: we had to focus on campuses, from sexual harassment to protecting women's rights.[4] They're all interwoven. But most of us in this room are thinking about our response to the overturn of *Roe v. Wade*.[5] It's 49 years . . . 50

---

3 *Roe v. Wade* 410 U.S. 113, Appendix A.

4 Catherine Clinton, "The Southern Social Network," *Journal of Southern History* 83, no. 1 (February 2017): 7–36.

5 *Dobbs v. Jackson Women's Health Organization* 597 US (2022), Appendix B.

years in 2023. And that's my response. I was elated. Now, we'd like to hear your reflections.

DE LONDRAS: That is actually such a great question. I love it.

WULF: Yes. It is a great question.

DE LONDRAS: Very nice.

WULF: I was nine years old in 1973, living in Pittsburgh. My mom was a classic white middle-class lady engaged in the feminist politics of that era via the National Women's Political Caucus and other groups. She was super engaged with the Equal Rights Amendment [ERA].

I don't remember learning about *Roe*, per se. What I remember is that women's bodily autonomy and sexuality were always connected to equal rights and always connected to law. When my mom and her friends and colleagues were agitating for the Equal Rights Amendment—a huge, huge part of my childhood—when the kind final collapse came, we moved to Florida partly because my Mom was lobbying the Florida state legislature.

The collapse of the ERA was a really big deal for us. But I don't remember when *Roe* and the ERA, and women's rights and sexuality being regulated by law, was ever *not* a part of my consciousness.

And as a historian, I became super interested in why and how the state is always invested in regulating families and regulating women's sexuality in different contexts. So in my case— early America—I was like, *why* are these empires always focused on women? Why are they *always* focused on regulating women's sexuality? Why is *that* the business of government, from the time that I'm interested in the eighteenth century?

COOPER OWENS: Yeah, it's a good question 'cause I have no date to pinpoint. I was born in 1972. I've always known a world where *Roe v. Wade* was just a part of the lexicon. But I do remember I started school in Washington, D.C. So, my parents, especially my father, looked at many news programs. I would hear these things dealing with women and abortion. And my mother has a degree in science, so she taught me technical terms. But much of my thinking around *Roe v. Wade*, quite honestly, came more from the church and conversations in Black churches around whether it was sinful or not. And *it* means *abortion*.

When I was in college and went to a Black women's college in Greensboro, North Carolina, Bennett College, we had much more extensive conversations. I'm not going to say they were necessarily nuanced, but they were extensive. I was able to understand cell development biologically. I was able to talk with women who had abortions. And then I remember this conversation pivoted towards the center when Supreme Court nominee Clarence Thomas and attorney Anita Hill had the hearings [1991], and sexual harassment and abortion came to the forefront. It seemed all of those things were intertwined.

And so that was the first moment, I think, where I started to think of myself as a feminist. And I still kind of wonder whether I was a womanist or not.[6] 'Cause that was the other part of it, this was the early 1990s. But to really *think* of myself as a feminist and what abortion might mean for me on a very personal level. By the time I got to a Ph.D. program in the early 2000s, I was pretty clear on the history of it.

I *never* thought for a moment *Roe* would be overturned. And so that's something that I'm reconciling now.

---

6 A form of feminism that emphasizes women's natural contribution to society—used by some in distinction to the term *feminism* and its primary association with white women.

How do you teach it to students? How do you teach this thing that always was to you but has now become past?

SCHOEN: I was born in 1963 and grew up in Germany. And I was going to look up when abortion became legal in Germany because you asked the story, and I don't know. But suffice it to say that from my earliest consciousness, abortion was always legal. And I always knew and was very aware that, should I ever get pregnant and not want the pregnancy, I could have an abortion, and it wouldn't be an issue. And contraceptives were pretty accessible, so there was no issue about getting them. Then I came to the U.S. for graduate school. I came to Chapel Hill, North Carolina. I came out, and somehow I became a feminist. It's not that I wasn't a feminist before, but it was like this whole world change, and it was a whole epiphany.

I came to the U.S. because I wanted to study U.S. women's history. Somebody sent me to the Southern Oral History Collection. And they have all these interviews with textile workers, and these textile workers all had ten children. For me, as a German, that was just weird. I was like, "Where is the birth control? Where is everything else?" And so that's how I got to study birth control, and then sterilization and abortion fell just into it.

I really came to an understanding and meaning of it all through an intellectual path more than anything else. Because I spent most of my life dating women, the issues that have to do with "Am I pregnant?" are not issues for me. The one thing that was really interesting to me, and kind of funny, is that I wrote the book about the history of abortions since *Roe* never having had or seen an abortion. I became friends with a number of abortion providers, including a physician who is now retired but who provided abortion care first in George Tiller's clinic and then in Albuquerque.

So, she performed abortions for fetal indication patients, for instance, often later in pregnancy.[7]

And after the book came out, she said, "Oh, you should come and shadow me." And I went down there and shadowed her for three days. And I was really interested to see the difference between the products of conception from an early abortion compared to a fetus from an abortion later in pregnancy. I remember being curious about the differences, observing it all, and being relieved that seeing fetal remains at different stages of pregnancy did not lead me to change my mind about abortion. And I didn't think it was going to—but you never quite know. And that was something that only happened about a decade ago.

DE LONDRAS: So, in contrast, I think, and strangely for someone who also didn't grow up in the U.S., *Roe* v. *Wade* has *always* been part of my life. I was born in Ireland in 1980. And in 1983, we had a referendum, which obviously I couldn't vote in—I was only two!—that introduced into the Irish Constitution a prohibition on abortion—the eighth Amendment—and established the "equal," as it said, the "equal right to life of the unborn with the mother."[8]

From two and a half years of age until thirty-eight, I lived in a country where abortion was almost completely illegal. And that connects with *Roe* because, in Ireland, *Roe* became seen as the salutary lesson of what would happen, at least for some conservative activists (which in the eighties was *everybody* in Ireland); *Roe* became the lesson of what happens if you didn't intervene and

---

7 George Tiller, a physician in Wichita, Kansas, was a nationally recognized abortion doctor who ran one of the only clinics providing late-term pregnancy termination. He was assassinated in 2009 by an anti-abortion terrorist while at church.

8 Fiona de Londras and Mairead Enright, *Repealing the 8th: Reforming Irish Abortion Law* (Bristol: Policy Press, 2018).

prevent 'judicial activism' that would permit or develop access to abortion.

So, of course, abortion was unlawful. It had been since 1861.[9] There was never a debate in Ireland since we got our independence about legalizing abortion. But we had had a case in '73, the case of *McGee v. the Attorney General*, where contraception was legalized for married people in Ireland.[10] And, of course, the argument was that *Griswold*[11] led to *Roe*; therefore, *McGee* will lead to something like a *Roe* in Ireland.

So, the entire country that I lived in, everything about reproduction was really dominated by Augustinian Catholic doctrine because of how Ireland was at the time, but it also had this kind of shadowy imprint of *Roe* all over it. And as I got older, I began to see that it wasn't that shadowy. Some anti-abortion activists in America quickly identified Ireland as a country where they could try to prove that you could do what they had failed to do here in the U.S.: namely, a constitutional amendment that would protect fetal life.

We can talk about it later. But anti-abortion activists came over from the U.S.; they did lessons, they taught activists, and they wrote drafts of the Amendment. Ireland's Eighth Amendment is a product of *Roe*. So, at eight years old in school, being shown *The Silent Scream* as a child is a product of *Roe*.[12] And then, at nine-

9 Offenses against the Person Act 1861, U.K. Public General Acts 1861 c. 100

10 *McGee v. The Attorney General* (1973) IR 284, a case in the Irish Supreme Court recognizing a right to marital privacy.

11 *In Griswold v. Connecticut* 381 U.S. 479 (1965), the Supreme Court ruled that a state's ban on contraceptives violated the right to marital privacy.

12 *The Silent Scream* is a 1984 anti-abortion short film depicting an abortion through an ultrasound recording. The film director Jack Daniels and the narrator

teen, during the first year of law school, doing constitutional law, the Eighth Amendment, where did it come from? *Oh*! We learned from America. It was presented as if that was just totally normal at the time, of course. So yeah, I feel like I grew up in a kind of anti-*Roe* world, even though it wasn't expressly articulated in that way in everyday life.

BARNES: Jim Downs is the Series Co-Editor with Catherine. Jim, do you want to share when you first learned about *Roe v. Wade*?

DOWNS: I was born the day before *Roe v. Wade*! So, I also didn't really know a world without it. But I don't want to disrupt the transcription. If you want coffee, just please raise your hand.

BARNES: Well, you can hop in whenever you do have something to say.

DOWNS: Thank you so much for doing this. I just want to say this is really a wonderful group. Say whatever you want to say whenever you want to say it. If you need anything, just let me know. Alicia's on her way, so I'm going to meet her downstairs in two seconds.

SCHOEN: Thank you so much for getting us coffee!

CLINTON: Your turn, Rhae Lynn.

BARNES: *Roe v. Wade* was only ever framed as a religious and political war. I was born into Reagan-era Orange County.

CLINTON: California?

Bernard Nathanson claimed that the fetus can be visibly seen making cries and screams of pain proving fetal life. It was widely shown by churches, schools, and anti-abortion campaigns internationally to children and teenagers to argue for abstinence until marriage and to recruit for the anti-abortionist activist cause. It rhetorically shifted abortion debates away from the safety for women post-*Roe*, now that they could receive proper medical care after the era of back alley abortions, onto a claim that regardless of the mother's situation, the fetus is being tortured to death (and thus, was alive since conception).

BARNES: Correct. Orange County, California. I didn't understand what abortion was until I was much older. Abortion was framed as an unmentionable thing I would hear about in whispers. My grandmother, who was very active in the Baptist Church, would allude to the fact that she had a sister who died in her mid-twenties during the Great Depression. I was told this sister was married, had a daughter or two, and found out she was pregnant again. They struggled financially during the Depression and couldn't provide for another child. And so, some sort of botched home abortion took place when it was illegal in the United States, but the family said an ectopic pregnancy exacerbated it. I remember looking at photographs of her. She was gorgeous. But her life was always presented with a strange warning.

I also remember my grandma conveying that her sister's cause of death was controversial and that her family wouldn't discuss it, but they were grateful that the death certificate did not reveal how she died. There was thankfulness that this coroner concealed the actual cause of death. As a historian, I think about how they changed the official historical record, but the story of what happened to her came down to me through oral history from women in my family.

And growing up in Orange County in the moment I did was quite strange. Most people have a particular idea through cultural representation of it being this hyper-white, rich, blonde beach town place. Yes, I was in the Orange County that loved John Wayne and Ronald Reagan. But I was living in and spending most of my time between Anaheim, Santa Ana, and Garden Grove, which are very diverse. Santa Ana, where I attended high school, is majority Mexican American. Westminster is where a significant number of Vietnam War refugees were relocated. I attended a wide range of church services, from Lutheran to Baptist, and bounced between megachurches. Extended family were members of Saddleback or the Crystal Cathedral, and then going with Black neighbors to places like Melodyland, where I was getting different denominations' interpretations of the Bible and what abortion was and could mean. Ultimately my parents left the Baptist and Catholic churches they were raised in due to gender and LGBTQ issues. Our political values in women's rights and faith did not fit in with those denominations. And so that was always very confusing. There were stories about disco abortions in the seventies! Just wild warning stories, especially in youth groups or in Christian summer Bible school camps.

But when I formally learned about *Roe v. Wade* as a legal and existing constitutional right that belonged to me, I was 14. I met Helen Thomas [a journalist and White House Press Corps member from the Kennedy to Obama administrations] in Washington, D.C. My Mom knew I loved history and would buy me women's history books. And that was the beginning of learning the intellectual tradition of not just *Roe v. Wade* but the Equal Rights Amendment, women's suffrage, and the social and legal history of women's rights.

TILLET: I was born in 1975 in Boston, Massachusetts. And I think I first learned about *Roe* from my mother, and it was just in a general conversation about coming of age and sexuality. She didn't talk to me about abortion with any sense of stigma or shame, which I now fully appreciate. But, I do not know the exact moment that I learned of *Roe*, partly because it was always there as a right that I could freely exercise or take for granted. Either way, my understanding of it was shaped by my mother, who did have an abortion when she was an adult, as a matter of choice.

It was during my senior year of high school, from 1991 to 1992, that I became politically passionate about reproductive freedoms. First, that fall with the Clarence Thomas confirmation hearings and Professor Anita Hill's allegations of sexual harassment against him. I was only 17-years-old, but I was struck by how easily her story and her racial identity were dismissed. I had read Toni Morrison's *The Bluest Eye* and Alice Walker's *The Color Purple* for the first time the summer before hearings, so my feminist awakening had already begun that August but was sped up by the cruel disregard for Hill.

A few months later, I interned at the National Organization for Women [1966–present], also known as NOW, and I began organizing specifically around issues that impacted women, girls, and their families, and that's when I first learned of the legal and political history of *Roe v. Wade*. The all-white, all-male Senate judiciary committee that questioned Hill and the subsequent public backlash against her also sparked the "Year of the Woman," in which an unprecedented number of women ran for political office, and I worked on a congressional campaign too. In that context, *Roe* was not just something my mother believed was a fundamental right, but I did too. I left high school primed with language and policies of feminism.

But, during my first year in college, and then again when I went on a study abroad program during my junior year, I was sexually assaulted. I did not have to have an abortion due to either of those traumas, but it did make me even more of a zealot about women and girls having full bodily and sexual autonomy. My healing and activism also led me to move from *choice* as a framework to the more holistic model of what Loretta Ross calls *reproductive justice.*

I attended "The March for Women's Lives" in 2004 with a group of my Black feminist friends, including filmmaker Aishah Shahidah Simmons,[13] and I think even then, for all of us who grew up with *Roe*, we knew it was a possibility that we might lose this right, but also, it felt like it could never happen. I wear a hanger necklace as a daily reminder of where we've been and in protest of where we are now.

SCHOEN: I'm probably stating the obvious, but because we're all here and we are all women who have careers, all of us could get the education we wanted and then proceed with whatever we wanted to do. That was so much premised on the fact that we have access to reproductive choice.

CLINTON: At the same time, the protection by law and the issue of the law leads us into what the history of abortion has been. Most of us in the field know the great fabrications being done by. . . Injustice by justices. So, we thought it would be good if we could at least lay the groundwork for our later discussion about how the law changes culture and how the culture changes law.

If we could begin by looking at the early American example, we can maybe ask you, Karin, if you—

SCHOEN: And Karin, can you do me a favor? One of the things that always irked me about the majority decision in *Dobbs* is that when they did their legal research, they looked for the word "abortion."

---

13 Simmons produced, wrote, and directed the film: *NO! The Rape Documentary*: a 2006-released, Ford Foundation-funded, groundbreaking feature-length film that focuses on intra-racial rape of Black girls and women, healing, and accountability through the first-person testimonies, scholarship, spirituality, activism, and cultural work of Black people in the United States.

So maybe, among many other things, you can talk about the words that were used.

COOPER OWENS: Yes.

WULF: Yeah, yeah, sure. There's so much to say. So, you're going to have to give me this!

BARNES: Go for it!

WULF: And, because I am on such a quest. "Have soapbox, will travel!" with passion about the importance of early America because I feel like there's so much about this early period that's foundational in the United States. And it's foundational for the kind of polemical understanding of America in the United States, but it's actually also structurally foundational.

I've brought my soapbox right here! I think there's a lot to say about the early history of abortion in early America. The key thing is that women have *always* sought reproductive control.

And we can find that, even in the very limited source materials that directly address what we would now call abortion. That is, that if you try to find a history of something that is not recorded in traditional histories, then you can't just say the history didn't exist. What you say is that the source material doesn't speak to it.

But we know from the kinds of sources that we have that, of course, women have always sought reproductive control.

There are great examples. I could give you an example of a woman who was a medic in mid-eighteenth-century Philadelphia who kept a medical recipe book, who wrote in the 1750s about when she was a young woman in the 1720s, maybe 1730s, and discovered she was pregnant before quickening. So maybe at the very end of the first trimester.

BARNES: Can you explain what quickening is?

WULF: Quickening was the idea in early America before we had the clear medical understanding that we now have of what pregnancy is, that no one knew they were pregnant *for sure* until they felt the child move. And for those of us who have felt pregnant, it is a very weird feeling. It feels like butterflies in your stomach, except they are bigger butterflies! But it's this moment of quickening, this notion that you could *feel in your body* that you were actually pregnant and not something else going on.

And I think that's a key thing because women didn't always know. A million things are going on with women's bodies.

Anyway, this woman had a sense that she was pregnant and that it wasn't a healthy pregnancy. And so, she combined herbs and did a whole variety of different things, and as she said very directly in this recipe book, which is held at the College of Physicians in Philadelphia, "the child came away . . ."

COOPER OWENS: Mmm hmm.

WULF: Many examples exist of women asserting reproductive control in this early period. The history of abortion, women deciding to conclude a pregnancy, is clear even in our limited records. The challenge comes when we try to talk about the law and what the law actually says. I don't know if you want to dive into law now. But women have always asserted reproductive control.

CLINTON: A lot of the arguments about the legal issues in the early republic are quite facetious, in a way. Is that a fair characterization?

WULF: I think they are deceptive.

CLINTON: Deceptive?

WULF: Because of the way that the majority opinion in *Dobbs* is written, it describes a *legal* right to abortion. Then it slides around to talking about whether abortion existed or is a legal right.

But if you don't have a legal prohibition, is a *legal right* the same as a lack of *legal prohibition*?

CLINTON: Mmm hmm.

WULF: I think the language in the *Dobbs* decision is very deceptive about history, both of abortion and the history of the law around women's reproduction in America.

Women's care for their reproductive bodies takes place in the context of a legal regime that thoroughly subordinated women. Under the law of coverture—and important from British law, which to some extent held on through the 1970s—married women could not be treated as independent legal subjects but rather as under the control—under the cover—of their husbands. Men were understood to be the head of the family, and they were empowered legally to act for their wives in a whole host of ways. The logic of coverture, women as subordinate to men, often extended even to unmarried women not technically under this set of laws. The law is also obsessed with legitimacy, so policing women's sexuality to determine or to try to ensure that a baby was born from married parents was intense.

What's so odd then about the history in *Dobbs* is that it doesn't take account of this legal context, which so constrained women and which we have largely discarded, but it does try to focus on a law against abortion, for which there is so little evidence.

CLINTON: As we go into the nineteenth century, there's so much fascinating evidence that women were seeking control. Joanne Freeman comments on early advertisements for remedies that clearly said, "Do not take this if you are pregnant because it could interfere with the pregnancy."[14] What is that but a telegram to medicinal remedy?

14 Heather Cox Richardson and Joanne Freeman, "Encore: Abortion, Whose Choice," *Now and Then* podcast, https://podcasts.apple.com/us/podcast/encore-abortion-whose-choice/id1567665859?i=1000577765842.

WULF: You can see by the 1790s advertisements for not just herbal or plant-based remedies for an unwanted pregnancy but rather interference in the woman's uterus. You can see the so-called French Syringe is being advertised in Philadelphia by the 1790s. In other words, reproductive technology is age-old, usually plant-based, but there is also an increasing advertisement development that is easily aware in print culture by the 1790s.

CLINTON: What about the Civil War? You know all about it, Deirdre.

COOPER OWENS: Yeah. no. Look, everybody comes to me for this. It's interesting because I study enslaved women. Karin brings up a wonderful point. The source material is ambiguous, and it depends on who captured the stories and how it was written. And at least in some of the slave narratives, some of the case books of nineteenth-century doctors . . . then I will move into the Civil War.

But there is this sense, of course, that Black women were blamed for abortions because they had no bodily autonomy.

Everything was controlled by the government, by their masters, by overseers. And the ways enslaved women (and then newly freed Black women) seek out that control is through the search for root doctors and sacred healers. If there has to be an intervention by a formally trained white male physician, Black women are looking at ways where they can at least have a say in what they're ingesting. And so, they're looking for these kinds of herbicides.

I only know about the cotton root that folk used to stop pregnancy. And so often, this is where the source material becomes frustrating for somebody who studies slavery and that period after enslavement. People ask me, "Well, what did they use?" And I am like, "It's *supposed* to be a secret!"

GROUP: Laughter

COOPER OWENS: They don't want us to know! That was the whole point.

You have a gaze and a kind of lens on you. They don't want people to know the actual ingredients. And so that's where Sharla Fett's wonderful book, *Working Cures,* talks about the kind of sacred healing that's integrated.

By the Civil War [1861–1865], you largely have a formalized obstetrics and gynecology field. And so Black women in that really weird space, a limbo between freedom, fugitive, and enslavement, still don't want white medical intervention.

And they're still seeking out Black midwives and nurses. And they're looking at—Karin brings up a great point about reproductive control—but also reproductive *diversity* in terms of the means and methods for controlling your body. Because the one thing they have never controlled, I mean have never had ownership of, was their own bodies. That really doesn't even become a thing; it's not tangible even after slavery ends.

And so, what this conversation historically for me means is that all other women, not just white women, but *all* other women maybe besides indigenous women, are really understanding now, I think in a very real sense, how the history of Black women's bodily control has always been in this nation. In fact, the country has always been invested in Black women having children because of the price tags on their heads. And so now, all of a sudden, people are like, "Wait, what are we going to do?" And it's only been a few centuries since Black women actively controlled their bodies.

WULF: I think part of what's so important here about this early history is that we're actually talking about multiple historical trajectories. We talk about the history of abortion; we're really talking about the development of medicine as a field. We're talking about any kind of scientific understanding of biology, never mind reproductive biology. The history of race, racial regulation, the history of regulating women generally. So, there are multiple things when you talk about the history of abortion; you're really talking about all these conjoined histories. And that's what makes it really complicated to put a finger on some period in the American past and say, "Oh, abortion was like X."

We have to remember that stemming from English common law, married women's bodies, their legal personality was subsumed by that of their husbands under colonial law. Also, in 1662 legislators in Virginia declared that a child born to an enslaved mother inherited the mother's status, regardless of the father's status.

[Alicia Gutierrez-Romine enters.]

GUTIERREZ-ROMINE: And if I could just make a comment.

CLINTON: Please! We're so pleased to have you.

BARNES: Yes, please, welcome.

GUTIERREZ-ROMINE: Sorry, I just got off a plane.

CLINTON: Please, introduce yourself. We also asked everyone when they first learned about *Roe*.

GUTIERREZ-ROMINE: My name's Alicia Gutierrez-Romine. I'm an associate professor of history at La Sierra University. My book is *From Back Alley to the Border: Criminal Abortion in California, 1920 to 1969*.

I was born in 1989. I had never given abortion much thought. I grew up in a religious household and don't remember ever hearing about abortion. Strangely, I remember seeing girls in my religious high school who got pregnant and disappeared as soon as they started to show, but abortion was never discussed. Abstinence was preached regularly! But abortion, no. I had to research and find out how to access birth control independently when I was in college.

I knew abortion was legal, and I knew it was an option, but I never really thought about *Roe* or how it affected women until I began doing my dissertation research. When I began uncovering documents about "illegal operations" in the archives, and once I realized that the term referred to abortion, I suddenly had a flurry of questions come to mind about what *Roe* actually meant and what *Roe* could have done for the many women I ended up writing about.

It just unlocked this whole Pandora's box of questions that I really wanted to answer.

What I was just going to mention is part of the difficulty, I think, in describing what is going on here when we're talking about the history of abortion is not just the time period and all of these interconnected historiographies that we're dealing with, but to speak to something that Deirdre was mentioning earlier, that these are supposed to be "secrets." Not just in terms of what drugs they're using, but this is not a history that we should know and that we are only finding out because we are finding the documentation of instances when things went poorly.

At least in my research, I was using coroners' records. I was using newspaper documents and court records. So had these women had successful and safe abortions, they would have been invisible from the historical record. There is this question "is this my story to tell? How do we do this in a way that is respectful and understanding of the difficult decisions that these women made?" But then also, "What right do people have to be forgotten? And what right do I have as an historian to tell and divulge these stories?" And hopefully, something can be learned and gleaned from it. But it's something that I've been considering ethically since my book came out. I wrote the book. I was so happy it came out. And then, I started understanding some of the ethical questions and debates of my "outing" some of these women and the details of what happened and their death. The very intimate details of their death.

DE LONDRAS: I just had a quick thing to say: the complexity of the histories is also reflected in the legislative record . . . So the court says, "We'll just look at legislation, we'll look at the statutes." But, of course, the statutes, as you said, are not always using the language of "abortion."

They use "child destruction" or "procurement of miscarriage" or other terminologies that are not always sought out in the legal research clerks do for the court.

But the other thing is that because the deployment of history in this kind of reasoning is instrumental, there is no intellectual integrity to uncovering a history's complexities. So that history becomes deployed in this kind of, if I may say, idiosyncratically American jurisprudential tradition of a certain kind of "originalism" as the truth of what the law was at X foundational date.[15]

There is no *truth* about what the law was *per se*. It ignores legal, sociological realities that the law is not just what's written down but also *what happens* with what's written down. And then it ignores the sociological reality of everyday life outside, within and against the law as well. And persons who are not addressed by the law or not recognized in the law.

15 "Originalism is a theory of the interpretation of legal texts, including the text of the Constitution. Originalists believe that the constitutional text ought to be given the original public meaning that it would have had at the time that it became law." See Stephen G. Calabrese, "On Originalism in Constitutional Interpretation," National Constitution Center, https://constitutioncenter.org/the-constitution/white-papers/on-originalism-in-constitutional-interpretation.

SCHOEN: Or, who has no role in making the law.

DE LONDRAS: Of course. Absolutely. No hand in making the law. And one of the interesting things, when I look at abortion law in the United States, is its continuity with this movement in the last couple of decades to really make originalism "the right way" to do constitutional law—which, as I said, is idiosyncratic. But secondly, it goes back again to the kind of legal entrepreneurs in the 1800s in this country. Like Anthony Comstock [1844–1915], who said, "Do you know what? I'm just going to write a law, then I'm going to take it to Washington. I'm going to get these men to pass it."[16] And suddenly, you have a raft of obscenity laws that some guy and his pals just came up with. And that then becomes the historical record...

CLINTON: He saw the male community and invented obscenity issues. And then, all at once, it struck a nerve, and all at once it could serve larger purposes. And remember, you had women without men, thousands. And the marriage possibilities reduce. And women form these communities and flock to settlement houses and become independent from men. And next thing you know, they want to go to college.[17] And...

DE LONDRAS: Where would we be *then*?

SCHOEN: They'll end up in a room at Harvard talking about this.

DE LONDRAS: The horror!

16 Anthony Comstock was an anti-vice crusader who designed laws to prevent the circulation of materials on sexuality, birth control. His "Comstock Law" of 1873 was part of a national campaign to legislate morality.

17 Settlement houses were housing projects established mainly in nineteenth-century American industrial centers to provide educational, recreational, and other social services for low-income and often immigrant families. They were founded and staffed in the main by white educated women seeking social welfare careers.

BARNES: I think Salamishah might be able to speak to how novelists have tried to reckon with this historical absence and the secrets we've been talking about. Do you want to talk about Alice Walker, Tony Morrison, or Zora Neale Hurston's work?

TILLET: I was thinking about this while you were talking and how—and Deirdre's earlier point about how some communities consider abortion a sin? This is especially important when discussing these issues within the context of conservative Black churches—whose members might overwhelmingly vote Democrat but be pro-Dobbs too.

But these debates are not new. There was an emergence of a Black feminist discourse in the 1970s and 1980s around *choice.* Audre Lorde's memoir *Zami: A New Spelling of My Name*, which came out in 1982, but it's really set in the 1950s. Alice Walker's 1976 novel *Meridian*, and then that same year, Ntozake Shange's play *For Colored Girls Who Consider Suicide When the Rainbow's Not Enough*. You have these different instances in which abortion is presented as a *viable* option and a *reasonable choice* for these Black women protagonists.

I think it's interesting to think about this idea of Black women being a historical "ground zero" for all women in our nation who are facing the reality of living without the right to choose—or at least most women in those states that have systemically limited their options and access to abortion.

These Black women writers received considerable backlash for their depictions of gender-based violence and abortion. Because they were writing in and coming out of the Black Power era, in which they were a lot of legitimate emphasis on saving the Black family in the face of white supremacy. Unfortunately, much of the focus was about preserving traditional gender roles, and of course, women being able to control their reproductive fate upsets patriarchy. And our country's history of racial eugenics increased the skepticism about abortion too.

So, to have an abortion risked being seen not just as a sin but a disservice to the Black family and to Black unity. And I think for those Black women writers and activists, like Shirley Chisholm or Flo Kennedy, who were publicly pro-choice, there was always a sense that they were going against the Black community—even as they knew they were trying to save Black women's lives.[18] Fortunately, for a generation of people like me, who grew up with *Roe* and read these books, I began understanding that ending racism meant you had to be pro-choice.

Black women having control over their sexuality and reproduction continues to be a direct challenge to American racism. We cannot forget that our enslaved foremothers and their children were automatically counted as property for white enslavers.

What does it mean that we still fully *haven't* embraced Black feminist discourse around *choice*? This is why I brought up the Anita Hill testimony from 1991—what a missed opportunity for us as a nation to really contend with racism and sexism in real time. And now, look at the Supreme Court. Our inability to think, theorize, and organize *intersectionality* has fractured a constituency and a voting bloc that is pretty liberal.

Abortion is not necessarily a galvanizing topic. But, in

18 Florynce Kennedy (1916–2000) was a lawyer, civil rights activist, and radical feminist, and Shirley Chisholm (1924–2005) was the first African American woman elected to the U.S. Congress, serving seven terms from 1969–1983. Chisholm was also the first African American woman to run for President in 1972.

Mississippi, where Jackson Women's Health Organization is, most of the women getting abortions are Black. So, why did they target that health clinic in *Dobbs*? Because those women were extremely vulnerable and invisible. Abortion is the biggest civil rights issue of our time—but our inability to build anti-racist, anti-sexist coalitions in the age of *Roe*, especially in communities of color, has led us to *Dobbs*.

BARNES: To expand the lens of popular culture, the source base is prolific when mentioning abortion under different names in the nineteenth century. To bridge what Karin was saying with what Deidre was saying—in the 1790s, you do have this flourishing of almanacs. But with the industrial revolution, the use of slave-based cotton, and cotton-based rags that now allow for the ability to make cheap paper, the penny press rose by the 1830s. And there is an explosion of print culture, especially newspapers and magazines, in places like New York City that publish the *Sun* and the *Herald* at an incredibly cheap rate, expanding readership at the moment of mass urbanization.

What I find interesting as someone who studies blackface and popular culture is that there is a rash of daily and weekly papers that are coming out in most urban cities like New York, Philadelphia, and San Francisco, that's commonly called the *Flash Press* or the *Sporting Press*—written for an assumed male readership. Many of these papers are written and edited by blackface celebrities as their day job on the page. The Flash Press is where blackface minstrels—the number one entertainment form in the nineteenth century—are advertising their nightly performances and horse racing, gambling, boxing, and other masculine affairs in this era as the kind of theaters in which blackface is found are presumed male spaces.

In their performances at night on the stage, they are constantly making jokes about Black reproduction and slavery—while in blackface and drag for these predominantly white male audiences. But I want to focus on these newspaper advertisements. All around the performance announcements in antebellum newspapers are advertisements for abortifacients [substances used to terminate a pregnancy] or abortive medication.

Some of the phrases they use include "female monthly pills"; "menstrual regulation pills"; "preventative powders"; "relief pills"; "curing irregularity pills."

By the 1830s and the 1840s, names of women who claimed they could assist were published. Madam Restell is one well-known woman.[19] These ads are normally framed as helping women suffering from menstrual irregularity to "fix" *it*—but in a publication targeted to men! And so, if you were trying to go into a digitized database of newspapers as a researcher and just type in "abortion" into the search engine, you wouldn't get anything. But if you use any of these phrases, you would see that men and women were bombarded daily with an enormous amount of mail-away options that they could get sent to any street in any city, and there was pretty much no regulation of it for decades.

Then you have scintillating collections like *New York by Gaslight*, which are turning well-known prostitution houses into

19 Calling herself a "female physician" and "professor of midwifery," the British-born immigrant to New York began advertising her services in Manhattan papers in 1839. After her arrest for performing an abortion in 1847 and serving a year in jail, she continued a great mail-order business. She was notorious, and Anthony Comstock posed as a customer and bought contraceptives from her in 1878. Before she could be brought to trial, she ended her life. See Syrett, *The Trials of Madame Restell.*

forms of entertainment. They're very gossipy; they're very sensational. They identify notable women by name because, at this moment, women on the stage are considered "public women." Their sexuality and reproduction are recounted in these newspapers as entertainment. Abortions are an extension of that.

Then, as you briefly mentioned, the print culture language flipped around the 1870s because of Comstock Laws [1873] that criminalized the use of the U.S. Postal Service to circulate anything obscene, including content about contraception, sex toys, or abortifacients. There's regulation but not of abortion or abortion products. It's a regulation of what printed material can be sent in the mail. The content becomes vice. Exchanging knowledge becomes vice. So, the wording gets even stranger, and the phrasing vaguer to make it through the censors, but those advertisements are all still physically there. They will not go away in any capacity; it's just new names for abortion and information transmission that changes.[20]

WULF: That's such a great example of how print information in print does not equal either the *presence* of a phenomenon or the *absence* of a phenomenon. And that's true both because the *language* in which people are describing—basically abortion services—changes. The language is suppressed or elevated. But also, because print is either available or not available. So, in the eighteenth century, when there was less print culture, nonetheless, the print culture that is there *still* has evidence of abortifacients fully available.

Benjamin Franklin is publishing information and reproducing it from other sources. We can find this stuff all across the

20 *Griswold v. Connecticut* (1965) essentially nulled this law as it related to contraception.

eighteenth century. Print isn't the core evidence for us of whether abortion is available or not because of these complications with the sources. But when we look at the sources, we find evidence of abortion services across time in what would be the United States.

BARNES: And that it's very, very open.

CLINTON: And, of course, Comstock is so brilliant because he's criminalizing information—you criminalize the spread of information and how you name it. He goes after everything and says, we'll catch something in the net. But by the early twentieth century, especially in urban centers, the sporting life that you're talking about, becomes a center for this information. And it's—

BARNES: *The Police Gazette* alone, yeah.

COOPER OWENS: It's also very ethnic-based. And the new work by Debbie Applegate, *Madam: The Biography of Polly Adler* (2021), looks at that world. Seeing that reproduction is sort of tied in with sexuality in that period and that the women's culture in urban centers really comes out in some of this exciting new work. I learned a lot from Saidiya Hartman's book on Harlem [*Wayward Lives, Beautiful Experiments: Intimate Histories of Social Upheaval*, 2019].

We're learning about things because it's *there*; it's ever-present. Back to the archive. How do we get at it? It is a secret. It's a secret. But we are historians who have been through the secrecy. My first editor said, "Slaves didn't write letters!"

But really, this is it; look at the progress that's been made. But I do also want to get to some of these ideas about too much of the movement being stereotyped and—

SCHOEN: Can I interject, and can we briefly talk about *why* it became illegal in the late nineteenth century and when?

Because that is really important. To tie back into your points, I think it's the increasing publicity about women's sexuality and greater access to education. And the fact that women are moving out of the home and starting to work in the settlement houses that you mentioned before, among many other workplaces. That leads to panic about the women.

BARNES: The women adrift. *Sister Carrie.*[21]

SCHOEN: Yes, to control women and their reproduction. Then, in competition with the emergence of the medical profession, OB-GYNs, in particular, are trying to drive out the regular midwives who are providing legal abortion services, which leads to the slate of anti-abortion laws across the country.

And Karin mentioned earlier that there is no relationship between whether abortion is legal or illegal and whether women are getting abortions or not.

So, women continued to get abortions, and, indeed, until after World War II, they mostly didn't get prosecuted, and the abortion providers didn't get prosecuted. Indeed, especially during the Great Depression, but also before we have the emergence of this phenomenon of people who specialize in providing illegal abortion such as Rickie Solinger's... What was her name?

GUTIERREZ-ROMINE: Ruth Barnett

SCHOEN: Ruth! Thank you so much. Who provides tens of thousands of abortions to women and has an open practice that advertises and does safe abortions.[22] And it is only after World War

21 Joanne J. Meyerowitz, *Women Adrift: Independent Wage Earners in Chicago, 1880–1930* (Chicago: University of Chicago Press, 1987). *Sister Carrie* (1900) is a novel by Theodore Dreiser.

22 Rickie Solinger, *The Abortionist: A Woman Against the Law*, (New York: Free Press, 1995).

II, with the return of the soldiers, and this desire to have women return home and become mothers and be in the kitchen, that we see the systematic prosecution of illegal abortion providers. We see all the terrible outcomes of illegal abortion that eventually need reform. So, I think abortion being illegal doesn't really impact whether you can find the service. And for most of the time period when it's illegal, it is relatively safe. This, I think, is also really important.

COOPER OWENS: I think, too, just to add onto what Johanna said, and Catherine brought up something that I thought was really important when you asked the question around chronology. That's important. And so, I started taking all these notes, everything from my comps [comprehensive examinations for Ph.D. candidacy] spilling out to the page.

BARNES: Give it to us.

COOPER OWENS: I'm thinking antebellum era, when Rhae Lynn brings up the point about the rise of a salacious popular culture around women's sexuality and race. Walter Johnson writes in *Soul by Soul: Life Inside the Antebellum Slave Market* (1999) that there are seven sites of racial reification. And if I were to tweak it and more tightly define it, Walter Johnson is really talking about is the reification of what Blackness *is*, right? It's still ambiguous, but people are trying to figure it out.

And so those kinds of sites of popular communication act as a site of racial reification around Blackness. But also, right at the end of slavery and the rise of Reconstruction, you have the rise of the Ku Klux Klan—not the creation, but the rise of the KKK that happens.

And by the early twentieth century, you have another rise of the KKK. And it is founded on not just racial purity, but how do we control traditional white womanhood?[23] Because we certainly don't want white women acting like these promiscuous, loose Black women and ethnic white women and doing all of these things that give them independence.

So, chronology *matters* here.

And then when we think about the advertisements across the antebellum era through, I'd say, the first maybe quarter of the twentieth century, the first quarter, literacy and what that means for the Black vote. Oftentimes, they may not be the ones picking up the newspaper and reading it, but communication is really community-based.

BARNES: Not a coincidence. This is the moment of lithography, photography, and mass visual reproduction in print.

COOPER OWENS: And so, they're going to know! So, they network. I call it the "gossip grapevine;" and they provide the services you need. And the silence protects that person. It goes back to what Johanna says: these people are known, yet there's silence around it. And so that's, I think, important in that the late-nineteenth-century, early-twentieth-century abortion is just kind of considered this thing that women do. And all of a sudden, you have these very fundamentalist traditional white men and some Black men who then begin a campaign to politicize abortion negatively. And they really have now instituted themselves, not just as the medical providers but also as the moral majority. And that's important as well, to discuss . . .

---

23 See Nancy MacLean, *Behind the Mask of Chivalry: The Making of the Second Ku Klux Klan* (Oxford: Oxford University Press, 1994).

GUTIERREZ-ROMINE: Yeah, because of that . . .

COOPER OWENS: Go ahead.

TILLET: Based on what we've been talking about, it's fascinating to think about how silence and secrecy became stigma and shame. That's a really important distinction.[24]

Also, I've been thinking about how *Roe's* "right to privacy" language might have inadvertently led to feelings of stigma and shame that were then easily co-opted by conservatives. But here we are talking about these networks that used silence *as* resistance. Whose abortion stories should we know, share, and tell are deeply ethical questions. Coming from the anti-sexual violence movement, I appreciate how significant a movement like Me Too initially was.[25] Three years after the Me Too hashtag went viral in 2017, it was, according to the #MeToo Digital Media Collection at Harvard, still used regularly in 85 countries worldwide and in more than 32 million tweets, more than 32 million tweets. And then post-*Dobbs*, we've had moments when people came forward on Twitter and Facebook and posted, "I had an abortion when . . ." But, it is still not as watershed as #MeToo.

One of the most effective tools of the right or the Christian fundamentalists has been weaponizing shame. Abortion is a medical procedure that should come without guilt or stigma; the left needs to mainstream how commonplace abortion is and how many lives have been saved as a result.

24 Carol Sanger, *About Abortion: Terminating Pregnancy in Twenty-first Century America* (Cambridge: Harvard University Press, 2017).

25 In October 2017, the hashtag #MeToo spread across the globe. What began as a Hollywood sexual assault scandal sparked a public reckoning worldwide. With these two words on social media, many thousands identified themselves as survivors of sexual harassment and assault, calling for justice and legal reforms.

GUTIERREZ-ROMINE: Well, so going back to this idea of "is it stigma," "is it shame?" Is it resistance? I keep going back to some examples from my research where a lot of that has to do with class. There are always exceptions for *some* women.

I remember there was this one document. It was a mother who helped her daughter go to Ensenada [Baja California in Mexico] for an abortion in the fifties. And the police were doing an investigation, and the mother said, "Well, she's about to get married, so let her get married first, and then we'll talk to you." Because she slipped up while her boyfriend was out of town, and she "got pregnant by a goon." That was the exact phrase, so I could never forget it. And so, she "fixed it," and then she's on track to a respectable life. And so, for this young eighteen-year-old white woman with a mother who had the means and resources to help her cross the U.S.-Mexican border in the fifties.

It was not something for her to. . . It was not dealt with in the same way as if it was perhaps a woman of color or another woman where you would stigmatize their choice of having an abortion. And that you would read into it differently as proof of their deviance, their deviant sexuality, their racial difference or lower class.

So, this young white woman got a mulligan; she was able to get this scratched off so that she could go on and have her future. And she deserved that, in the eyes of the mother. But how would that situation be viewed differently if the identity of that young woman changed? If it was a young woman of color if it was a different woman who was also single? And so, I think how we look at resistance, shame, stigma, perceptions of abortions, and acceptance of abortion often has a lot to do with these kinds of fringe exceptional cases that are somehow different than I still want to regulate abortion, but this was okay, and this is just a one-off thing over here.

COOPER OWENS: Some of that is embedded in infanticide law early on in the seventeenth century. In some weird way, it doesn't apply to married women. It's like the infanticide law is targeted at unmarried women, particularly servant women. So, this is in England before we get to the period of transatlantic slavery. But infanticide law is targeted at unmarried servant women and not at married women.

There's a long and deep tradition here of excluding married women from regulating sexuality in the same way as unmarried women.

BARNES: We see that with the pill in *Griswold v. Connecticut* [1965]. Married couples have the right to privacy, to access oral contraception.

COOPER OWENS: And then, of course, disallowing marriage in the first place. Black men and women weren't allowed to get married for centuries. They weren't legally allowed to get married until after the Civil War. The Civil Rights Act of 1866 allows Black folk to enter into legal contracts.

So, there are such deep roots here. It's not just cultural. There is a legal framework.

GUTIERREZ-ROMINE: I studied California and the way that the first California laws were drawn. There were exceptions for physicians. So, it was only illegal if a "quack" performed an abortion.

It was not illegal if a physician performed an abortion. And so, it leaves a lot of room for, again, these women of a certain class or status who can negotiate with their physician a reason that their abortion is okay. And so, it creates all these barriers for lower-class women who cannot afford the services of a private physician, who would then, under California law, be able to provide them with a legal abortion. And so, we are constantly kind of reinstating and affirming these social statuses and differences through the law itself.

WULF: Like *Roe v. Wade*, obviously caused the *Hyde Amendment* to come out immediately. And I think of that as, again . . .

BARNES: Explain the *Hyde Amendment*.

WULF: The *Hyde Amendment* [1976] was a law championed by Congressman Henry Hyde [Republican, House of Representatives 1975–2007], who wanted to make sure that no federal funds would ever be spent on providing abortion care to women who are protected under Medicaid and other federal funding—like if they are a part of the military. And it goes with certain exceptions, but it goes from the 1970s right up to 2022. These laws are on the books and negotiated repeatedly: the control factor. And the class factor is so important. But in the popular cultural image, which we're also trying to deal with, it is always "young girls getting themselves pregnant."

CLINTON: It is always "young girls getting themselves pregnant" when we know, for example, Margaret Sanger and her campaigns were well aware that it was *mothers* seeking the majority of abortions in America; mothers trying to limit their families.

And the control factor is very much in the hands of the medical profession: they're able to do it legally, and they're able to choose it. And I remember right before *Roe v. Wade* passed; women were telling their abortion stories.

There was a slew of women in the fifties and sixties who, to have an abortion, had to say that they were depressed and possibly a "danger to themselves," which allowed them to get an abortion.

They had to claim they were depressed and would get their abortion based on their impaired mental health.

Then, years later, when a divorce came up, their husbands would go and take out these medical records, and the court would find them "unfit mothers" because they suffered from instability and depression.

Back again, to the fact that the reality of the *legal application* is very different from the *practical application.*

And the Everly Brothers song—referenced in Ricki Solinger's important book: *Wake Up Little Susie: Single Pregnancy and Race before Roe v. Wade* [1999] tells us about how pregnancy is portrayed in images.

As I said, I was thrilled with *Roe v. Wade* because I was raised in the Bible Belt... My mother was reared a Southern Baptist, and my stepfather was Catholic—and we had to juggle... Going from Baptist gospel to Catholic mass was quite nightmarish.

But as a young girl, I saw *The Cardinal* [1963], a film that none of you saw, and you've probably never heard of it. But in the film, the Cardinal's sister was pregnant in the hospital, and they could save the baby or the mother. Naturally, the Cardinal supported saving the life of the child!

So Irish, exactly like the case in Ireland, the death of Savita Halappanavar.[26]

DE LONDRAS: Ah, yes.

26 Savita Halappanavar died from sepsis in 2012 after her request for an abortion was denied on legal grounds because of the hospital's interpretation of the law, which only allowed for abortion if there was a "real and substantial risk to the life" of the pregnant person. In the wake of a nationwide outcry over her death and a Citizens Assembly on the possibility of constitutional change, Irish voters voted in favor of an amendment, which repealed the Eighth Amendment of the Constitution of Ireland and led to the legalization of abortion in Ireland.

CLINTON: So, the battle over balancing the life of the mother and the life of the child . . . "choice" was being supplanted in activism by "right to life."

And I remember this terrible sinking moment when I thought, "How could they get that slogan?" I mean, we're supposed to work against *life*? This is not where feminists want to be. And we look at how this crusade moves forward. And I just saw some new material on abolitionists in *The Nation*. [27]

And I remember quite distinctly in the 1980s when I wrote a piece on how amazing it was to me that during the 1850s, there was a movement to redefine slaves as *people*, not property. And it was an absolute, nothing to negotiate. And for Americans, this was redefining life.

And this struck me as what the pro-life movement was doing in the 1980s. And wasn't it dangerous? And shouldn't we look at it? Compare the parallel. And thank goodness this marvelous mentor of mine said, "You are not to publish that under any circumstance. You will be tarred by that." He saved me from cancellation. But at that very moment, I really believed, much like the early Equal Rights Amendment, there was a misstep; there was a real misstep of not realizing the focus on the fetus—the shift away from the mother, which is something Johanna . . .

SCHOEN: Yeah, I wanted to say that actually ties nicely back to Salamishah's earlier point because I think one of the things that's really important to remember is that the stigma that we've been talking about is *man-made*.

I am saying *man*-made here intentionally.

27 Linda Hirschman, "What the Anti-Abortion Movement Learned from Abolitionists," The Time of Monsters Podcast, *The Nation*, May 11, 2022, https://www.thenation.com/podcast/activism/time-of-monsters-linda-hischman/.

Even when it was still illegal, the kind of testimonies that women were forced to make, where their whole sexual lives get exposed in front of courts, is how Leslie Reagan describes it in *When Abortion Was a Crime.*[28] And the dying testimonies—women were forced to talk about the most intimate aspects of their life.

And then, especially once we get to the anti-abortion movement and particularly after Ronald Reagan's election with the rise of the religious right in the early 1980s, there's a very concerted effort to stigmatize the language that has to do with abortion and to call abortion clinics "death clinics" and to call escorts "deathcorts" and to call abortion providers "murderers," and "killers," and so on, and so on.

And to start using that language in front of abortion clinics and to yell at, to accost patients with those words and phrases, and to accost them with the pictures that anti-abortion people are carrying and trying to block patients' access to clinics. And to confront them physically and verbally, and following them home, and following abortion staff home, and protesting in front of abortion providers' home. And tracing license plate numbers!

And all those things they then start doing contribute to the stigmas and the fact that people don't want to talk about abortion. But they have done a lot of damage because not only do women start feeling guilty, but they also don't want protestors in their living room. They don't want protestors calling and telling everybody that they had an abortion.

And so, I think that we really take the stigma of abortion as

28 Reagan, *When Abortion Was a Crime.* See also Reagan's "'Caught in the Net,' in Top Ten Articles.

natural, and it's not natural. It is man-made, and it is *intentional*, and it gets worse and worse and worse as we move into the present time period.

DE LONDRAS: And can I...

SCHOEN: Oh, go ahead.

DE LONDRAS: I think part of the stigma as well, goes back even further than that—to the real attempt to assert medical control over abortion and to construct abortion as an inherently dangerous procedure. This is the basis upon which the argument is then made: that criminalization is required to protect women from something dangerous and that *only* physicians can provide safe abortions.

Abortion becomes the monster. It is this inherently dangerous thing, when in fact, for most of the time, it hasn't been. And what actually makes the difference between safe and unsafe abortion is the legal and regulatory context—and the availability of medical commodities rather than the procedure itself. If you want to call it that—it's not really a procedure anymore with medical abortion—but the thing you're doing.

CLINTON: But on that note of the procedure, since there is the issue now of abortion pills[29] and how you must go to a doctor, and the doctor must administer it, and you have to go make a return visit. And what about the timing so that people crossing state lines will be dealing with lengthy and excessive waiting periods? Is that class? Is that race? Is that just plain old misogyny writ large?

I mean, in other words, every time there is a moment where

29 Pam Belluck, "Abortion Pills Take the Spotlight as States Impose Abortion Bans," *New York Times*, June 27 2022, https://www.nytimes.com/2022/06/26/health/abortion-medication-pills.html.

there is an expansion of opportunity and access, there's a slam coming back. And it's done for the "good" of women, to "protect" them.

DE LONDRAS: Exactly.

CLINTON: I'm in a state [Texas] with a gun law on campus so *women* can "protect themselves." I mean. . . the *language* . . .

DE LONDRAS: The difference with oral medication is that all those attempts at legal regulation will ultimately be futile because you cannot control swallowing. It's a great line drawing on Sally Sheldon's work. Super line. The state cannot control swallowing.[30]

And, because these pills are very much like community provisions before women know how to use them. You can buy them; you can have them, you give them to each other, you support each other, and you become abortion doulas.

The state is going into this hyperactive legislative moment to do everything it can to make abortion more difficult to access because regulators know about the pill and its uncontrollability. And it has been in their sights since the first prototypes in the '70s and '80s.

Abortion medication is a *game changer*. The state cannot control abortion in the face of abortion medication.

TILLET: My answer is not related to a pill but to the history of genealogies and what it has meant for us to miss crucial political coalitions. Regarding Ronald Reagan, it might be helpful to think about those debates that were happening before his presidency and in the 1970s—during the *Roe v. Wade* decision within African American communities.

In 1969, the same year Shirley Chisholm became the first

30 Sally Sheldon, "How Can a State Control Swallowing? The Home Use of Abortion Pills in Ireland," *Reproductive Health Matters*, 24, no. 48 (2016): 90–101, doi: 10.1016/j.rhm.2016.10.002.

Black woman to serve in Congress, she was also the honorary co-president of the National Association to Repeal Abortion Laws (NARAL). Despite being attacked for her views, she understood the links between racial and gender justice and that she has the power to stand in for all the Black women who cannot publicly support abortion.

And so, what's interesting is then *Roe* occurs, and it's a victory. And then, by the time we get to the '80s, this notion of stigma really takes off from the right. But to me, these moments—if we could have learned from these—what are seen as internecine battles between Black people. These Black feminists and Black nationalists are arguing, or at least trying to protect Black women's bodies.

And someone like Shirley Chisholm is going on record saying that this is important for Black women's health. It's important for Black women's families. And she's going against the grain of what the political discourse of the Black Power movement is at the time.

But we don't necessarily pay heed to that when we're given this long history. We're not necessarily looking back and saying, "Well, there are these conversations that are happening within this community that can then help us shape maybe how our activism should be going forward."

During Obama's presidency, billboards sprang up everywhere in places like Dallas and Chicago about abortion being a genocide for the African American communities.[31] The divide seemed to be the Black religious right versus Black reproductive justice health experts, advocates, and activists. But really, Republicans were

31 A billboard announced in 2010, "Every 21 minutes, our next possible LEADER is aborted," with an image of Obama's profile. The Catholic Church also sponsored a billboard campaign with an image of a fetus in the womb. One of these advertisements proclaimed: "A baby is a person, no matter how small."

using the same Black nationalist discourse from the 1970s to then create a new groundwork for *Dobbs*.

And I guess when you said Reagan in the '80s, I thought, "Well, but there's also the genealogy of the '60s and '70s with the Black nationalist and the Black feminists really trying to, in a way, duke it out around choice. That, I think, again, is a missed moment" because *Roe* is a victory.

And so, when you have a victory, sometimes you miss the moment to organize properly. But I do think the moralizing that happens in the '80s is learning from that Black nationalist discourse around Black women . . . This idea that Black women shouldn't get abortions because it's harmful to the Black family gets picked up differently by the religious right . . . They're cousins to each other. And I think it becomes nationalized, even though it was seen as internecine in the '60s and '70s.

CLINTON: Alicia, I have students who write about Latinas and their discourse in the 1970s and '80s and grappling with this notion of where reproductive rights fall within that community. Could you comment on that period?

GUTIERREZ-ROMINE: Yeah. I think especially what Alex Stern and Natalie Lira have discussed previously . . . about when we're looking at Chicana feminism in the 1960s and 1970s.[32] And if we're thinking about the feminist movement of the 1970s, it often is framed as this pro-choice movement, when in reality, for a lot of these women of color for Latinas, especially in California, there is this desire for reproductive autonomy because they

32 See Stern, *Eugenic Nation*; and Natalie Lira, *Laboratory of Deficiency: Reproductive Justice: A New Vision for the 21st century* (Berkeley: University of California Press, 2021).

are undergoing sterilization, coerced sterilization practices in California at this time, like with the *Madrigal v. Quilligan* case.[33] Although the judge ruled in favor of the doctors, the case led to better-informed consent for patients, especially those who are not native English speakers.[34]

And so, it is putting them at odds with some of this larger discussion about choice and abortion access when these Chicana feminists want waiting periods for sterilizations when white feminists want sterilization on demand. And I think a lot of this centers on what control you have previously had over your own body that then frames how you are approached or received in the medical field.

And for a lot of these women of color who are coming into the medical field at odds with their physicians or with physicians, professionals of medicine who have this certain perspective of nonwhite women's bodies and their fecundity and their reproduction writ large—that is then framing how those physicians are reading them and their bodies: what choices and decisions they [medical professionals] should make for them, versus what white women are experiencing as they're going into professional medicine as well.

BARNES: That really connects to the Shirley Chisholm example. Someone I think about when we teach forced sterilization is

33 United States District Court for the Central District of California no. CV 75-2057-JWC (1978)

34 *Madrigal v. Quilligan* (1978), a class action suit involving the sterilization of ten Latina women by doctors without the women's consent. The judge ruled in favor of the doctors, but it ushered in an era of reform concerning forced and coerced sterilization of non-English speaking women.

Fannie Lou Hamer.[35] And so, in this Jim Crow era, but a larger Jim Crow that's impacting Latinas, Asian Americans, and Native American women, many don't have a choice. You can see the trajectory of Black reproduction before and after slavery—and Jim Crow, with her biography. Fannie Lou Hamer was one of 20 children. And then, she goes to see a white doctor who gives her what she calls "the Mississippi appendectomy," rendering her sterile.

Even though she's a movement mother, representationally, she can't have biological children with her husband. And so, I think it's worth exploring more in our conversation the role of these limited choices before we get to *Roe v. Wade* about who could even conceive because of medical intervention by the state.

COOPER OWENS: You know, all your points made me think about the rhetoric of racial annihilation, particularly during times of, "Oh gosh, there's multiculturalism or racial diversity that's happening. All of these people of color, these foreigners," insert whatever bad racial group, "They're going to wipe out the white race."

And so, it's very natural for women to be seen as mothers. Personally, I'm talking about myself as a cis heterosexual woman who is married. Even at fifty [and that's because I look young], the enduring question I get is, "Why don't you have children? Why don't you have children?"

GROUP: What! Who would ask you that?

COOPER OWENS: *Everybody*. From my trainer to people you meet, they're like, "Oh, how old are your kids?" And I'm like, "I don't

35 Born the daughter of sharecroppers in the Mississippi Delta, Fannie Lou Hamer was a voting rights activist and civil rights warrior. A co-founder of the Freedom Democratic Party in Mississippi, which she represented at the 1974 Democratic National Convention. See Keisha Blain, *Until I am Free: Fannie Lou Hamer's Enduring Message to America* (Boston: Beacon Press, 2021).

have any. I have a cat." And they are astounded because they see my wedding ring. I'm married to a man, and it just doesn't make sense. It is unnatural.

And then there's also this conversation around controlled death that is also seen as unnatural, bad, and sinful. Euthanasia is bad. Suicide is bad. Abortion is bad. And so, men must be the ones to be able to control those things, to create laws to keep a natural balance.

It is often interesting to me that these women if they're doing this unnatural imbalanced thing, are destroying the race. Yeah, it becomes deeper when you're talking about women of color. But more broadly, this affects *all* women. I can't wait until my hair is gray and I have a face full of wrinkles so I can finally stop being asked, "Why don't I have kids?" And then I said, "Go read the back of my book." And then, "Oh gosh! I'm so sorry. You really can't have children." But there is something that seems *unnatural* about women not being mothers.[36]

WULF: This goes back to the bigger question of what we mean by autonomy and why women can't have autonomy. There are many forms of autonomy and why women are obligated, whether it's to race or to the principle of marital unity, the understanding that somehow women are underneath their husband's control and husbands represent their household. So why would women need to vote, for example, or why would women need to own property? Or why would women need to do anything their husbands can do on their behalf?

But this notion that women can never be separable, women

36 See Deirdre Cooper Owens, "More Than a Statue: Rethinking J. Marion Sims's Legacy," in *Confederate Statues and Memorialization*, ed. Catherine Clinton (Athens: University of Georgia Press, 2019).

can never be separate and autonomous and make their choices for themselves, their bodies included. And I think that's so deeply embedded in these discussions about how the law instantiates reproductive control.

And it goes to the question of why shame? Because it's a choice for autonomy. And what strikes me about the *Dobbs* decision is how much the word liberty arises, and yet autonomy is somehow contrasted. Right? It's like you can't have autonomy and liberty in the same life.

SCHOEN: And not only that, but also the kind of protective language that legislators and judges have used in recent decisions. They have to protect women from their own choices.

WULF: From themselves.

SCHOEN: From choosing abortions. Women actually cannot make those decisions on their own.[37]

WULF: Oh, my God! The sixteen-year-old who couldn't possibly make this choice got pregnant by sexual assault, not old enough to make the decision for an abortion.

GUTIERREZ-ROMINE: But by all means, let her become a mother!

WULF: Exactly. Yeah.

TILLET: So, *what is it*? Patriarchy?

DE LONDRAS: Please.

TILLET: . . . *really*. Before *Dobbs*, in Utah, Mississippi, and Oklahoma, a woman who has been raped must first file a police report before

---

37 For the history of woman-protective anti-abortion arguments, see Reva B. Siegel, "The Right's Reasons: Constitutional Conflict and the Spread of Woman-Protective Anti-abortion Argument," *Duke Law Journal* 57 (2008): 1641–1692; and Reva B. Siegel, "The New Politics of Abortion: An Equality Analysis of Woman-Protective Abortion Restrictions," *University of Illinois Law Review* 3 (2007): 991–1054.

being able to get an abortion. Mississippi even denied girls and women access to abortion in the case of incest!

These laws are not only just about people thinking that women aren't intelligent enough to make decisions about their own reproductive health. There's something much more insidious that goes back to and how women and women of color's bodies were originally treated at our nation's founding. But I don't understand what's happening in 2022—saying that rape and incest are no longer exclusions or exceptions.

CLINTON: You have a woman gubernatorial candidate saying that . . .[38]

GUTIERREZ-ROMINE: Michigan.

CLINTON: She supports pregnancy, even after rape, saying it's important to have a "healing process."

GUTIERREZ-ROMINE: Yes. Yes.

CLINTON: Back to the mother. Back to the insistence a pregnancy will not be interfered with . . . is very *Handmaid's Tale*. It is very frightening for some of us—back here in Cambridge . . . looking at Margaret Atwood's world . . . fictional worlds. Sorry.[39]

GUTIERREZ-ROMINE: I think two things. The sixteen-year-old, for example: she's not mature enough to make this decision. But underlying that is this natural biologic notion of women being

38 Tudor Dixon, a gubernatorial candidate (who lost her bid) and anti-choice advocate. See Yelena Dzhanova, "GOP Candidate and Anti-Abortion Advocate Running for Michigan Governor Said Rape Victims Find 'Healing' by Being Forced to Have a Baby," *Insider*, August 20, 2022, https://www.businessinsider.com/michigan-gop-governor-candidate-said-having-baby-healing-rape-victims-2022-8.

39 Reference to Margaret Atwood's 1985 dystopian novel, *The Handmaid's Tale*, which was made into a 1990 film and a mini-series (2017–2022), and has won numerous awards. The fictional Gilead is centered in Cambridge, Massachusetts where executed dissidents are hung on the walls of Harvard University.

mothers. She may not *think* she wants to be a mother, but it might come naturally to her when she is. She just needs to nurture something in her, and then that will be fine.

Is that patriarchy? Is it relying on these misconceptions about the naturalization of women as mothers? I think both of those things are there.

And what I also think is interesting about these exceptions for rape and incest. When we were revising our laws in California, there was a lot of legal discussion about this. If we believe that fetuses have some semblance of rights, then abortion restrictions that leave exceptions for rape and incest are violations of the fetus's Fourteenth Amendment.

Because if we're saying these fetuses—again, if we're relying on the argument—it was found void for vagueness, but if we're saying that these fetuses can be aborted, but *these* fetuses cannot, then we are discriminating against certain fetusus.

And so, that was one of the reasons we could not have this abortion statute with those exceptions. And ultimately, we found the statute void for vagueness. We decriminalized it. We never created a legal right to it immediately, but we decriminalized abortion because the existing language of the law didn't work legally.

CLINTON: How the originalists understand rights: go back to *Dobbs*.

GUTIERREZ-ROMINE: So, there was no concept of fetal rights,[40] but this was part of the back-and-forth discussion if we presented this model code. We had these exceptions. And then, ultimately, we picked the law apart and said, "Well, it doesn't work for this because it's a violation of this. It doesn't work with these exceptions

40 See W. A. Bowes Jr and B. Selgestad, "Fetal Versus Maternal Rights: Medical and Legal Perspectives," *Obstet Gynecol* 58, no. 2 (August 1981): 209–214. See also "A Push to Recognise the Rights of the Unborn is Growing in America, " *The Economist*, July 7, 2022, .

because it's a violation of fetus rights." And all of these different reasons coalesced to say this abortion law doesn't work ultimately. So, we can't use it! And so we're just decriminalizing abortion because the law doesn't work. It's void by vagueness.

BARNES: Can you give us a year?

GUTIERREZ-ROMINE: 1967 for the original trial. The appeal where the court found it void was in 1969.[41]

WULF: Sorry. Go ahead.

SCHOEN: I would argue that what you call the naturalization of women as mothers is *patriarchy*. That is exactly what it is. And the whole debate around both abortion and, in general, women's reproductive rights—it's really a battle between women and men about control over women's bodies. I think that's really at the core of it.

LONDRAS: But there are women, too. I mean . . .

SHOEN: Yeah! But they are living in a patriarchal society. That's the point.

DE LONDRAS: Yeah, it's true.

SCHOEN: It doesn't mean that they don't adopt those concepts.

DE LONDRAS: Yes.

COOPER OWENS: It's patriarchy, but it's a more nuanced patriarchy. It made me think of this thing I heard when I was a Christian and growing up in the church. Because I've been out of the church for so long, I had to Google it, but "there is no respect of persons with God."[42] So all of these unborn children are the same. And it goes to Alicia's point about this legal definition.

BARNES: "Before I formed thee in the belly I knew thee; and before

41 *People v. Belous*, 458 P. 2d 194 (1969)—a California case that marked the first time a patient's constitutional right to abortion was upheld in the courts.

42 Romans 2:11 and repeated in Acts 10:34: "Then Peter opened this mouth, and said, Of a truth I perceive that God is no respecter of persons," in King James Version of the Holy Bible.

thou camest forth out of the womb I sanctified thee . . . "[43]

COOPER OWENS: Right. If God is no respecter of persons, whether that "child," and I'm using air quotes, is seen or unseen, in order to restore the balance, you have to allow the child to be born. And that is at the heart of it.

As academics, I do have to say this is a liberal space that I now occupy and have occupied for a really long time.

And there are lots of ways that people are saying it's not. But I got my Ph.D. at closer to 40 than not. And so, I've worked in a world that was not as protected as academia, where people proselytized you. In academia, you are allowed to be an atheist. You are allowed not to be a Christian. You're allowed to be in a space where you can say, "Oh, my wife," if you are a woman or a non-binary person.

And people don't bat their eyes, or at least they are trained well enough not to say anything. But the general American public is Christian—and they are *religious*.

And even if you are Jewish, even if you are Hindu, even if you are a Muslim, at the end of the day, people understand what "controlled death" means. And that means, and I'm saying it in that way because I can tell you often I am in the minority when it comes to these kinds of issues around my high school friends and some of my college friends. After all, I was coming out of a Black women's college that was Christian and religiously affiliated.

And so, in many ways, you are returning this nation to its Christian roots. And that's what we hear when we say, "Oh, I know you were raped. I know it was incest and sexual assault, and that's really horrible, but at least somebody can adopt the children," or

43 Jeremiah 1:5 in the King James Version of the Holy Bible.

perhaps people will, they'll grasp onto that in the ways that, for us, I'm not saying it doesn't make sense. *Intellectually*, we understand it, but it's such an oppositional part of our philosophical way of being and thinking that we are just like, "How?"

TILLET: But it is a new moment because you wouldn't have had a woman running for governor against another woman in Michigan saying that. Right? And I think this is why #MeToo is important because we're on the fifth anniversary of #MeToo. And so, you have this explosion—a new discourse and a potential shift in how we think about sexual harassment, sexual assault.

Then you have the ongoing backlash against that. So, you have this historic, unprecedented seismic shift in how we think about sexual assault and sexual harassment, globally and nationally, across institutions and industries. That's the potential.

And then you have ways in which that will be regulated, controlled, and not fully operationalized in law or in different institutions. There was true feminist potential with #MeToo, but how has that been contained?

How are sexual freedoms now being controlled? How do you make sure it doesn't fully transform society? And then you have *Dobbs*. And I'm figuring out how you can have #MeToo, and then you can have *Dobbs*. Ultimately, most Americans want democracy and see reproductive justice as crucial to our shared fates.

COOPER OWENS: It's because they feel like they're losing power.

GROUP: Yes. Yeah. Exactly.

COOPER OWENS: They're losing power in the Christian Church. Studies show that young people are not joining the church. People are walking away from Christianity. It's a loss of power.

WULF: This extreme version has led to *Dobbs* and the extreme version that's expressed in the Alito opinion: it's not a majority. I mean, *it's a majority of the Supreme Court* at the moment, but it's not a majority opinion among Americans. We can see that. And I think—

BARNES: Seventy-seven percent support some sort of access. What was it?

WULF: Yes. A lot of people. The kinds of logic which led to this decision would be shocking to them. The kind of logic of husbands' control over wives, their property, their money, and their ability to make choices for their bodies: medically, in terms of reproduction or any other choices. People would be *shocked* by that.

People were shocked by the *Dobbs* decision, but they'd also be shocked by the other implications of the underlying legal and cultural logic of it. I hear you that there is a kind of liberal bubble and that there's a world outside, but I think that world outside *also* has its limits.

BARNES: It's more liberal than the Supreme Court.

COOPER OWENS: Sure. Definitely.

CLINTON: But the headlines have been prescient—dealing with the issue of this as a civil rights issue. We are seeing movement in the polls: I mean, certainly with the state of Kansas.[44] [Kansas voters defeated an amendment—59 percent to 41 percent—to remove abortion rights from the state's constitution in the 2022 primary election.]

SCHOEN: Yeah. I was thinking about Kansas, too.

CLINTON: I mean, so with *Dobbs*, we went from *Roe* to *Dobbs*. Were we sleeping? Did we just wake up? Because all of us were

---

44 The first ballot initiative on abortion law following *Dobbs* was held in Kansas on August 2, 2022. Kansas voters rejected the removal of abortion rights from the state's constitution. However, Republican leaders warned that Kansas might become "an even bigger destination site for abortion tourism," and conservative lawmakers passed more restrictive anti-abortion legislation.

saying, it couldn't happen. And, we're historians; how did it slip by?

DE LONDRAS: I think people everywhere else were saying *it absolutely could happen.*

We were talking earlier about when we first heard about *Roe.* I want to bet that most people have never read *Roe.* It's not really a women's rights decision. It's a *doctor's* right decision. It's about medicalization.

Right? The reasoning isn't really about. . . It's not about women's autonomy or agency or privacy. It's about the right of a woman *with her doctor* to decide on medical care. And to say that the state's interest in fetal life or the preservation of fetal life is only strong enough to intervene once you get to the end of the first trimester, strengthening then further as the pregnancy progresses. Then you have the *Casey* decision, which doesn't get talked about much, but it's just as important, saying that when they regulate abortion, they can't impose undue burdens.[45]

So actually, when you read *Roe,* it is not really a women's rights decision. And from the outside–from outside of the United States–one of the things that's always been really interesting is a kind of complacency one could observe about the *settledness* of *Roe* because even if they actually didn't overturn *Roe,* even if they

45 *Planned Parenthood of Southeastern Pennsylvania v. Casey* 505 U.S. 833 (1992) affirmed the core holding of *Roe* but held that the state could regulate abortion prior to viability provided these regulations do not impose undue burdens on pregnant people (a lower standard than 'strict scrutiny' which had been applied under *Roe*). Also, holding that the state's interest in preserving fetal life is strong enough to prohibit abortion from fetal viability onwards provided there is an exception where the life of the pregnant person is at risk. Essentially, *Casey* eliminated the *Roe* framework of the "first trimester" in favor of a "viability" assessment.

just looked at the internal logic of *Roe* itself, we know that they could restrict abortion really, really *significantly*. Even within what *Roe* provides for in the law.

SCHOEN: I was going to say they already are!

DE LONDRAS: Exactly. They were already doing it. And when you then look at what happened immediately after *Roe* . . . To be honest, the pro-life side, as they call themselves, are very, very, very good lawyers. And they immediately, after *Roe*, organized legal defense funds, trained amazingly talented lawyers, and had endless resources. And they just intervened in everything. They intervened in every case. They intervened at the state level and with legislation.

CLINTON: Wasn't a state-level *key*. I mean . . .

DE LONDRAS: State level is key. They could experiment. They could develop legislation that would then get tested. They could push the boundaries. They could very quickly get a case that they don't win but which they could build on. Sandra Day O'Connor, one of her first cases, *Akron*: they don't win it. But if you read Sandra Day O'Connor's dissent in the *Akron* case in 1983, and then you read *Dobbs*, it's not a big leap from what she says in '83.[46]

And remember, she's the first justice being appointed who gets monstered by the pro-life side for not being anti-abortion *enough*. So, they have developed legislation at the state level. They intervene in all these cases. They experiment with arguments and know

46 *City of Akron v. Akron Center for Reproductive Health*, 462 U.S. 416 (1983). In Akron, the Supreme Court invalidated an ordinance of the City of Akron imposing seventeen requirements for the performance of abortion, such as requiring first-trimester abortions to be done in hospitals, requiring parental consent where an unmarried minor sought abortion, and imposing a 24-hour wait period. The court found these were clearly intended to direct women away from choosing an abortion.

they don't have to win right now. All they have to do is keep pushing, keep pushing, pushing, pushing the boundaries.

And then, they set up the structure where they have a majority on the Court. It takes 40 or 50 years. That's fine. They're in this for the long game, and they are not finished *yet.* It's really, really interesting to see from the outside the extent to which, of course, everyone was shocked in a way by *Dobbs,* but actually, we shouldn't have been. From the day after *Roe* happened, *this* was the destination.

SCHOEN: I think what Fiona is saying is important. So, one of the questions was: what were the most important events leading to *Dobbs*? And my response would also be, "There isn't *one.* Right? It's a concerted attack that starts the day after *Roe.* And the first real event was the *Hyde Amendment* in 1976, where we defunded poor women trying to get access to abortion.

And it actually starts *before* that. I mean, how abortion providers were trying to open abortion clinics in the 1970s, the local regulations, and things that they had to fight against even to open the clinics once abortion became legal are totally underappreciated.

Anything from having to prove a certificate of need wasn't legally required for abortion clinics but which local authorities still demanded, to zoning laws, to building permits, to building inspectors—it wasn't easy. It was a fight all along the way.

And then, in the 1980s, as we talked about earlier, how the religious right started to protest against abortion clinics. And then barriers to access: spousal consent and parental consent, counseling requirements, and waiting periods—the fact that people had to return after counseling to have an abortion.

The way that courts began to treat women as needing protection against abortion. The TRAP laws [targeted regulations of abortion providers] made it expensive for abortion providers to provide abortion care because of all the regulations that abortion clinics had to meet that didn't serve any purpose aside from making abortion more difficult to access.[47]

I think all these things came together over the course of the past few decades. Then, as you noted, it's the fact that the Supreme Court changes in ways that we didn't anticipate or appreciate, and now they're going to be devastating for years.

This morning, I saw a post by a friend that the Supreme Court just accepted a personhood case...

COOPER OWENS: I lived in Mississippi . . . Go back to *Dobbs*, and then we'll deal with personhood. Thomas Dobbs was the state health officer of the Mississippi Department of Health, and he filed suit against the Jackson Women's Health Organization. I taught at the University of Mississippi from 2009 until 2014. I was a board member of the Southeast Region's Planned Parenthood, so personhood was really important. Even before Thomas Dobbs sued the Jackson Women's Health Organization, Mississippi politicians wanted to get personhood on the Mississippi state constitution.

That essentially means that life begins at conception, so personhood was about legally recognizing that life begins at conception. It would have been the country's most anti-abortion law nationally in terms of national implications. In late 2010 through 2011, we had these groups, powerful anti-abortion groups that descended on Mississippi trying to get *Amendment 26* passed.

47 "Targeted restrictions on abortion providers"—laws that require abortion providers to fulfill requirements—such as hospital affiliation—are designed to prohibit or shut down facilities that terminate pregnancy.

I remember being doxxed, trolled, and cyber-harassed before I knew what those words meant.[48] Having my face, my image, and my voice on video and being very ashamed to go back to that because social media wasn't as huge back then, so you didn't want people to know what you were doing. I thought I could lose my job because I wasn't changing. You're out there by yourself. November came around, and overwhelmingly, Mississippi voters did not vote for personhood, and white Mississippians were shocked.

I remember Black Mississippians were not—because we kept joking with each other, "all those white girls dating those Black boys don't want to have those little Black babies." When I told this story to my white colleagues and friends, they hadn't considered it. I said, "But your daughters did because we see them dating all the Black athletes at Ole Miss at nighttime when nobody can see them publicly," so that was a part of it to bring in the religious component.

This article by the *Mississippi Free Press*, Ashton Pittman, November 12th, 2021, not even a full year ago, says, "ten years after Mississippi's rejected personhood, federal life at conception efforts were underway." So, they lost. Those national groups galvanized just like Fiona said, and this is the declaration that then-Governor Phil Bryant made in 2011. He said, "the evil dark side in this world is taking hold. If Mississippians reject the personhood amendment at the polls" the next day, he warned, "then Satan wins."

SCHOEN: I think one of the things that I find so fascinating and tragic

48 Doxxing means to search for and publish private or identifying information about (a particular individual) on the internet, typically with malicious intent, while trolling is to instigate conflict, hostility, or arguments in an online social community—and cyberharassment is to use the internet to target and harm an individual.

about Mississippi and the Jackson Women's Health Organization is that Susan Hill started that clinic.

COOPER OWENS: That's right.

SCHOEN: . . . who was one of the first. . .

COOPER OWENS: That's right.

SCHOEN: Susan Hill was one of the first people who basically tried to open abortion clinics in underserved areas across the country and who ran that clinic where African American women were at the forefront of the reproductive rights movement.[49] One of the long-serving abortion providers at Jackson Women's Health was an African American woman, Dr. Helen Barnes, who had delivered all the babies in Jackson and started providing abortion care there early on. Mississippi today is one of the states with the highest infant maternal mortality rates among Black African Americans.[50]

COOPER OWENS: Yeah.

SCHOEN: It is a state that doesn't give a shit about the health of Black women and the health of Black infants.

COOPER OWENS: Yeah. Yes.

SCHOEN: I don't know; it just leaves me speechless. But it is also the confluence between so many of the Black women who are getting abortion care and those who are providing abortion care

---

49 Susan Hill (1948–2010) from North Carolina was president of the National Women's Health Organization in her state and advocated for reproductive rights throughout her career.

50 Dr. Helen Barnes (b. 1928 in Jackson Mississippi), former professor of obstetrics and gynecology at the University of Mississippi Medical Center, was one of the first African American female physicians to practice medicine in Mississippi and was the first African American board-certified OB/GYN to practice in Mississippi. She has been an advocate for women's reproductive rights, an educational and medical leader within her community and state.

and also for African American male physicians who really see this as an extension of civil rights activism and as part of fighting for a healthier African American community and a healthier future. What that means politically in terms of Mississippi politicians to kind of clamp down again and make abortion illegal—it is a slap in the face of providing a better future for the Black community.

COOPER OWENS: It happened, but that's the thing. You could only get an abortion if you lived within 25 miles of Jackson, so you had to live within the county. The abortion services were provided once or twice a week.

Now, this is what I remember from my own advocacy working there. It was *difficult* to get an abortion. In terms of the fear, you had the escorts being terrorized and patients seeing this and also being terrorized. It was tough to still get an abortion at the Jackson Women's Health Organization, and yet they chose it, and a part of the political messaging, particularly for the Black community and the Christian community in Mississippi, was, "You see *these* white folks? These are white folk who are the architects of this message. These white folk are trying to kill Black babies."

Once again, it goes into the genocide issue, but also the civil rights issue. They're taking away Black people's civil rights by focusing on killing the babies.

SCHOEN: Yeah. Legally. . . I'm so sorry. Legally, you didn't have to be within 25 miles, but I think in practice, women from further away often found it difficult to get to the clinic.

COOPER OWENS: That was the practice.

SCHOEN: Practice because of the waiting period if you came from the Mississippi Delta. Right.

COOPER OWENS: Yes.

SCHOEN: I remember Susan Hill telling me stories about how

women who came from the Mississippi Delta would come in their cars and they would sleep in the parking lot in their cars so they could get the counseling, and then they would stay in the parking lot in their cars with their entire families to be able to get the procedure 48 hours later or whatever the waiting period was.

COOPER OWENS: Mmm hmm.

TILLET: This goes back to *Dobbs v. Jackson*. It's like a culmination of all these events, but Brett Kavanaugh and Clarence Thomas's appointments were significant.[51]

I want to return to Clarence Thomas and Anita Hill, not only because it was a rite of passage and a significant watershed moment for all of us in this room but because that was a turning point. You see this division in which Black women are not women; they're not Black. They're in this 'no man's land' of not having race and not having gender. Anita Hill was doubly vulnerable in the public imagination because it was seen as unreasonable and unlikely that someone like Clarence Thomas could sexually harass her even though he had had a longstanding pattern of harassing other colleagues who were ready to testify, but ultimately were not allowed to in 1991.

I'm bringing this up because that was a lost opportunity. Imagine if of those who came out against him: the ACLU, NOW, the NAACP.

COOPER OWENS: Black academics . . .

TILLET: The Black *women* academics Elsa Barkley Brown, Debra King, and Barbara Ransby, organized 1,600 black women as signatories for the full page ad: "African American Women In

---

51 Clarence Thomas was appointed to the Supreme Court in 1991, and Brett Kavanaugh joined the court in 2018.

Defense of Ourselves," in the *New York Times*.[52] What if they had all formed a grassroots campaign to block his nomination? In contrast, Clarence Thomas's approval ratings skyrocketed *after* he invoked the 'high-tech lynching.'

To me, that was a failed opportunity, but it reveals how Black women are rarely seen as symbols of racial or gender oppression that can catalyze a mass movement. I think it's sad even that with *Dobbs v Jackson*, the public discourse does not know that Black women were specifically targeted. That's not a story the media seemed ready to explore or cover in that way.

COOPEROWENS: That's right.

TILLET: In this age of Black Lives Matter, *Dobbs* must be a galvanizing racial justice. But the bigger questions are: how do we *really* center Black women in particular and women of color in general within the larger reproductive movement? Of course, it means we are using a reproductive justice framework that includes choice but also protects women to raise the children they do chose to have with dignity and in safe, healthy, and supportive environments. This means we need to include, but not only engage, suburban white women as those most enraged by *Dobbs* or our most vocal electorate. Our movement should be led by those who are the most vulnerable, and we should learn from our failed lessons from the past. And that brings us back to Clarence Thomas; he's done a real number on us.

BARNES: His first vote on the court was for *Casey*.

COOPER OWENS: That's right.

52 African American Women in Defense of Ourselves," Fractals, November 17, 1991, https://fractals.blackfeministfuture.org/fractal/aawidoo-african-american-women-in-defense-of-ourselves/.

BARNES: It's right there. Immediately.

TILLET: There might be ongoing repercussions around birth control and marriage equality too.

SCHOEN: I think one of the things that I find really fascinating about the current moment . . . and in a way to say that "it's fascinating," is an academic privilege . . .

TILLET: Yeah, it's horrible . . .

SCHOEN:. . . is that many African American reproductive rights activists have always criticized the fact that we only focus on the abortion issue. In a way, it does provide us with an opportunity to sit back and look at it in a reproductive justice framework and to say, okay, yes, access to abortion is important, but what is *also* important is maternal healthcare and infant healthcare.[53]

COOPER OWENS: That's right.

SCHOEN: And the right to be able to raise a child in a respectful environment where parents can provide for all of those kinds of things that really are tied up with the framework of reproductive justice.

I think, especially many in the white community, many did not really see this as a crucial political issue. Part of me is curious to see where we will be in ten years and whether we have made progress in all the other issues or whether we will still get stuck in terms of abortion rights.

BARNES: Karin, you have been trying to jump in.

WULF: Yeah. I'm so sorry.

BARNES: No, no, no.

WULF: I've got 20 things since then.

53 See, for instance, Loretta Ross and Rickie Solinger, *Reproductive Justice: An Introduction* (University of California Press, 2017).

BARNES: Unload it.

WULF: One of them was about contraception and about just going back to this point about the unacceptable. I think the broad American majority of the logic that's led to *Dobbs*... and the logic that's led to *Dobbs* leads, of course, to regulating contraception much more tightly. This, I think, is something really worth talking about because regulating contraception, I think, exposes what's really at the heart here, which is that kind of control over women. It's not about personhood. It really is about denying women autonomy essentially. I wonder what you think about the next step in contraception regulation. We've seen this with medical abortion and the effort to regulate access to that and describe it as abortion rather than as preventing contraception, for example.

CLINTON: Is it privacy? Who gets privacy? Privacy is a privilege, not a right, in all this regulation. Earlier, Alicia talked about certain fetuses being given rights and others not. On privacy, when we look at issues like gay marriage . . . when we look at new language for pronouns and identifiers . . . and new designations for bathrooms. . . . We are still fighting laws involving regulation of public bathrooms!

WULF: It's like the Equal Rights Amendment. Remember, that was a debate. If you let women have this Equal Rights Amendment, *there won't be any male and female bathrooms.* What is this obsession with bathrooms?

DE LONDRAS: It's anti-gender ideology, anti-contraception, anti-sex. In Ireland, we just said anti-fun. It was all just anti-fun. No happiness, no desire, no freedom, no nothing. Of course, that's patriarchy as well, but . . .

SCHOEN: It also goes back to the point you made earlier about Roe's weaknesses. There was this other case that I'm now teaching to my students, Susan Struck, that was about a woman who was in the military, Susan Struck, who got pregnant and who wanted . . . [54]

LONDRAS: Was this the Hyde Amendment challenge?

SHOEN: No, this was just before *Roe,* and I know that Ruth Bader Ginsburg really wanted *that* case to become the abortion case because that case was grounded in equal rights and not in privacy. If it's grounded in equal rights, then it is much easier to make a strong argument for it.

CLINTON: There was a cultural crest, because I think of the Anti-War movement, the Civil Rights movement, and the Women's Rights movement. After *Roe v. Wade*, what was next? Maybe pay equity? Maybe the ERA?

Now getting back to *Dobbs*, what's next? We talk about a coalition. We know that we must avoid making the same mistakes . . .

TILLET: I'm an optimist. We rarely think about one of the good things that came out of Hillary Clinton's attempt to change the healthcare system,[55] but one of those is when the Black Women's Health Imperative was formed in 1994, and the idea of reproductive justice came out of their meeting in Chicago.

54 Airforce Capt. Susan Struck, a nurse serving in Vietnam, fought the military rule which forbade servicewomen to remain in the ranks when pregnant. Her attorney was Ruth Bader Ginsburg. The Supreme Court ultimately declined to hear the case, yet Ginsburg's skills led to the Air Force reversing its policy. See *Struck v. Secretary of Defense*, 460 F.2d 1372 (9th Cir. 1971). See also a segment of *On The Media*, "Instead of Roe: The Case that Could Have Defined Abortion Law," discussing the case, https://www.wnycstudios.org/podcasts/otm/segments/case-debate-almost-defined-abortion-law-roe-on-the-media.

55 In 1993, President Bill Clinton appointed First Lady Hillary Clinton to head a task force aimed at healthcare reform and introduce universal healthcare for all Americans.

The term reproductive justice gives us more valence and more room to think about rights within that framework, but we also need to think about maternal mortality and how Black women and women of color, and feminists of color have been advocating for that to be a topline racial justice issue too.

That is the potential. Big organizations like Planned Parenthood may have started to use more of these kinds of models. That was always the potential of adopting a kind of Black feminist framework in the larger "choice" movement.

What's interesting, too, is that these things have obviously been pitted against each other. I was thinking about earlier when you were like "womanist" versus "feminist." Those are actually just sister conversations. They're not distinct or competitive movements. They're just people organizing and trying just to have conversations with each other and create coalitions. That's the good thing. That's where we could go.

For me, it's been disheartening that it hasn't risen to the big occasion of a racial justice issue. But I've just been paying attention because the other movement that's the backdrop to us is Black Lives Matter. If you have *Dobbs*, you have #MeToo, and then you have Black Lives Matter. Where does *Dobbs* fit into the Black Lives Matter movement? It's unclear if there's momentum, if there's urgency, or even if there's a way to create coalitions within Black Lives Matter. Activists are doing it, but in terms of the national discourse, it feels like there's little room for that to happen.

The other thing I would like to say, though is in popular culture, I do feel like even though we've been focusing on the law—and this is why I think pop culture attitudes have changed significantly in terms of the vast majority of Americans believing in choice—is because we have *seen* it. Our culture has depicted women and girls having access to abortion quite differently, with sympathy and empathy.

Then you go up to something like, more recently, something like *Scandal* where you have Olivia Pope just having an abortion, and she has it, and she doesn't even tell Fitz—who impregnated her and is the President of the United States.[56] It's a commonplace decision for her, and we, as an audience, must move on with her. That's an important note. In popular culture, it's not as fraught. That means there's more room for people to have empathy. Also, our cultural imagination has shifted significantly. The conservative backlash feels out of step with where American culture is. That is important.

CLINTON: Yeah. We see #MeToo tied into testimony—people telling their stories about their abortions . . . [57] Alicia?

GUTIERREZ-ROMINE: Well, it doesn't speak to that, but I think there's also an opportunity for those in the reproductive justice camp to use the fact that the pro-life arguments are antiquated. They're based on abortion as surgery, medical treatment: so now that we're relying on pills, there's an opportunity to change the imagery, change the language, change how we're discussing abortion.

But then also if we're coming down to this issue where it's being legislated state by state, by state . . . We saw this in the past where

56 The award-winning broadcast series *Scandal*, created by Shonda Rhimes, starring Kerry Washington (Olivia Pope) and Tony Goldwyn (Fitzgerald Grant III) from 2012–2017.

57 See Uma Thurman, "The Texas Abortion Law is a Human Rights Crisis for American Women," *Washington Post*, September 21, 2021; Nicole Walker, "My Abortion at Eleven Wasn't My Choice, It was My Life," *New York Times*, August 18, 2022; and Danielle Campoamor, "39 Abortion Stories Show Just How Important Abortion Access Is," *Teen Vogue*, January 9, 2020.

women cross the border to go to Mexico or to go to other places to get these procedures. It proved to be a challenge for law enforcement, so do we want federalism or not? Do you want states' rights or not?

Are we then talking about restricting women's movements?

I think there's a lot to unpack and try to figure out; I think we've seen a lot of this before. There were efforts to restrict women's movements to procure abortions with the Mann Act, but those ultimately failed.[58] We need to revisit the tools and language that we've used in the past.

We need to figure out how to stay on top of it because the pro-life movement is very good at litigating. They're very good at creating good slogans and things like that. So, I think the reproductive justice group needs to engage more with that, to counter the language they're using and the arguments they're making.

WULF: Slightly different question is about what histories we need now. That brings us here, and what histories are we missing? What are we saying about the histories that we have or don't have? We should be saying more! Full-throated! Especially to young people...

SCHOEN: I have to say, as a medical historian, one of the things that we often miss is the true understanding of the implications of overturning *Roe v. Wade*. It is, of course, not just about whether we can continue college or have a career. It's also about women's health in general. It's also about the ability to treat women who have miscarriages. It's about the ability to treat women who have ectopic pregnancies.

---

58 The Mann Act (also known as the White-Slave Traffic Act) was a federal law passed in 1910, which criminalized the transportation of "any woman or girl for the purpose of prostitution or debauchery, or for any other immoral purpose."

It's about the ability to treat women who see rheumatologists and oncologists—where treatments frequently have a negative impact on the developing fetus, so patients need to have access to abortion care. Physicians need to be able to refer women and ensure that the people who provide that care don't feel that they're going to be prosecuted.

The *Dobbs* decision is so callous: not just about women's ability to control their reproduction, but about their general health. The larger health complications are not just about reproduction but about many kinds of medical treatment.

CLINTON: It's the protection of the womb—because the womb is the patriarch's organ.

SCHOEN: Yes.

DE LONDRAS: The result of it, in Ireland, to be honest, with the fetal personhood thing, was that the whole idea of a successful pregnancy legally, not medically, but given the constraints placed on medics, was very simple: a woman is alive when a baby is born. That is effectively what it was reduced to. If you were *alive*, the state had done everything it was obliged to do in respect of you.

Exactly the things you're talking about happened. Women died because they could not get cancer treatment. Their medics were not allowed to prescribe treatment that might endanger the fetus if they were pregnant, and they were not allowed to access an abortion. Even though abortion was lawful if the woman's life was in "real and substantial danger," this kind of situation was not considered clear enough under the law.

If you're thinking about what comes next, that is what they want to come next. . . . The question is, what are the techniques needed: Argumentatively? Legally? Normatively? Politically? to ensure that you don't get to a situation where just being alive is all the state must do for you if you're pregnant. It's just really grim.

COOPER OWENS: I thought about something Salamishah, Karin, and Catherine said about coalition building, but also, it's this post-*Roe v. Wade* moment.

What can *we* do as scholars, historians, intellectuals, and activists who know the historical record? I've taken it very seriously, and this is a part of, I think. . . . I'm a two-time HBCU graduate, but this is really a part of that political tradition. You go outside of traditional academic roles and teach.

The opportunities I've been given as an individual have allowed me to speak in many different places, but I keep thinking *I'm an educator*. I've chosen to be an educator. How do I use education politically in ways that I might not be able to do so in a university classroom? That's allowed me to help with curriculum design from grassroots birth working groups. Doulas all across the nation, largely Black, whether it's in the South or in urban areas, I've been able to go to really powerful medical institutions and schools and help redesign curriculum. Most proudly at Jefferson Medical College in Philadelphia, where James Marion Sims graduated![59]

GROUP: Laughter

CLINTON: Where his ghost follows . . .

COOPER OWENS: Oh, his ghost always follows me. But how does the individual historian commit herself or themselves to the mission of educating? I speak to people from big to small. I still joke that I do a Chitlin' Circuit because I realize people want to know. They feel shaded when you explain a thing, and they're like, "*Wait*, why didn't I know this? This isn't even hard. Oh, wait."

59 See Owens, *Medical Bondage*; and Owens, "More than a Statue."

I need to take all of those things that we joked about today. "Oh, this is comp's knowledge" [a comprehensive exam a PhD candidate must complete]. But to be able to roll that out and say, "Okay, let's make sure we're on the same page using the language that we all understand."

That doesn't mean dumbing things down, but to be able to say, "Okay, *this* is what abortion meant in the nineteenth century."

Words change over time. Meanings change over time. How was it meant? How was it meant in the twentieth century or the twenty-first century? We need to be able to contextualize things.

On an elementary level for all of us, that can come through the kind of beautiful writing that Salamishah does with the *New York Times*, and she was being modest. She won a *Pulitzer*! Put *that* in that transcript!

But that kind of writing, from the op-eds we all do, to the talks that we do, to the workshops that we give. Education is key. People often don't know, and we have all this knowledge. They want to know. Make it accessible.

CLINTON: We're told to put all our knowledge between two covers, work on it for years, and dedicate ourselves to it and hope . . .

BARNES: Those of you that are tenured can work to change that!

CLINTON: Yeah. What can I say? I did not believe it until I got tenure . . . in my late fifties.

We have a public history program at the University of Texas at San Antonio [UTSA], and the students and faculty want to be involved in organizations and the community.

At first, I wondered why we are doing all this in San Antonio? What about the world? Then I realized that people can really connect to their community. Fifty percent of our students are Latinos and fifty percent are first-generation college students, and less than a third of the people in San Antonio have a college degree. We're here—reaching out. And I'm especially interested in training women who are committed to the ideology of change and how you talk about the maternal.

Today we discussed how to bring maternity into the "abortion movement." Can we not change the language? It's not about abortion. It's about *choices.* It's about women's autonomy, but maybe we need more campaigns.

We started out thinking about bringing on board a lot of people in the entertainment industry who are spokespeople who speak to younger women. Is this not something that our students connect to? Young people today! We have a president [Joe Biden] who, despite his religion [Catholic], is supportive of the right to a woman's choice. Yet I read less than 10% of the people between 18 and 29 support him.

I was in Ireland during the election of Obama and came back here for the election of the one whose name I won't speak. We are talking about *that* backdrop, right?

About education: if we are in an era when people get their news and their headlines, not even from the newspapers, the Penny Press, what can we do? We have a History News Network, but what can we do to get history out to a general audience, so they understand: a right is being taken away?

COOPER OWENS: Medical care.

CLINTON: . . . medical care is being taken away.

WULF: It's so frustrating to see powerful people denigrating the value of history. When we know how potent history is as an instrument for change. Really, understanding history is so deeply important.

We should be advocating for the significance of history and the humanities—and it's brought us reach and application and all those things. too. Anyway, we should be advocating for history.

CLINTON: Rhae Lynn, you're doing cultural history on the front lines and combining disciplines. How do you feel?

BARNES: Well, this was referenced before, but it's important. None of us would be in this room together thirty or forty years ago at this institution. We wouldn't have the lives that we have, the jobs we have, the ability to travel. Many of us in this room wouldn't be married to the people that you're married to. I think there are very recent examples of how we can apply history to try to make a change.

I think a prime example of history being applied through education helping was here in Cambridge during Prop 8 and the use of Laurel Thatcher Ulrich's work, Nancy Cott's work, George Chauncey's work as part of the expert witness testimonies by historians to get marriage equality in America.[60]

I'm with Salamishah. I think that in popular culture, it's increasingly accessible. I grew up in a world where *Dirty Dancing* played on TNT almost every weekend. It was constant.

It is a relatively positive representation of choice and a woman being supported by people in her community to make that choice, the danger of trying to get an abortion in the pre-*Roe* era, and never being shamed for it.

In music, especially, we see an expanding cultural conversation. It was active in country music in the '60s and '70s. Female

---

60 See Ulrich, *A Midwife's Tale*; Nancy Cott, *The Grounding of Modern Feminism* (New Haven: Yale University Press, 1987); and George Chauncey *Gay New York: Gender, Urban Culture, and the Makings of the Gay Male World, 1890–1940* (New York: Basic, 1994)

singer-songwriters like Dolly Parton and Loretta Lynn put women's issues like reproduction, abortion, and desertion part of their storytelling. All kinds of alternative bands in the 90s sang about abortion. I have a list because I'm fascinated.

These were all male groups with releases in 1997 and 1998: The Goo Goo Dolls (*Slide*), The Verve Pipe (*Freshman*), and Ben Folds Five (*Brick*) all sing about, from the male perspective, having to get an abortion for their partner . . . and the anti-abortion songs "In America" that same year in 1997 by Creed and "Retrospect for Life" by Common. Then also in hip-hop, Lauryn Hill's "Zion" deals with both sides of the issue. I tried to go through recently how many films featured abortion, and in the last fifteen years, it's exploded. What's interesting is it's quite intergenerational. Lily Tomlin, for example . . .

DE LONDRAS: Oh yeah, *Grandma*!

BARNES: Exactly. *Grandma*. You have women who were very active in the '70s and '80s fighting for equal rights and reproductive rights now in positions of power in Hollywood working with younger stars like Julia Garner to explain this history and move it forward in American culture. It's always a pendulum, it swings wider and further, but here we are. We're back to the fight.

As the speakers were preparing for a photograph—the news was released that Queen Elizabeth II of the United Kingdom, the longest-reigning British Monarch in history, had died during our round table. As we packed up, we discussed what her death meant for world history, the future of women globally, and the forms of cultural representation her life perpetuated and reshaped.

Top Ten Articles

How the Right to Legal Abortion Changed the Arc of All Women's Lives

KATHA POLLITT

The New Yorker, May 24, 2019

Katha Pollitt is an American poet, essayist, and critic. She is the author of four essay collections and two books of poetry. Her writing focuses on political and social issues, including abortion, racism, welfare reform, feminism, and poverty.

I've never had an abortion. In this, I am like most American women. A frequently quoted statistic from a recent study by the Guttmacher Institute, which reports that one in four women will have an abortion before the age of forty-five, may strike you as high, but it means that a large majority of women never need to end a pregnancy. (Indeed, the abortion rate has been declining for decades, although it's disputed how much of that decrease is due to better birth control, and wider use of it, and how much to restrictions that have made abortions much harder to get.) Now that the Supreme Court seems likely to overturn *Roe v. Wade* sometime in the next few years—Alabama has passed a near-total ban on abortion, and Ohio, Georgia, Kentucky, Mississippi, and Missouri have passed "heartbeat" bills that, in effect, ban abortion later than six weeks of pregnancy, and any of these laws, or similar ones, could prove the catalyst—I wonder if women who have never needed to undergo the procedure, and perhaps believe that they never will, realize the many ways that the legal right to abortion has undergirded their lives.

Legal abortion means that the law recognizes a woman as a person. It says that she belongs to herself. Most obviously, it means that a woman has a safe recourse if she becomes pregnant as a result of being raped. (Believe it or not, in some states, the law allows a rapist to sue for custody or visitation rights.) It means that doctors no longer need to deny treatment to pregnant women with certain serious conditions—cancer, heart disease, kidney disease—until after they've given birth, by which time their health may have deteriorated irretrievably. And it means that non-Catholic hospitals can treat a woman promptly if she is having a miscarriage. (If she goes to a Catholic hospital, she may have to wait until the embryo or fetus dies. In one hospital, in Ireland, such a delay led to the death of a woman named Savita Halappanavar, who contracted septicemia. Her case spurred a movement to repeal that country's constitutional amendment banning abortion.)

The legalization of abortion, though, has had broader and more subtle effects than limiting damage in these grave but relatively uncommon scenarios. The revolutionary advances made in the social status of American women during the nineteen-seventies are generally attributed to the availability of oral contraception, which came on the market in 1960. But, according to a 2017 study by the economist Caitlin Knowles Myers, "The Power of Abortion Policy: Re-Examining the Effects of Young Women's Access to Reproductive Control," published in the *Journal of Political Economy*, the effects of the Pill were offset by the fact that more teens and women were having sex, and so birth-control failure affected more people. Complicating the conventional wisdom that oral contraception made sex risk-free for all, the Pill was also not easy for many women to get. Restrictive laws in some states barred it for unmarried women and for women under the age of twenty-one. The *Roe* decision, in 1973, afforded thousands upon thousands of teen-agers a chance to avoid early marriage and motherhood. Myers writes, "Policies governing access to the pill had little if any effect on the average probabilities of marrying and giving birth at a young age. In contrast, policy environments in which abortion was legal and readily accessible by young women are estimated to have caused a 34 percent reduction in first births, a 19 percent reduction in first marriages, and a 63 percent reduction in 'shotgun marriages' prior to age 19."

Access to legal abortion, whether as a backup to birth control or not, meant that women, like men, could have a sexual life without risking their future. A woman could plan her life without having to consider that it could be derailed by a single sperm. She could dream bigger dreams. Under the old rules, inculcated from girlhood, if a woman got pregnant at a young age, she married her boyfriend; and, expecting early marriage and kids, she wouldn't have invested too heavily in her education in any case, and she would have chosen work that she could drop in and out of as family demands required.

In 1970, the average age of first-time American mothers was younger than twenty-two. Today, more women postpone marriage until they are ready for it. (Early marriages are notoriously unstable, so, if you're glad that the divorce rate is down, you can, in part, thank *Roe*.) Women can also postpone childbearing until they are prepared for it, which takes some serious doing in a country that lacks paid parental leave and affordable childcare, and where discrimination against pregnant women and mothers is still widespread. For all the hand-wringing about lower birth rates, most women—eighty-six per cent of them—still become mothers. They just do it later, and have fewer children.

Most women don't enter fields that require years of graduate-school education, but all women have benefitted from having larger numbers of women in those fields. It was female lawyers, for example, who brought cases that opened up good blue-collar jobs to women. Without more women obtaining law degrees, would men still be shaping all our legislation? Without the large numbers of women who have entered the medical professions, would psychiatrists still be telling women that they suffered from penis envy and were masochistic by nature? Would women still routinely undergo unnecessary hysterectomies? Without increased numbers of women in academia, and without the new field of women's studies, would children still be taught, as I was, that, a hundred years ago this month, Woodrow Wilson "gave" women the vote? There has been a revolution in every field, and the women in those fields have led it.

It is frequently pointed out that the states passing abortion restrictions and bans are states where women's status remains particularly low. Take Alabama. According to one study, by almost every index—pay, workforce participation, percentage of single mothers living in poverty, mortality due to conditions such as heart disease and stroke—the state scores among the worst for women. Children don't fare much better: according to *U.S. News* rankings, Alabama is the worst state for education. It also has one of the nation's highest rates of infant mortality (only half the counties have even one OB-GYN), and it has refused to expand Medicaid, either through the Affordable Care Act or on its own. Only four women sit in Alabama's thirty-five-member State Senate, and none of them voted for the ban. Maybe that's why an amendment to the bill proposed by State Senator Linda Coleman-Madison was voted down. It would have provided prenatal care and medical care for a woman and child in cases where the new law prevents the woman from obtaining an abortion. Interestingly, the law allows in-vitro fertilization, a procedure that often results in the discarding of fertilized eggs. As Clyde Chambliss, the bill's chief sponsor in the state senate, put it, "The egg in the lab doesn't apply. It's not in a woman. She's not pregnant." In other words, life only begins at conception if there's a woman's body to control.

Indifference to women and children isn't an oversight. This is why calls for better sex education and wider access to birth control are non-starters, even though they have helped lower the rate of unwanted pregnancies, which is the cause of abortion. The point isn't to prevent unwanted pregnancy. (States with strong anti-abortion laws have some of the highest rates of teen pregnancy in the country; Alabama is among them.) The point is to roll back modernity for women.

So, if women who have never had an abortion, and don't expect to, think that the new restrictions and bans won't affect them, they are wrong. The new laws will fall most heavily on poor women, disproportionately on women of color, who have the highest abortion rates and will be hard-pressed to travel to distant clinics.

But without legal, accessible abortion, the assumptions that have shaped all women's lives in the past few decades—including that they, not a torn condom or a missed pill or a rapist, will decide what happens to their bodies and their futures—will change. Women and their daughters will have a harder time, and there will be plenty of people who will say that they were foolish to think that it could be otherwise.

Reproductive Justice, Not Just Rights

DOROTHY ROBERTS

Dissent, Fall 2015.

Dorothy Roberts is an acclaimed scholar of race, gender, and the law, who joined the University of Pennsylvania as its fourteenth Penn Integrates Knowledge Professor with a joint appointment in the Department of Sociology and the Law School where she also holds the inaugural Raymond Pace and Sadie Tanner Mosell Alexander chair. Her pathbreaking work in law and public policy focuses on urgent contemporary issues in health, social justice, and bioethics, especially as they impact the lives of women, children and African-Americans. Her major books include *Killing the Black Body: Race, Reproduction, and the Meaning of Liberty* (1998). She is the author of more than one hundred scholarly articles and book chapters.

The last time I was filled with euphoric confidence that the left would win the battle for reproductive freedom was when I linked arms with black women activists at a march in Washington, D.C. in 2004. My elation stemmed partly from a victory of one of the co-sponsors, SisterSong: it had shifted the march's focus from "choice" to "social justice." This shift was dramatically symbolized by deleting the words "freedom of choice" from the march's original name—Save Women's Lives: March for Freedom of Choice—to rename it the March for Women's Lives.

For too long, the rhetoric of "choice" has privileged predominantly white middle-class women who have the ability to choose from reproductive options that are unavailable to poor and low-income women, especially women of color. The mainstream movement for reproductive rights has narrowed its concerns to advocate almost exclusively for the legal right to abortion, further distancing its agenda from the interests of women who have been targets of sterilization abuse because of the devaluation of their right to bear children.

A caucus of Black feminists at a 1994 pro-choice conference coined the term "reproductive justice," a framework that includes not only a woman's right not to have a child, but also the right to have children and to raise them with dignity in safe, healthy, and supportive environments. This framework repositioned reproductive rights in a political context of intersecting race, gender, and class oppressions. The caucus recognized that their activism had to be linked to social justice organizing in order to gain the power, resources, and structural change needed for addressing the well-being of all women. Back in 2004, SisterSong brought a reproductive justice approach to the march's leadership and helped to mobilize busloads of newly energized, diverse supporters, making the march one of the largest of its kind in U.S. history. The success of the March for Women's Lives demonstrates a winning strategy; under the leadership of women of color, the left needs to ditch the dominant reproductive rights logic and replace it with a broader vision of reproductive justice.

The language of choice has proved useless for claiming public resources that most women need in order to maintain control over their bodies and their lives. Indeed, giving women "choices" has eroded the argument for state support, because women without sufficient resources are simply held responsible for making "bad" choices. The reproductive rights movement was set on this losing trajectory immediately after *Roe v. Wade*, when mainstream organizations failed to make funding for abortion and opposition to coercive birth control policies central aspects of their agenda. There was no sustained major effort to block the Hyde Amendment, which has been attached to annual appropriations bills since 1976 and excludes most abortions from Medicaid funding. Mainstream reproductive rights organizations practically ignored the explosion of government policies in the 1990s, such as welfare "family caps" and prosecution for using drugs while pregnant, principally aimed at punishing childbearing by Black women who received public assistance. This myopia not only alienated women of color, but also failed to address the connection between criminalization of pregnant women and abortion rights. Today, a resurgence of prosecutions for crimes against a fetus makes crystal clear a unified right-wing campaign to regulate pregnant women—whether these women plan to carry their pregnancies to term or not. There is little to distinguish criminal charges against women for "feticide" and for abortions.

The impediment to winning is not just the current right-wing onslaught of state laws; also pernicious is a nasty, resilient strain of thinking within the left that views birth control as a means of addressing social and environmental problems like poverty and "overpopulation." On one hand, the right has recently exploited the history of eugenics to falsely portray abortion as a form of Black "genocide" and to ban abortions intended to avoid having a baby with Down syndrome. On the other hand, however, the left has yet to purge its advocacy of family planning of some of its racist and eugenicist roots, which can be traced back to the early twentieth century when progressives promoted controlling reproduction of "unfit" populations. Margaret Sanger allied with eugenicists to further her crusade for women's access to birth control, entangling the issue of reproductive rights with both liberating and oppressive aims.

Today, the mainstream reproductive rights movement has failed to confront liberals' promotion of birth control as a way to save taxpayer money spent on unintended, welfare-dependent children. For example, the *New York Times*, *Slate*, and the *American Journal of Public Health* recently published articles recommending increased use of provider-controlled long-acting contraceptives among low-income populations in order to reduce poverty, high school drop-out rates, and Medicaid costs. The troubling legacy of the U.S. biologist Paul R. Ehrlich is also perpetuated today by some environmentalists like Population Connection (formerly Zero Population Growth) and the Sierra Club's Global Population and Environment Program, which continue to see birth control as a way of addressing global "overpopulation." Framing birth control as a cost-reducing and problem-solving measure masks its potential for racial and class bias and coercion, as well as the systemic and structural reasons for social inequities.

Moreover, pro-choice groups have used the "tragedy" of fetal anomalies as an argument for supporting abortion rights without considering discrimination against people with disabilities or the potential for alliances with disability rights activists to improve the wellbeing of women and children, or the history of approved therapeutic abortions and unapproved elective abortions. The liberal notion of reproductive choice aligns with a neoliberal market logic that relies on individuals' purchase of commodities to manage their own health, instead of the state investing in health care and the other social needs of the larger public. The rhetoric of choice obscures the potential for reproductive and genetic selection technologies to intensify regulation of women's childbearing decisions in order to privatize remedies for illness and social inequities. While we should point a finger at right-wing legislators for creating wedge issues, the dominant framework for reproductive rights advocacy has created colossal political chasms within the left all by itself.

A reproductive justice framework can attract support from tens of thousands of women alienated by the mainstream agenda—poor and low-income women, women of color, queer women, women with disabilities, and women whose lives revolve around caregiving. In addition, the movement's social justice focus provides a concrete basis for building radical coalitions with organizations fighting for racial, economic, and environmental justice, for immigrant, queer, and disabled people, and for systemic change in law enforcement, health care, and education. True reproductive freedom requires a living wage, universal health care, and the abolition of prisons. Black women see the police slaughter of unarmed people in their communities as a reproductive justice issue. They recognize that women are frequent victims of racist police violence and that cutting short the lives of Black youth violates the right of mothers to raise their children in healthy, humane environments. The reproductive justice movement and Black Lives Matter are likely allies because, at their core, both insist that American society must begin to value Black humanity. Black, Latina, Asian-American, and indigenous reproductive justice organizations have a history of solidarity, exemplified by SisterSong, and they have begun to forge links with other social justice movements.

The galvanizing impact of reproductive justice extends beyond these mobilization and coalition-building strategies. The movement articulates the rationale for reproductive freedom in positive moral and political terms, as a requirement for social justice, human rights, and women's well-being. Reproductive justice activists treat abortion and other reproductive health services as akin to the resources all human beings are entitled to—such as health care, education, housing, and food—in an equitable, democratic society.

In January 2015, the leaders of five Black reproductive justice organizations launched a national initiative called In Our Own Voice: National Black Women's Reproductive Justice Agenda to mobilize Black women, initially highlighting three key policy issues: abortion rights and access, contraceptive equity, and comprehensive sex education. The initiative plays off Black women's unique strategic position: they have a long legacy of grassroots organizing for reproductive justice and they are the most progressive voting block in the nation's electorate. Reproductive justice initiatives spearheaded by women of color are important, not because they allot these women a marginalized voice within the same losing reproductive rights agenda, but because they let women of color lead a reproductive justice movement that can win.

Reproductive Rights, Slavery, and *Dobbs v. Jackson*

JENNIFER MORGAN

Black Perspectives (African American Intellectual History Society), August 2, 2022.

Jennifer Morgan, is professor of social and cultural analysis and history at New York University, the author of the prize-winning *Reckoning with Slavery: Gender, Kinship and Capitalism in the Early Black Atlantic* (2021) and of *Laboring Women: Gender and Reproduction in the Making of New World Slavery* (2004). She is the co-editor of *Connexions: Histories of Race and Sex in America* (2016). Her research examines the intersections of gender and race in the Black Atlantic. Morgan is the past-vice president of the Berkshire Conference of Women Historians and is a lifetime member of the Association of Black Women Historians.

In 1662, the Virginia legislature cast a cold, calculating eye on Black women's children. Never mind that fewer than 150 Black women were enslaved there at the time, those legislators recognized that control of women's reproductive bodies yielded both profits and policing that would be at the heart of their wealth and the colony's future. In doing so, they set in motion a precedent for violent state involvement in the bodies of dispossessed women that we are viscerally encountering today some 360 years later.

Their intent was to rectify an error on their predecessors' part. Six years earlier, a Black woman named Elizabeth Keye had successfully sued for her freedom on the basis of the fact that while her mother had been an enslaved Angolan woman, her father had been a free, white, property-owning Englishman who, not incidentally, was also a member of the Virginia legislature. Based on her paternal inheritance she claimed a freedom that was, indeed, logically hers based on centuries of Anglo-European juridical notions of both descent and the prerogatives of Christianity. Keye used the laws of descent against them—and now they needed to clarify the relationship between their power and her mother's womb.

Six years later, after she had slipped away from the bondage that she had labored under for the first twenty-six years of her life, the Virginia legislators realized that something about their concession to her sat poorly with them. In the 1660s, they represented the political and economic interests of about 15,000 English settlers among whom lived a mere 300–500 Africans—some enslaved, some free. Still, the implications of Keye's freedom suit were alarming. Their brethren to the south in the colonies of Antigua and Barbados had already begun to carve enormous wealth out of the land using the labor of Black workers. Their Blackness was increasingly the key symbol of their enslavability—conveying through the color of their skin and the texture of their hair an astonishing range of claims that we now clearly understand as racism. And so, with eyes set on a horizon in which their wealth and power would be guaranteed through the relentless labor of other people, the Virginia legislators reconsidered their earlier decision and wrote, "Whereas some doubts have arisen whether children got by any Englishman upon a negro woman should be slave or free . . . all children borne in this country shall be held bond or free only according to the condition of the mother." The Act cemented hereditary racial slavery, overturned long-standing laws that regulated fatherhood, and incentivized rape for capitalism.

The connecting tissue between 1662 and 2022 are fundamentally rooted in the history of slavery and reproduction. In his concurrence to *Dobbs v. Jackson Women's Health Organization*, Clarence Thomas mobilizes, as he has since he joined the Bench, his opposition to substantive due process. This is the clause in the Fourteenth Amendment that says that "no state shall make or enforce any law which shall abridge the privileges or immunities of citizens of the United States; nor shall any State deprive any person of life, liberty, or property, without due process of law; nor deny to any person within its jurisdiction the equal protection of the laws." It is from here that the notion of privacy as a protected right emerges—much to the dismay of conservative jurists like Thomas.

Thomas has long marshalled the history of slavery and racism to buttress his deeply conservative politics. Thus, Thomas gestures to Moynihan's "tangle of pathology" as he laments the damage slavery did to Black manhood, lambasts birth control and abortion as the strategy of eugenicists trying to control Black populations, and cites the failures of Reconstruction and its aftermaths to argue for the importance of gun ownership and the sacrosanct nature of the Second Amendment. But his fundamental opposition is rooted in rejecting the notion that the autonomous body is constitutionally protected.

As Corey Robin has recently written, Thomas has played a central role in the demise of *Roe v Wade*, and his stance against substantive due process is at its heart. For Thomas, past misreading of the Fourteenth Amendment has led to the explosion of what he defines as "unenumerated" rights—those rights not listed in the Constitution and thus not guaranteed by it. Thomas argues this proliferation of rights has eroded traditional authority, denying Black men of their opportunity to be strong father figures. Abortion is just the tip of the iceberg for this interpretation. Birth control, state support for single mothers, the rights of the incarcerated, same sex marriage—all of these are in the sights of not just Thomas, but also the conservative religious right. "To reverse the downward spiral of social decadence and patriarchal decay, conservatives must undo the liberal culture of rights, starting with the unenumerated rights of substantive due process." This is the fundamental issue. Only rights enumerated in the Constitution—like the right to bear arms—are those whose tradition and text must be upheld. Rights rooted in privacy, or worse, in bodily integrity, are not the business of the federal government.

It might be argued that the right to privacy is a modern concern. One that, as Thomas himself argues, emerged in the aftermath of the "rights revolutions" of the 1960s. And yet, the legal case of Elizabeth Keye reminds us that women's struggles over bodily autonomy are at the foundation of our modern political and economic institutions. Racial slavery pitted women's reproductive capacities against the interest of the state, introducing a conflict between a woman's identity as a parent and the child's identity as a commodity—enacting, most brutally and decisively, the notion that the fetus's worth was paramount, and that the mother's corporeal integrity was immaterial. The 1662 case should remind us that the founding legislators of this country were erecting a legal system in which, among other things, the expansion of the slave economy rendered women's reproductive lives as matters of political, legal, and economic intervention. The absence of the right to bodily integrity for the formerly enslaved should have been rectified in the aftermath of the Civil War and the Emancipation Proclamation. Instead, we have seen the erosion of such claims to autonomy—rooted in the experience of the enslaved—expanding exponentially into the lives of poor and dispossessed Americans across the racial spectrum. The Supreme Court has just put the rights of a fetus above those of the person who carries it. Where is the precedent for the appropriation of a person's body by the state? Where did we learn in this country that the state could define a fetus as a distinct matter of law and property and state intervention? We learned that from the long and violent history of hereditary racial slavery. The laws of our country laid a clear path towards the utter dispossession of rights bearing subjects at the hands of the state. Elizabeth Keye saw it coming in 1656. Every woman in this country now understands it too, as a matter of deep and relentless dispossession at the hands of those whose agendas have always been to rewrite American law to erase the impact and implications of the history of slavery.

'Caught in the Net': Interrogated, Examined, Blackmailed: How Law Enforcement Treated Abortion-Seeking Women Before *Roe*

LESLIE REAGAN

Slate, September 10, 2021.

Leslie J. Reagan is a professor at the University of Illinois and specializes in the history of American medicine and public health, women, gender, and sexuality, disabilities, and visual culture. In 2012, she was named a University Scholar, the highest award the University gives for scholarship, teaching, and service. Her most recent book, *Dangerous Pregnancies: Mothers, Disabilities, and Abortion in Modern America* (2010), has won several awards, including the Joan Kelly Award from the American Historical Association and the Eileen Basker Memorial Prize from the Society for Medical Anthropology of the American Anthropology Association.

Twelve police officers with walkie-talkies and binoculars hid in the nearby fields and in the farmhouse next door, waiting and watching. It was dark. After seeing a car drive up carrying two women, who then went inside the house, the officers unlocked the front door and went in. They walked down the halls and into the bedrooms, where they found one woman wearing only a slip in one room, two lying in bed in another, and two more who, having removed their skirts and underwear, sat waiting for their abortions in a third. The police questioned, photographed, and fingerprinted each woman. Then they drove them in police cars to a doctor, to be vaginally examined while in police custody.

This is the beginning of a true story of a raid on an underground abortion clinic by Pennsylvania state troopers in the late 1950s. It began when a suspicious neighbor called the police after listening on her party-line phone and overhearing her neighbor's conversation about a pregnancy. The raid was easy: Since the landlord had given the police a key, they walked in and surprised everybody there. The police didn't act in response to reports of injury or deaths. Abortion was simply illegal, and police raids based on reports from suspicious neighbors or doctors were standard methods of enforcing the law.

Standard, too, was the approach of capturing women in the midst of an abortion procedure and gynecologically examining them for evidence. Women who sought abortions were not targeted for prosecution (although some states allowed it). Prosecutors who tried to go after women who sought abortions in the nineteenth century had quickly learned that juries refused to convict and shifted to pursuing abortion providers when women died. By the 1940s and 1950s, though, police were shutting down providers even if they were safe. The law treated aborting women as "victims" and used them for evidence. Being captured, examined, interrogated, occasionally jailed, and forced to testify in court, however, punished women for seeking abortions even if they were never prosecuted or convicted of a crime.

The Texan abortion ban that took effect last week is designed to encourage private citizens to spy and report on suspicious people and activities, in the same way that the Pennsylvania woman reported her neighbor in 1958. In fact, the Texas statute permits *only* nonstate actors to bring civil lawsuits against individuals or organizations they suspect have "aided" or "abetted" any abortion that occurs after six weeks. This unusual law excludes state officials and police from enforcement—typically their job, of course—in order to make challenging its constitutionality difficult. And the Texas statute, like those in some states before *Roe*, doesn't allow women themselves to be sued for getting abortions. This tactic allows anti-abortion activists to claim they are "on women's side," and don't intend to harass them, but rather to target what they call the "abortion industry."

There are a few things standing between women in Texas and the kind of invasive enforcement that happened in the past. Right now, Texas police can't conduct raids or force medical exams under the statute, because the law depends on citizen enforcement. This new law does not require proof that an abortion occurred; *intention* to help or to perform an abortion past the six-week mark is enough. But if a judge assessing claims under the present statute wanted more evidence of an abortion taking place than that offered by anti-abortion volunteers, judges could conceivably order examinations, just as some have ordered C-sections or specific medical care. And if the Supreme Court, in formally overturning *Roe*, allows other state laws banning abortion to take effect (including Texas's own "trigger" law), police raids like those that took place in Pennsylvania in 1958 may happen again.

In the 1950s and 1960s, police raided the offices and apartments where abortion providers worked, with the goal of catching practitioners and patients both. In the Pennsylvania case I described above, state troopers put the women in police cars and brought them to a male doctor to determine whether a "surgical procedure" had been performed. Late on a Friday night, the women submitted to a vaginal examination by the doctor, who then named them and testified about their bodies in court.

Let's look at reality rather than hiding behind fairly innocuous medical terms like "examine." The doctor's examination in search for evidence required each woman to remove her clothing, spread her legs, and allow the doctor to touch and look at her genitals, and physically invade her vagina with a medical instrument—a cold speculum—through which he viewed her cervix and uterus. In the name of collecting evidence of a crime, the doctor performed a coercive exam. And even if he was polite and kind, these were humiliating, voyeuristic, and frightening procedures performed not for the benefit of the woman, but for the police. Prenatal care and annual gynecological exams included pelvic exams, but at that time, many patients found them uncomfortable and avoided them in order to avoid exposure and embarrassment. We can imagine the horror of captured women forced to undergo such exams. We also now know that such exams can be particularly traumatizing for people who have been sexually abused.

Following the examinations of the women in Pennsylvania, the police took them to their headquarters. The police searched for other evidence as well: they collected envelopes of cash and gathered anything that appeared to be part of the abortion process, taking medications, rubber tubing, medical gloves and masks, a table, gauze, surgical instruments, and more. They photographed the abortion specialist and his two assistants, and the rooms of the house. What was set up as a clinic was now photographed and presented in court as a "crime scene." When the case against the abortionist and his assistants came to trial, the doctor and one of the patients testified. The doctor reported his findings: in two women he found vaginal bleeding and "packing." The cotton gauze packed into the uterus, he explained, was intended to irritate the cervix and thereby induce a miscarriage.

The state went after abortion providers, not aborting women, and in this case all three defendants were sentenced to prison. Nonetheless, in this case and in others from the pre-*Roe* era, women who aborted were punished, shamed, and physically violated through the processes of capture, gynecological examinations, interrogation, and being forced to testify in a public courtroom. If women who had sought abortions refused to cooperate, they risked threats and being sent to jail, as happened to one Chicago woman in 1949. When she refused to testify about her abortion, the judge cited her for contempt and sentenced her to six months in jail. One night in jail convinced her to talk. In other cases, there's evidence that prosecutors released photographs to the press or threatened women caught in raids with prosecution in order to win cooperation from hostile witnesses.

Women who traveled for abortions before *Roe* also faced versions of this invasive enforcement of the law. Mexico decriminalized abortion this week, one week after Texas's abortion ban went into effect. Online commenters immediately grasped that Texans would be crossing the border for safe, legal abortions in Mexico. They also wryly suggested that Texas Gov. Greg Abbott would place guards on the border to check all Texans leaving the state, in order to stop abortions. This nightmare scenario may seem utterly ridiculous, but it has been done before. In the 1960s, thousands of American women from California, Texas, Arizona, and nearly every other state went to Mexico for safe (but illegal) abortions. Attempting to stop them, San Diego border patrol agents would question young women closely when they crossed the border, looking for people who might be leaving for an abortion or returning afterward. They wouldn't allow women under the age of eighteen to cross the border without parental permission, when alerting parents was, no doubt, what some of these young people wanted to avoid.

Given that the state has demonstrated its hostility to the autonomous decision-making of pregnant women, it is not at all unlikely that Texas—or vigilante citizens acting in the state's place—will attempt to stop women from accessing abortions outside the state. Still, even if Americans cross the border for legal, safe abortions in Mexico—in the same way that Americans go to Mexico to buy pharmaceuticals, alcohol, gas, and other items and services for less—not everyone will be able to go there. Not only does travel to Mexico take money and time, many cannot easily leave the U.S. because they are minors, have green cards, or are undocumented.

History offers grim examples of what making abortion a crime means for women whose lives and bodies are invaded by law enforcement. If this history is a guide, they are likely to be shamed, traumatized, and victimized, in the name of their own protection. Black, brown, and poor women will be hit the hardest—both because of their disproportionate use of abortion, and because of the overpolicing of people of color. Almost half of the states now have laws on the books ready to make abortion a crime again if the Supreme Court rules in the anti-abortion movement's favor. For women who will pursue abortions anyway, and end up shamed, roughly handled by law enforcement, traumatized, and (in some states) prosecuted, it's a disaster in the making.

The Abortion Fight Has Never Been About Just *Roe v. Wade*

MARY ZEIGLER

The Atlantic, August 14, 2022.

Mary Ziegler holds the Martin Luther King Jr. Professor of Law at the University of California Davis School of Law. She is an expert on the law, history, and politics of reproduction, health care, and conservatism in the United States from 1945 to the present. A 2023 Guggenheim fellow, she is the author of numerous articles and six books on social movement struggles around reproduction, autonomy, and the law, including *Reproduction and the Constitution* (2022), *Dollars for Life: The Anti-Abortion Movement and the Fall of the Republican Establishment* (2022) and most recently *Roe: The History of a National Obsession* (2023).

This week, the Supreme Court agreed to hear a case that could result in the overruling of *Roe v. Wade*. The case, *Dobbs v. Jackson Women's Health Organization*, involves a Mississippi law that bans abortion starting at the fifteenth week of pregnancy. Significantly, the statute draws the line before fetal viability—the point at which survival is possible outside the womb. The Court has previously held that before viability, "the state's interests are not strong enough to support a prohibition of abortion or substantial obstacle to the woman's effective right to elect the procedure." To uphold Mississippi's law, the Court would have to rewrite the rules—perhaps just the opportunity it needs to overturn Roe altogether.

If that happens, it will represent the culmination of decades of work by anti-abortion-rights activists. But for those activists, gutting *Roe* would be just the beginning.

Ever since *Roe*, abortion-rights foes and their Republican allies have been asking the Court to reverse course—to acknowledge that the Constitution has nothing whatsoever to say about abortion, either in favor of or against it. Antonin Scalia, the Supreme Court justice arguably most beloved by conservatives, routinely stated that the Constitution is silent on abortion. Republicans have railed against the Court's judicial activism in *Roe*, insisting that the justices robbed the American people of the opportunity to decide the abortion issue for themselves. In this account, *Roe* did not just destroy valuable opportunities for compromise on abortion; the decision did fundamental damage to America's democratic principles, removing one of the most controversial issues from representative legislatures and resolving it by judicial fiat.

But within the anti-abortion-rights movement, there is not so much talk about democracy anymore. Now some abortion-rights opponents are quite literally looking for a *Roe* of their own, asking the Court to recognize fetal rights under the Fourteenth Amendment. Remember that overturning *Roe* wouldn't make abortion illegal; it would mean that states could set their own abortion limits, which would no longer be subject to constitutional review. That will never be enough for anti-abortion-rights activists, though. In the conservative magazine *First Things*, John Finnis, a professor emeritus at the University of Notre Dame, recently made an argument that could provide the framework an anti-abortion-rights Supreme Court could use to outlaw abortion across the country: that the legislators who wrote the Fourteenth Amendment viewed unborn children as persons. If the Constitution recognizes fetal personhood, then unborn children would have the right to equal protection under and due process of the law. Abortion would be unconstitutional in New York as well as in Alabama. Other leading anti-abortion-rights scholars have made the same argument.

Finnis's article has provoked debate across the ideological spectrum. The conservative attorney Ed Whelan has taken issue with the substance of Finnis's claim, suggesting that unless the anti-abortion-rights movement first wins over public opinion, Finnis's approach will backfire. Progressives have been far harsher, unsurprisingly. Writing in *The New York Times*, the columnist Michelle Goldberg denounced what she calls an authoritarian turn in anti-abortion-rights advocacy—one more sign that the GOP has changed fundamentally in the post-Trump era.

The abortion debate has never been about just *Roe*—and it's never been about letting a popular majority have a say. What's new is that this argument now meets a receptive Supreme Court for the first time in more than a generation.

The anti-abortion-rights movement mobilized in the 1960s, pre-*Roe*, as states began loosening criminal abortion laws. From quite early on, abortion-rights foes defined their cause as a constitutional one—a defense of the rights of unborn children. Anti-abortion-rights lawyers argued that everything from "the Declaration of Independence [to] the United States Declaration of Human Rights" protected a fetal right to life. Then as now, anti-abortion-rights lawyers paid particular attention to the Fourteenth Amendment. One of the post–Civil War provisions passed during Reconstruction, the amendment guarantees "persons" equal protection under the law and due process of the law. Quite clearly, the amendment extended those protections to recently freed Black people. Long before *Roe*, anti-abortion-rights leaders insisted that the Fourteenth Amendment did the same thing for unborn children. Their argument was simple: If fetuses qualify as persons under the Fourteenth Amendment, the Constitution itself prohibits abortion.

The appeal of this personhood argument to those who believe that a fetus is a person created in God's image or is otherwise sacred is obvious. When states proposed laws allowing abortion only in cases of rape, incest, fetal abnormality, or a severe threat to the mother's health, anti-abortion-rights activists almost universally rejected them. Believing that unborn children have a right to life, the movement's leaders rejected any middle-ground law as unconstitutional and immoral.

But arguments for personhood under the Fourteenth Amendment also attracted support partly because, leading up to *Roe*, abortion-rights foes viewed the courts as a potential ally. Across the country, lawyers went on the offensive, asking courts to appoint them the guardians of unborn children or to reinstate criminal laws that legislatures had wiped away. Their optimism seemed reasonable until the Supreme Court decided *Roe*. While recognizing a privacy right to end a pregnancy, the Court also rejected the case for personhood under the Fourteenth Amendment.

In recent decades, strategies like Finnis's have rarely dominated national conversations. That's not primarily because abortion-rights opponents changed their mind about the meaning of the Fourteenth Amendment. Instead, talking about personhood seemed to be a waste of time. After all, following *Roe*, the courts appeared to be antagonists rather than allies.

Moreover, by the early 1980s, the anti-abortion-rights movement had come to rely on the Republican Party, which Ronald Reagan had made the "party of life." And the Fourteenth Amendment argument did not work as well for the movement's new Republican allies. GOP leaders had mocked the Court for inventing rights from whole cloth and stripping the people of the power to decide for themselves whether abortion should be legal. If a conservative Court effectively outlawed all abortions, people could easily accuse the justices of committing the sin that the GOP had long decried.

So instead, abortion-rights opponents argued that *Roe* was a prime example of judicial activism, out of step with the original, publicly understood meaning of the Fourteenth Amendment.

In this, they found allies in the Reagan administration, which was well served by arguments about judicial activism. The president and his allies accused the Court of overreaching in *Roe*—and doing real damage to the country. The administration suggested that an imperial judiciary was riding roughshod over American democracy. Christian conservatives had hoped that the president would appoint judges who openly opposed abortion. But Reagan, who had vowed to depoliticize the judiciary, could hardly fulfill that promise without seeming hypocritical. Labeling *Roe* an activist decision—and calling for a more restrained approach to constitutional interpretation—signaled that the Reagan administration was looking for anti-*Roe* judges while allowing the president to say that his judges would never impose their own policy preferences on the American people. Besides, when it came to a fragmented GOP coalition, almost everyone disliked something that the Court had done recently. Hatred of judicial activism united Reagan Republicans who disagreed about much else.

So for years, anti-abortion-rights activists lambasted the *Roe* Court for failing to uphold democracy. But recently, their leaders seem far less concerned about popular opinion. Some states have passed sweeping laws curtailing abortion rights—many without rape or incest exceptions—even though polling suggests that the public does not support them. Talk has turned away from protecting democracy and toward maximizing protection for fetal life.

This is partly because abortion-rights opponents are optimistic about the Supreme Court—and with good reason. Donald Trump chose three new justices, creating a supermajority that seems likely to reverse *Roe* and perhaps go much further. The movement doesn't feel that it has to settle anymore. The Court's decision to take *Dobbs* certainly suggests that *Roe* is not long for this world.

Another factor is that changes to the GOP have made it easier for abortion-rights foes to pursue a personhood strategy. In past years, the Republican Party (like the Democratic Party) shied away from arguments that could expose it to charges that it had embraced extremism. In the post-Trump era, however, the GOP has been more inclined to try to energize the base or shrink the electorate than win new supporters. In earlier decades, the anti-abortion-rights movement might have hesitated to promote Finnis's argument for fear of alienating voters—Gallup recently found that seventy-nine percent of Americans think that at least some abortions should be legal. Today's Republican Party does not concern itself much with popular majorities in the first place.

Is the anti-abortion-rights movement correct that a personhood argument could be welcomed by the Court? Even the most ardent supporters of a Fourteenth Amendment strategy recognize its perils. Finnis himself acknowledges that the Court would face "unimaginable resistance" if it followed his advice. Overturning *Roe* is one thing; recognizing fetal personhood is another. Doing so would force the Court to continue taking abortion-adjacent cases, as it might need to figure out what personhood means across a wide variety of legal domains, such as whether a fetus can make personal-injury claims and how fetuses figure into the tax code. Finnis and his allies respond to this counterargument by saying that a personhood strategy still makes sense: social movements rarely succeed unless they fight for what they really want—and persuade the public to embrace their view of the world.

Anti-abortion-rights groups may have forgotten the most important lesson of all, though, one that pro-abortion-rights groups learned the hard way in the aftermath of *Roe*: Winning in the Supreme Court gets you only so far. Harry Blackmun, the author of the *Roe* decision, kept a clipping of a poll suggesting that the large majority of Americans believed abortion to be a decision between a woman and her doctor. In writing the *Roe* decision, he hoped to tamp down the controversy surrounding abortion and maybe even pave the way to a less acrimonious debate. We all see how that worked out.

The Reconstruction Amendments Matter When Considering Abortion Rights

PEGGY COOPER DAVIS

Washington Post, May 3, 2022

Peggy Cooper Davis is the John S. R. Shad Professor of Lawyering and Ethics at New York University and the author of *Neglected Stories: The Constitution and Family Values* (1997).

On Monday night, *Politico* reported that a Supreme Court made significantly more conservative by President Donald Trump's appointments had voted in an initial conference on a Mississippi abortion case to overturn the line of decisions beginning with *Roe* v. *Wade* in 1973 that provide the right to have an abortion. The bombshell report also included a draft opinion that it said Justice Samuel Alito had written.

The Founders may not have intended in 1789 to secure for the people of the United States liberty to choose whether to continue a pregnancy. The framers of the original Constitution and the Bill of Rights are not known to have contemplated abortion choice as it relates to the balance between individual and family autonomy on the one hand and state power on the other.

But, the Constitution underwent a radical transformation after the Civil War. A document that had tolerated human bondage and been interpreted to deny Black people the privileges of citizenship was amended to embrace principles of human equality and republican freedom. The Thirteenth Amendment secured the blessings of liberty by ending slavery. The Fourteenth Amendment protected against unwarranted invasions of human liberty.

The lawmakers who implemented those changes did so in direct response to slavery's heartless separations of families and to enslavers' brutal practices of human breeding.

Speaking on the Senate floor in 1866 to the civil rights that the Reconstruction Congress meant to protect, Sen. Jacob Howard of Michigan, a member of the Committee on Reconstruction, noted that the enslaved had no right to be a spouse or parent in the eyes of the law and were "not at liberty to indulge the natural affections of the human heart" for children or partners. "What definition," he asked, would you attach to the word freedom without these rights?

Howard and others understood that slavery had denied enslaved people familial rights and control over their reproductive choices. "Slave narratives," written by people who had been enslaved but found freedom, spoke movingly of the loss of reproductive control. J.W. Loguen's narrative told of his determination not to partner because, as he put it, slavery would "never own a wife or child of mine." The narrative of Henry Bibb contained these words: "If there was any one act of my life while a slave, that I have to lament over it is that of being a father and a husband of slaves." Bibb vowed that the daughter whom he left in slavery was "the last . . . that ever I will father, for chains and slavery on this earth."

Enslaved women seized control of their reproductive capacities in more direct ways. Some were abstinent or used substances and devices to prevent conception or to induce abortion. Herbert Gutman, the historian of slavery who compiled the most extensive evidence of these practices, details physicians' reports that abortion and miscarriage occurred with inordinate frequency among enslaved women.

One doctor found that during slavery "all country practitioners . . . [were] aware of the frequent complaints of planters about the unnatural tendency in the African female to destroy her offspring." Another physician reported that some enslaved women tried "to effect an abortion or to derange menstruation" by medicine, violent exercise and "external and internal manipulation."

Enslaved women also used abortifacients, including vaginally inserted rags, and ingested tansy, rue, roots and seed of the cotton plant, pennyroyal, cedar gum and camphor. There is little doubt that these actions were enslaved women's efforts to exert control over their bodies and their progeny. In a biographical booklet published in 1897 by a daughter of her former enslaver, Jane Blake was said to have refused to bear children for enslavement. As the author of Blake's biography commented: "If all the bond women had been of the same mind, how soon the institution [of slavery] could have vanished from the earth."

Freedom meant the right to have families on one's terms. A childless enslaved woman was sold as "unsound" in 1857, presumably because she was barren; she had three children after emancipation. Following and even during the Civil War, emancipated couples that previously were unable to have their unions legally recognized rushed to claim legal status for their families.

Historian James McPherson documented this rush to marriage.

An agent of the federal government's Freedmen's Bureau reported legalizing seventy-nine Black marriages in a single day. A Black Union soldier told the government official of the many prayers he had made for legal recognition of his family, calling that recognition a mark of respect and a sign that those formerly enslaved had been "established as a people." A Mississippi regiment chaplain who had legalized forty-three marriages reported that emancipated people considered the Civil War not only an exodus from bondage, but a "road to Responsibility; Competency; and honorable Citizenship."

The Reconstruction amendments were inspired by antislavery beliefs, and they were designed to extend to all people the right to have autonomous life choices of the kind that slavery had so cruelly restricted. In the words of Sen. Lyman Trumbull of Illinois, an author of the Thirteenth Amendment, their authors designed the amendments to assure that liberty was restrained only so far as necessary for the public good. "And no further."

Other members of the Reconstruction Congress made clear that this liberty principle extended to the realm of partnering and reproduction. Rep. John Creswell of Maryland decried the fact that enslaved people could not claim their spouse, their child or even their own bodies. Rep. Robert Elliott of South Carolina noted that because partners could be separated at an owner's will slavery "could not know a home," and that no act could secure freedom if it did not contemplate "the security of home." Sen. Henry Wilson of Massachusetts said that upon passage of the 13th Amendment "the sharp cry of the agonizing hearts of severed families will cease to vex the weary ear of the nation."

For more than two-hundred years, America lived with slavery and felt the brutality of its disregard of enslaved people's family ties and of their reproductive autonomy and choice. As a consequence, the United States amended its Constitution to strengthen its commitment to human liberty in the formation and families and the conduct of family life. This history frames today's debates about reproductive freedom.

The Racist History of Abortion and Midwifery Bans

MICHELE GOODWIN

ACLU Online Journal, July 1, 2020

Michele Bratcher Goodwin is a Chancellor's Professor at the University of California, Irvine and founding director of the Center for Biotechnology and Global Health Policy. She is the 2022 recipient of the American Bar Association's Margaret Brent Award and held the Abraham Pinanski Visiting Professorship of Law at Harvard University in 2023. Dr. Goodwin is also the recipient of the 2020–2021 Distinguished Senior Faculty Award for Research, the highest honor bestowed by the University of California and the 2021–2022 Provost's Distinguished Visiting Faculty Fellow at the University of Pennsylvania. She is an elected member of the American Law Institute as well as an elected Fellow of the American Bar Foundation and the Hastings Center (the organization central to the founding of bioethics). Dr. Goodwin is the author of the award-winning book, *Policing The Womb: Invisible Women and the Criminalization of Motherhood.*

In 1851, Sojourner Truth delivered a speech best known as "Ain't I A Woman?" to a crowded audience at the Women's Convention in Akron, Ohio. At the time, slavery remained in full force, a vibrant enterprise that fueled the American economy. Various laws protected that system, including the Fugitive Slave Act, which resulted in the abduction of "free" Black children, women, and men as well as those who had miraculously escaped to northern cities like Boston or Philadelphia. Bounty hunters then sold their prey to Southern plantation owners. The law denied basic protections for Black people caught in the greed-filled grasps of slavery.

Ms. Truth condemned this disgraceful enterprise, which thrived off not only uncompensated labor, but also physical and psychological terror. Most will remember Ms. Truth's oration for its vivid descriptions regarding physical labor; Black women were forced to plough, plant, herd, and build—just as men. Yet far too little attention centers on her condemnation of that system, which made sexual chattel of Black women, and then cruelly sold off Black children. This was human trafficking in the American form, and it lasted for centuries.

Ms. Truth pleaded: "I have borne 13 children, and seen most all sold off to slavery, and when I cried out with my mother's grief, none but Jesus heard me! And ain't I a woman?"

Following the Supreme Court's decision in *June Medical Services v. Russo* this week, it is worth reflecting on the racist origins of the anti-abortion movement in the United States, which date back to the ideologies of slavery. Just like slavery, anti-abortion efforts are rooted in white supremacy, the exploitation of Black women, and placing women's bodies in service to men. Just like slavery, maximizing wealth and consolidating power motivated the anti-abortion enterprise. Then, just as now, anti-abortion efforts have nothing to do with saving women's lives or protecting the interests of children. Today, a person is 14 times more likely to die by carrying a pregnancy to term than by having an abortion, and medical evidence has shown for decades that an abortion is as safe as a penicillin shot—and yet abortion remains heavily restricted in states across the country.

Prior to the Civil War, abortion and contraceptives were legal in the U.S., used by Indigenous women as well as those who sailed to these lands from Europe. For the most part, the persons who performed all manner of reproductive health care were women—female midwives. Midwifery was interracial; half of the women who provided reproductive health care were Black women. Other midwives were Indigenous and white.

However, in the wake of slavery's end, skilled Black midwives represented both real competition for white men who sought to enter the practice of child delivery, and a threat to how obstetricians viewed themselves. Male gynecologists claimed midwifery was a degrading means of obstetrical care. They viewed themselves as elite members of a trained profession with tools such as forceps and other technologies, and the modern convenience of hospitals, which excluded Black and Indigenous women from practice within their institutions.

History would later reveal that it was literally on the backs of Black women's bodies that such tools were developed. Dr. Marion Sims famously wrote about his insomniac-induced "epiphanies" that stirred him to experiment on enslaved Black women, lacerating, suturing, and cutting, providing no anesthesia or pain relief. Only recently have the terrors that Black women endured through nonconsensual experimentation by gynecologists of the 19th and 20th centuries been acknowledged.

Successful racist and misogynistic smear campaigns, cleverly designed for political persuasion and to achieve legal reform, described Black midwives as unhygienic, barbarous, ineffective, non-scientific, dangerous, and unprofessional. Dr. Joseph DeLee, a preeminent

20th century obstetrician and fervent opponent to midwifery, stated in a much-quoted 1915 speech, "Progress Toward Ideal Obstetrics": "The midwife is a relic of barbarism. In civilized countries the midwife is wrong, has always been wrong. . . . The midwife has been a drag on the progress of the science and art of obstetrics. Her existence stunts the one and degrades the other. For many centuries she perverted obstetrics from obtaining any standing at all among the science of medicine. . . . Even after midwifery was practiced by some of the most brilliant men in the profession, such practice was held opprobrious and degraded."

At the root of these stereotypes were explicit efforts to destroy midwifery and promote white supremacy. As the surge of lynchings, "separate but equal" laws, police violence, and the decimation of successful Black communities during Jim Crow revealed, Black Americans post slavery suffered greatly due to white supremacy, as did Chinese and Japanese workers and their families. Indeed, the racist campaigns launched by doctors against Black midwives extended to anti-immigration legislative platforms targeted at Chinese and Japanese workers. The Page Act, which restricted Chinese women from entering the United States, is a part of this shameful legacy. This broader 20th century anti-Chinese campaign became known as "yellow peril." DeLee and Horatio Storer urged white women to "spread their loins" across the nation, a dog whistle about the threat of too many Blacks and Asians in the U.S.

Gynecologists explicitly revealed their motivations in undermining midwifery: They desired financial gains, recognition, and a monopoly. As Dr. DeLee wrote in a 1916 article published in the American Journal of Obstetrics & Disease of Women & Children, "There is high art in obstetrics and that it must pay as well for it as for surgery. I will not admit that this is a sordid impulse. It is only common justice to labor, self-sacrifice, and skill." They believed that men should be paid, but not women—particularly not Black women.

To better understand racial injustice in the anti-abortion movement, remember that American hospitals barred the admission of African Americans both in terms of practice and as patients. And, the American Medical Association (AMA) barred women and Black people from membership. The AMA, founded in 1847, refused to admit Black doctors, informing them, "You come from groups and schools that admit women and that admit irregular practitioners." For this reason, Black doctors formed the National Medical Association in 1895.

In 2008, the organization issued a public apology for its active campaigns to close Black medical schools, deny Blacks membership, and other efforts to marginalize Black patients and practitioners. Gynecologists pushed women out of the field of reproductive health by lobbying state legislatures to ban midwifery and prohibit abortions. Doing so not only undercut women's reproductive health, but also drove qualified Black women out of medical services. For these groups, there was no meaningful path to the formalized skill set DeLee claimed necessary.

Abortion was an expedient way to frame their campaign to create monopolies on women's bodies for male doctors. The American Medical Association explicitly contributed to this cause through its exclusion of women and Black people.

Today, as people debate whether anti-abortion platforms benefit Black women, the clear answer is no. The U.S. leads the developed world in maternal and infant mortality. The U.S. ranks around 50th in the world for maternal safety. Nationally, for Black women, the maternal death rate is nearly four times that of white women, and 10 to 17 times worse in some states.

In the wake of both *Whole Woman's Health* and *June Medical Services v. Russo*, keep in mind that both Texas and Louisiana, where these cases originated, are considered the deadliest in the developed world for a woman to give birth.

Sadly, pregnancy has become a death sentence for many in the very places that make reproductive health care access the most fraught and hard to reach. Many of these states (though not all) are former slave states, such as Texas, Louisiana, Mississippi, Alabama, and Arkansas. As Black people in these states continue to fight for equal access the reproductive care they need, Sojourner Truth's 1851 speech continues to resonate. And as the Supreme Court demonstrated this week, the fight for justice in reproductive health care and equality in abortion access is far from over. The decision does not advance the equality of poor Black women—it maintains all other burdensome restrictions already in place. We have much more work to do such that not only DeLee's words, but also his racist and exploitative viewpoints, are relegated to history.

Supreme Court's Selective Reading of U.S. History Ignored 19th-Century Women's Support for 'Voluntary Motherhood'

LAUREN THOMPSON

The Conversation, September 6, 2022

Lauren Thompson is an assistant professor of History and Interdisciplinary Studies at Kennesaw State University and a faculty fellow at the Georgia State University College of Law's Center for Law, Health, and Society. Her book, *Rivals and Rights: Mary Dennett, Margaret Sanger, and the Making of the American Birth Control Movement* is forthcoming from Rutgers University Press.

The history of abortion in the U.S. guided some of Supreme Court Justice Samuel Alito's arguments in the *Dobbs v. Jackson Women's Health Organization* decision. Alito argued that abortion has never been a "deeply rooted" constitutional right in the United States. But as a historian of medicine, law and women's rights, I think Alito's read of abortion history is not only incomplete, it is also inaccurate.

Alito argued in the opinion that abortion has always been a serious crime, but there were no laws about abortion at all in Colonial America. Beginning in the 19th century, most states barred it only after "quickening," when a pregnant woman can first feel the fetus move, typically around the fourth to sixth month of pregnancy.

Abortion is indeed deeply rooted in the American experience and law. American women have always tried to personally determine the size of their families. Enslaved Black women used contraception and abortion as specific strategies of resistance against their physical and reproductive bondage.

The very passage of the Thirteenth and Fourteenth amendments, which ended slavery and guaranteed citizenship for all, is evidence that the Constitution actually does protect bodily autonomy. The Fourteenth Amendment's due process and equal protection clauses have long been the legal basis for gender equality cases. If, as the Supreme Court's ruling suggests, the right to abortion is not constitutionally protected via the Fourteenth Amendment, it opens up the possibility that other settled law concerning gender and racial equality also has the potential to be reversed.

Instead of examining abortion through the lens of past cases of gender law, however, Alito instead refers to the opinions of seventeenth-century male legal theorists, who believed in witches and the right of husbands to rape their wives. He also cites as evidence the passage of 19th-century state abortion laws by all-male legislatures, which criminalized abortion and birth control. The Comstock Postal Act of 1873 also made possessing or selling all sexual information and contraceptive items a federal crime.

Meanwhile, Alito's opinion does not discuss the women's rights movement in the 1800s or women's ordinary, daily perspectives on abortion at the time. In this landmark decision, the court has skipped one of the biggest parts of U.S. history on abortion, creating a glaring gap in an understanding of how abortions and abortion law in the country worked in the past.

Considering how suffragists like the Black journalist and activist Ida B. Wells and other prominent women's rights activists in the nineteenth century thought about rights to their own bodies is an overlooked part of this history.

Suffragists in the nineteenth century focused on a woman's right to vote—and did not openly support legalizing abortion or birth control.

The reason why reproductive rights were omitted from the suffragist campaign is complex.

Suffragists argued that legalizing birth control and abortion would hurt women, who already had few legal rights at the time. They said that men would then use these legal freedoms to further abuse and control women.

Instead, suffragists embraced an idea they termed "voluntary motherhood." This meant that women had the right to reject unwanted sex and could choose if and when they had children.

Even in happy marriages, many women in the 1800s could not necessarily control the number of pregnancies they had. Marital rape was legal, and enslavers had total control over enslaved women's bodies.

The idea of voluntary motherhood—meaning that women should have full control over their own bodies—was a powerfully radical idea. This notion appealed to women across race and class lines, and it helped drive the emergent women's rights movement, beginning in the 1840s.

Suffragist reformers recognized that the right to vote meant little if they did not have control of their bodies or reproductive lives. Black suffragists like Wells and Frances Ellen Watkins Harper, for example, spoke eloquently about the constant dangers Black women faced from white men raping and assaulting them. They and White women suffragists like Lucy Stone argued that gaining the right to vote would help women have more power to combat these problems.

These activists recognized that women turned to contraceptives and abortion to control their own reproduction. But they also said that unscrupulous manufacturers and people who performed abortions sometimes took advantage of women, by selling them ineffective or harmful contraceptives or charging them large sums for abortions. Substances used to induce abortion, or abortifacients, also often contained harmful and poisonous ingredients that killed women, while surgical abortions were incredibly risky in an era where germ theory and understandings of infection were rudimentary at best.

Reformers also openly blamed harsh anti-abortion laws for contributing to these problems—driving women to desperate measures while still allowing men to have sex freely and shirk their responsibilities of fatherhood. Suffragist Matilda Joslyn Gage agreed, writing in a suffrage newspaper in 1868 that "this crime of . . . abortion . . . lies at the door of the male sex."

Today, some anti-abortion rights women's groups look to the suffragist movement to make the case that abortion should be limited or banned. Feminists for Life and Susan B. Anthony Pro-Life America, for example, have long rested their funding and advocacy campaigns on attempting to prove that suffragists were "pro-life." But research shows that their argument is an incomplete reading of suffragists' complex views of abortion, while also falsely presuming that suffragists would have supported current laws banning abortion today.

There is ample primary source evidence in suffrage newspapers like "The Revolution" or in the private letters of the suffragists showing that they repeatedly insisted that anti-abortion laws punished women, without actually eliminating the practice of abortion.

White suffragists like Anthony held overtly racist and eugenic views, and their support for women who sought abortions often incorporated ideas of eliminating disability and what they deemed undesirable offspring. They prioritized rights for white, middle-class women and ignored or outright rejected Black reformers' urgent pleas for reproductive justice. But that messy, complex past nonetheless remains central to understanding Americans' experiences with abortion and abortion law.

Alito wrote that women's role in abortion history is too "conflicting" to be useful. Yet considering women's historical attitudes about reproductive rights—and the reasons behind these views—was a critical omission in the court's historical considerations of the role of abortion in Americans' lives.

Letters from an American

HEATHER COX RICHARDSON

Letters From an American, January 21, 2023

Heather Cox Richardson is an American historian, author, and educator. She is a professor of history at Boston College, where she teaches courses on the American Civil War, the Reconstruction Era, the American West, and the Plains Indians. Her impressive list of scholarly books includes *The Death of Reconstruction, West from Appomattox, To Make Men Free: A History of the Republican Part* and, most recently: *Democracy Awakening: Notes on the State of America.* Her weekly podcast "Now and Then" (with Joanne Freeman) covers historical perspectives on contemporary politics and her daily online *Letters From an American* attracts over a million subscribers.

Tomorrow marks the fiftieth anniversary of the *Roe v. Wade* decision. On January 22, 1973, the Supreme Court decided that for the first trimester of a pregnancy, "the attending physician, in consultation with his patient, is free to determine, without regulation by the State, that, in his medical judgment, the patient's pregnancy should be terminated. If that decision is reached, the judgment may be effectuated by an abortion free of interference by the State."

It went on: "With respect to the State's important and legitimate interest in potential life, the 'compelling' point is at viability. This is so because the fetus then presumably has the capability of meaningful life outside the mother's womb. State regulation protective of fetal life after viability thus has both logical and biological justifications. If the State is interested in protecting fetal life after viability, it may go so far as to [prohibit] abortion during that period, except when it is necessary to preserve the life or health of the mother." The wording of that decision, giving power to physicians—who were presumed to be male—to determine with a patient whether the patient's pregnancy should be terminated, shows the roots of the *Roe v. Wade* decision in a public health crisis.

Abortion had been a part of American life since its inception, but states began to criminalize abortion in the 1870s. By 1960, an observer estimated, there were between 200,000 and 1.2 million illegal U.S. abortions a year, endangering women, primarily poor ones who could not afford a workaround.

To stem this public health crisis, doctors wanted to decriminalize abortion and keep it between a woman and her doctor. In the 1960s, states began to decriminalize abortion on this medical model, and support for abortion rights grew.

The rising women's movement wanted women to have control over their lives. Its leaders were latecomers to the reproductive rights movement, but they came to see reproductive rights as key to self-determination. In 1969, activist Betty Friedan told a medical abortion meeting: "[M]y only claim to be here, is our belated recognition, if you will, that there is no freedom, no equality, no full human dignity and personhood possible for women until we assert and demand the control over our own bodies, over our own reproductive process...."

In 1971, even the evangelical Southern Baptist Convention

agreed that abortion should be legal in some cases, and vowed to work for modernization. Their convention that year reiterated the "belief that society has a responsibility to affirm through the laws of the state a high view of the sanctity of human life, including fetal life, in order to protect those who cannot protect themselves" but also called on "Southern Baptists to work for legislation that will allow the possibility of abortion under such conditions as rape, incest, clear evidence of severe fetal deformity, and carefully ascertained evidence of the likelihood of damage to the emotional, mental, and physical health of the mother."

By 1972, Gallup pollsters reported that 64% of Americans agreed that abortion should be between a woman and her doctor. Sixty-eight percent of Republicans, who had always liked family planning, agreed, as did 59% of Democrats.

In keeping with that sentiment, in 1973 the Supreme Court, under Republican Chief Justice Warren Burger, in a decision written by Republican Harry Blackmun, decided *Roe v. Wade*, legalizing first-trimester abortion.

The common story is that *Roe* sparked a backlash. But legal scholars Linda Greenhouse and Reva Siegel showed that opposition to the eventual *Roe v. Wade* decision began in 1972—the year before the decision—and that it was a deliberate attempt to polarize American politics.

In 1972, President Richard Nixon was up for reelection, and he and his people were paranoid that he would lose. His adviser Pat Buchanan was a Goldwater man who wanted to destroy the popular New Deal state that regulated the economy and protected social welfare and civil rights. To that end, he believed Democrats and traditional Republicans must be kept from power and Nixon must win reelection.

Catholics, who opposed abortion and believed that "the right of innocent human beings to life is sacred," tended to vote for Democratic candidates. Buchanan, who was a Catholic himself, urged Nixon to woo Catholic Democrats before the 1972 election over the issue of abortion. In 1970, Nixon had directed U.S. military hospitals to perform abortions regardless of state law, but in 1971, using Catholic language, he reversed course to split the Democrats, citing his personal belief "in the sanctity of human life—including the life of the yet unborn."

Although Nixon and Democratic nominee George McGovern had similar stances on abortion, Nixon and Buchanan defined McGovern as the candidate of "Acid, Amnesty, and Abortion," a radical framing designed to alienate traditionalists.

As Nixon split the U.S. in two to rally voters, his supporters used abortion to stand in for women's rights in general. Railing against the Equal Rights Amendment, in her first statement on abortion in 1972, activist Phyllis Schlafly did not talk about fetuses: "Women's lib is a total assault on the role of the American woman as wife and mother and on the family as the basic unit of society. Women's libbers are trying to make wives and mothers unhappy with their career, make them feel that they are 'second-class citizens' and 'abject slaves.' Women's libbers are promoting free sex instead of the 'slavery' of marriage. They are promoting Federal 'day-care centers' for babies instead of homes. They are promoting abortions instead of families."

A dozen years later, sociologist Kristin Luker discovered that "pro-life" activists believed that selfish "pro-choice" women were denigrating the roles of wife and mother. They wanted an active government to give them rights they didn't need or deserve.

By 1988, radio provocateur Rush Limbaugh demonized women's

rights advocates as "feminazis" for whom "the most important thing in life is ensuring that as many abortions as possible occur." The complicated issue of abortion had become a proxy for a way to denigrate the political opponents of the radicalizing Republican Party.

Such threats turned out Republican voters, especially the evangelical base. But support for safe and legal abortion has always been strong. Today, notwithstanding that it was overturned in June 2022 by a Supreme Court radicalized under Republican presidents since Nixon, about sixty-two percent of Americans support the guidelines laid down in *Roe v. Wade*, about the same percentage that supported it fifty years ago, when it became law.

References

https://news.gallup.com/poll/350804/americans-opposed-overturning-roe-wade.aspx

Linda Greenhouse and Reva B. Siegel, "Before (and After) Roe v. Wade: New Questions About Backlash," *The Yale Law Journal*, 120 (June 2011): 2028–2087, at https://www.jstor.org/stable/41149586

https://awpc.cattcenter.iastate.edu/2016/02/02/whats-wrong-with-equal-rights-for-women-1972/

https://www.nytimes.com/interactive/2023/01/21/us/abortion-ban-exceptions.html

https://www.law.cornell.edu/supremecourt/text/410/113

https://www.washingtonpost.com/history/2022/05/15/abortion-history-founders-alito/

https://www.pewresearch.org/politics/2022/07/06/majority-of-public-disapproves-of-supreme-courts-decision-to-overturn-roe-v-wade/

https://www.theguardian.com/commentisfree/2015/oct/01/feminazi-feminists-women-rights-feminism-charlotte-proudman

Kristin Luker, *Abortion and the Politics of Motherhood* (University of California Press, 198)

A Major Problem for Minors: Post-Roe Access to Abortion

TRACEY WILKINSON, JULIE MASLOWSKY,
AND LAURA LINDBERG

STAT, June 26, 2023

Tracey Wilkinson is a pediatrician and an assistant professor of pediatrics at Indiana University School of Medicine. Julie Maslowsky is an associate professor of community health sciences at the University of Illinois Chicago School of Public Health. Laura Lindberg is a professor of urban-global health at Rutgers School of Public Health.

Now that the Supreme Court has overturned constitutional protection to abortion access, more than two dozen states will ban or severely restrict abortion access. Young people, especially those under age eighteen, will be disproportionally affected by this decision.

The existing barriers to legal access to abortion, already insurmountable for many people, serve as a preview of what to expect and the inequities that will further be exacerbated. In Indiana, for example, consent for a minor to have an abortion requires a notarized parental consent form to be completed; in-person, state-directed counseling; an ultrasound; and an eighteen-hour waiting period.

Given teens also face greater barriers to preventing pregnancy in the first place, including barriers to accessing contraception and limited access to comprehensive sexual health education, the door is closed for them at every turn.

Teens under age 20 make up 12% of individuals who have abortions nationally; minors, age 17 or younger, account for about 4% of all abortions in the U.S. This means at least 50,000 adolescents need abortion care each year in the United States. Further, teen pregnancies are more likely to be unintended and end in abortion than pregnancies among older individuals. This means teens will be disproportionately impacted by this legal decision.

Teens' rights to access safe and confidential abortions has been affirmed by the American Academy of Pediatrics, the Society for Adolescent Health and Medicine, and the North American Society of Pediatric and Adolescent Gynecology. Yet, abortion access for teens is more legally regulated than adults' access. Currently, minors lack access to confidential abortion care in 38 states, as parental notification or consent is required before obtaining an abortion. While judicial bypass is a legal option to obtain an abortion without parental involvement, the process is complicated, onerous and time consuming.

Even when young people can overcome legal obstacles, they face barriers related to economics, information, and access. The cost of an abortion, which is likely to rise in a post-Roe world, makes it inaccessible for many teens. Teens and their guardians are rarely familiar with existing federal and state legal restrictions on abortion care and coverage through insurance until an abortion is needed. There are federal restrictions to Medicaid plans, and various state restrictions on both public and private insurance plans.

The teen "abortion road trip" is already part of American cultural discourse in books and movies. These fictionalized versions will pale against the harsh realities of increasingly far distances to travel to obtain an abortion if the constitutional precedent of Roe is overturned. Illinois, New York and other states where abortion remains legal will become a "safe haven state" for people across the country seeking abortions, but many youths will not be able to travel hundreds of miles to get to a clinic.

Minors face restrictions in independently buying interstate bus, rail, or airline tickets. Covering the cost of travel is particularly difficult for youths who are not financially independent. Supportive adults may fear legal consequences if they assist with transporting a minor across state lines to seek abortion care. Existing laws that require waiting periods and multiple appointments make these trips more time consuming, costly, and challenging.

When combined with delays in recognizing that a pregnancy has begun and presenting for medical care, which are more common among teens, abortion regulations based on weeks of pregnancy will have a larger impact on teens' ability to access abortion care. Although telehealth can serve as an option for those desiring medication abortion, these services are almost entirely restricted to those 18 years and older in states that permit telehealth, leaving younger teens without this medically safe option.

The existing laws and barriers have outsized harm for teens as they contribute to unnecessary medical complications due to delays in care.

These barriers are compounded by poverty, race, and other social statuses. Teen pregnancy rates are higher among youths who are poor, people of color, LGBTQ+, and those in foster care or in the criminal justice system. They are also least likely to have resources and social networks to support them as they navigate barriers to abortion access—or as new parents. When young people give birth to children in the absence of a real choice about whether to become a parent, existing inequities grow.

As the right to make decisions about pregnancy and parenthood becomes more restricted, teens' rights to bodily autonomy and reproductive freedom must be protected so they can determine their own futures.

Immediate efforts must focus on supporting abortion funds that provide people with financial and logistical support and helping legal groups assist minors with obtaining judicial bypass and other legal. Policymakers in states with protected abortion access need to repeal forced parental involvement laws, as Illinois recently did. Access to medication abortion via telehealth should be expanded to minors in these states as well. And policymakers must be held accountable to ensure access to comprehensive sex education and the full range of contraceptive options for everyone in all states.

Teens deserve to have autonomy over their bodies. It is time to fight for this fundamental right.

Appendix A

Roe v. Wade Ruling (excerpts)

SYLLABUS

ROE ET AL. V. WADE, DISTRICT ATTORNEY OF DALLAS COUNTY

APPEAL FROM THE UNITED STATES DISTRICT COURT FOR THE NORTHERN DISTRICT OF TEXAS

no. 70–18. Argued December 13, 1971—Reargued October 11, 1972—Decided January 22, 1973

A pregnant single woman (Roe) brought a class action challenging the constitutionality of the Texas criminal abortion laws, which proscribe procuring or attempting an abortion except on medical advice for the purpose of saving the mother's life. A licensed physician (Hallford), who had two state abortion prosecutions pending against him, was permitted to intervene. A childless married couple (the Does), the wife not being pregnant, separately attacked the laws, basing alleged injury on the future possibilities of contraceptive failure, pregnancy, unpreparedness for parenthood, and impairment of the wife's health. A three-judge District Court, which consolidated the actions, held that Roe and Hallford, and members of their classes, had standing to sue and presented justiciable controversies. Ruling that declaratory, though not injunctive, relief was warranted, the court declared the abortion statutes void as vague and overbroadly infringing those plaintiffs' Ninth and Fourteenth Amendment rights. The court ruled the Does' complaint not justiciable. Appellants directly appealed to this Court on the injunctive rulings, and appellee cross-appealed from the District Court's grant of declaratory relief to Roe and Hailford. Held:

1. While 28 U. S. C. § 1253 authorizes no direct appeal to this Court from the grant or denial of declaratory relief alone, review is not foreclosed when the case is properly before the Court on appeal from specific denial of injunctive relief and the arguments as to both injunctive and declaratory relief are necessarily identical. P. 123.

2. Roe has standing to sue; the Does and Hallford do not. Pp. 123–129.

(a) Contrary to appellee's contention, the natural termination of Roe's pregnancy did not moot her suit. Litigation involving pregnancy, which is "capable of repetition, yet evading review," is an exception to the usual federal rule that an actual controversy must exist at review stages and not simply when the action is initiated. Pp. 124–125.

(b) The District Court correctly refused injunctive, but erred in granting declaratory, relief to Hallford, who alleged no federally protected right not assertable as a defense against the good-faith state prosecutions pending against him. Samuels v. Mackell, 401 U. S. 66. Pp. 125–127.

(c) The Does' complaint, based as it is on contingencies, any one or more of which may not occur, is too speculative to present an actual case or controversy. Pp. 127–129.

3. State criminal abortion laws, like those involved here, that except from criminality only a life-saving procedure on the mother's behalf without regard to the stage of her pregnancy and other interests involved violate the Due Process Clause of the Fourteenth Amendment, which protects against state action the right to privacy, including a woman's qualified right to terminate her pregnancy. Though the State cannot override that right, it has legitimate interests in protecting both the pregnant woman's health and the potentiality of human life, each of which interests grows and reaches a "compelling" point at various stages of the woman's approach to term. Pp. 147–164.

   (a) For the stage prior to approximately the end of the first trimester, the abortion decision and its effectuation must be left to the medical judgment of the pregnant woman's attending physician. Pp. 163, 164.

   (b) For the stage subsequent to approximately the end of the first trimester, the State, in promoting its interest in the health of the mother, may, if it chooses, regulate the abortion procedure in ways that are reasonably related to maternal health. Pp. 163, 164.

   (c) For the stage subsequent to viability the State, in promoting its interest in the potentiality of human life, may, if it chooses, regulate, and even proscribe, abortion except where necessary, in appropriate medical judgment, for the preservation of the life or health of the mother. Pp. 163–164; 164–165.

4. The State may define the term "physician" to mean only a physician currently licensed by the State, and may proscribe any

abortion by a person who is not a physician as so defined. P. 165.

5. It is unnecessary to decide the injunctive relief issue since the Texas authorities will doubtless fully recognize the Court's ruling that the Texas criminal abortion statutes are unconstitutional. P. 166.

314 F. Supp. 1217, affirmed in part and reversed in part.

BLACKMUN, J., delivered the opinion of the Court, in which BURGER, C. J., and DOUGLAS, BRENNAN, STEWART, MARSHALL, and POWELL, J. J., joined. BURGER, C. J., post, p. 207, DOUGLAS, J., post, p. 209, and STEWART, J., post, p. 167, filed concurring opinions. WHITE, J., filed a dissenting opinion, in which REHNQUIST, J., joined, post, p. 221. REHNQUIST, J., filed a dissenting opinion, post, p. 171.

Appendix B

Dobbs v. Jackson Ruling (excerpts)

October Term, 2021

Note: Where it is feasible, a syllabus (headnote) will be released, as is being done in connection with this case, at the time the opinion is issued. The syllabus constitutes no part of the opinion of the Court but has been prepared by the Reporter of Decisions for the convenience of the reader. See *United States* v. *Detroit Timber & Lumber Co.*, 200 U. S. 321, 337.

SUPREME COURT OF THE UNITED STATES

SYLLABUS

DOBBS, STATE HEALTH OFFICER OF THE MISSISSIPPI DEPARTMENT OF HEALTH, ET AL. V. JACKSON WOMEN'S HEALTH ORGANIZATION ET AL. CERTIORARI TO THE UNITED STATES COURT OF APPEALS FOR THE FIFTH CIRCUIT

no. 19–1392. Argued December 1, 2021—Decided June 24, 2022

Mississippi's Gestational Age Act provides that "[e]xcept in a medical emergency or in the case of a severe fetal abnormality, a person shall not intentionally or knowingly perform . . . or induce an abortion of an unborn human being if the probable gestational age of the unborn human being has been determined to be greater than fifteen (15) weeks." Miss. Code Ann. §41–41–191. Respondents—Jackson Women's Health Organization, an abortion clinic, and one of its doctors—challenged the Act in Federal District Court, alleging that it violated this Court's precedents establishing a constitutional right to abortion, in particular *Roe* v. *Wade*, 410 U. S. 113, and *Planned Parenthood of Southeastern Pa.* v. *Casey*, 505 U. S. 833. The District Court granted summary judgment in favor of respondents and permanently enjoined enforcement of the Act, reasoning that Mississippi's 15-week restriction on abortion violates this Court's cases forbidding States to ban abortion pre-viability. The Fifth Circuit affirmed. Before this Court, petitioners defend the Act on the grounds that *Roe* and *Casey* were wrongly decided and that the Act is constitutional because it satisfies rational-basis review.

Held: The Constitution does not confer a right to abortion; *Roe* and *Casey* are overruled; and the authority to regulate abortion is returned to the people and their elected representatives. Pp. 8–79.

(a) The critical question is whether the Constitution, properly understood, confers a right to obtain an abortion. *Casey*'s controlling opinion skipped over that question and reaffirmed *Roe* solely on the basis of *stare decisis*. A proper application of *stare decisis*, however, requires an assessment of the strength of the grounds on which *Roe* was based. The Court therefore turns to the question that the *Casey* plurality did not consider. Pp. 8–32.

(1) First, the Court reviews the standard that the Court's cases have used to determine whether the Fourteenth Amendment's reference to "liberty" protects a particular right. The Constitution makes no express reference to a right to obtain an abortion, but several constitutional provisions have been offered as potential homes for an implicit constitutional right. *Roe* held that the abortion right is part of a right to privacy that springs from the First, Fourth, Fifth, Ninth, and Fourteenth Amendments. See 410 U. S., at 152–153. The *Casey* Court

grounded its decision solely on the theory that the right to obtain an abortion is part of the "liberty" protected by the Fourteenth Amendment's Due Process Clause. Others have suggested that support can be found in the Fourteenth Amendment's Equal Protection Clause, but that theory is squarely foreclosed by the Court's precedents, which establish that a State's regulation of abortion is not a sex-based classification and is thus not subject to the heightened scrutiny that applies to such classifications. See *Geduldig* v. *Aiello*, 417 U. S. 484, 496, n. 20; *Bray* v. *Alexandria Women's Health Clinic*, 506 U. S. 263, 273–274. Rather, regulations and prohibitions of abortion are governed by the same standard of review as other health and safety measures. Pp. 9–11.

(2) Next, the Court examines whether the right to obtain an abortion is rooted in the Nation's history and tradition and whether it is an essential component of "ordered liberty." The Court finds that the right to abortion is not deeply rooted in the Nation's history and tradition. The underlying theory on which *Casey* rested—that the Fourteenth Amendment's Due Process Clause provides substantive, as well as procedural, protection for "liberty"—has long been controversial.

The Court's decisions have held that the Due Process Clause protects two categories of substantive rights—those rights guaranteed by the first eight Amendments to the Constitution and those rights deemed fundamental that are not mentioned anywhere in the Constitution. In deciding whether a right falls into either of these categories, the question is whether the right is "deeply rooted in [our] history and tradition" and whether it is essential to this Nation's "scheme of ordered liberty." *Timbs* v. *Indiana*, 586 U. S. ___, ___ (internal quotation marks omitted).

The term "liberty" alone provides little guidance. Thus, historical inquiries are essential whenever the Court is asked to recognize a new component of the "liberty" interest protected by the Due Process Clause. In interpreting what is meant by "liberty," the Court must guard against the natural human tendency to confuse what the Fourteenth Amendment protects with the Court's own ardent views about the liberty that Americans should enjoy. For this reason, the Court has been "reluctant" to recognize rights that are not mentioned in the Constitution. *Collins* v. *Harker Heights*, 503 U. S. 115, 125.

Guided by the history and tradition that map the essential components of the Nation's concept of ordered liberty, the Court finds the Fourteenth Amendment clearly does not protect the right to an abortion. Until the latter part of the 20th century, there was no support in American law for a constitutional right to obtain an abortion. No state constitutional provision had recognized such a right. Until a few years before *Roe*, no federal or state court had recognized such a right. Nor had any scholarly treatise. Indeed, abortion had long been a *crime* in every single State. At common law, abortion was criminal in at least some stages of pregnancy and was regarded as unlawful and could have very serious consequences at all stages. American law followed the common law until a wave of statutory restrictions in the 1800s expanded criminal liability for abortions. By the time the Fourteenth Amendment was adopted, three-quarters of the States had made abortion a crime at any stage of pregnancy. This consensus endured until the day *Roe* was decided. *Roe* either ignored or misstated this history, and *Casey* declined to reconsider *Roe*'s faulty historical analysis.

Respondents' argument that this history does not matter flies in the face of the standard the Court has applied in determining whether an asserted right that is nowhere mentioned in the Constitution is nevertheless protected by the Fourteenth Amendment. The Solicitor General repeats *Roe*'s claim that it is "doubtful . . . abortion was ever firmly established as a common-law crime even with respect to the destruction of a quick fetus," 410 U. S., at 136, but the great commonlaw authorities—Bracton, Coke, Hale, and Blackstone—all wrote that a post-quickening abortion was a crime. Moreover, many authorities asserted that even a pre-quickening abortion was "unlawful" and that, as a result, an abortionist was guilty of murder if the woman died from the attempt. The Solicitor General suggests that history supports an abortion right because of the common law's failure to criminalize abortion before quickening, but the insistence on quickening was not universal, see *Mills* v. *Commonwealth*, 13 Pa. 631, 633; *State* v. *Slagle*, 83

N. C. 630, 632, and regardless, the fact that many States in the late 18th and early 19th century did not criminalize pre-quickening abortions does not mean that anyone thought the States lacked the authority to do so.

Instead of seriously pressing the argument that the abortion right itself has deep roots, supporters of *Roe* and *Casey* contend that the abortion right is an integral part of a broader entrenched right. *Roe* termed this a right to privacy, 410 U. S., at 154, and *Casey* described it as the freedom to make "intimate and personal choices" that are "central to personal dignity and autonomy," 505 U. S., at 851. Ordered sets limits and defines the boundary between competing interests. *Roe* and *Casey* each struck a particular balance between the interests of a woman who wants an abortion and the interests of what they termed "potential life." *Roe*, 410 U. S., at 150; *Casey*, 505 U. S., at 852. But the people of the various States may evaluate those interests differently. The Nation's historical understanding of ordered liberty does not prevent the people's elected representatives from deciding how abortion should be regulated. Pp. 11–30.

(3) Finally, the Court considers whether a right to obtain an abortion is part of a broader entrenched right that is supported by other precedents. The Court concludes the right to obtain an abortion cannot be justified as a component of such a right. Attempts to justify

abortion through appeals to a broader right to autonomy and to define one's "concept of existence" prove too much. *Casey*, 505 U. S., at 851. Those criteria, at a high level of generality, could license fundamental rights to illicit drug use, prostitution, and the like. What sharply distinguishes the abortion right from the rights recognized in the cases on which *Roe* and *Casey* rely is something that both those decisions acknowledged: Abortion is different because it destroys what *Roe* termed "potential life" and what the law challenged in this case calls an "unborn human being." None of the other decisions cited by *Roe* and *Casey* involved the critical moral question posed by abortion. Accordingly, those cases do not support the right to obtain an abortion, and the Court's conclusion that the Constitution does not confer such a right does not undermine them in any way. Pp. 30–32.

(b) The doctrine of *stare decisis* does not counsel continued acceptance of *Roe* and *Casey*. *Stare decisis* plays an important role and protects the interests of those who have taken action in reliance on a past decision. It "reduces incentives for challenging settled precedents, saving parties and courts the expense of endless relitigation." *Kimble* v. *Marvel Entertainment, LLC*, 576 U. S. 446, 455. It "contributes to the actual and perceived integrity of the judicial process." *Payne* v. *Tennessee*, 501 U. S. 808, 827. And it restrains judicial hubris by respecting the judgment of those who grappled with important questions in the past. But *stare decisis* is not an inexorable command, *Pearson* v. *Callahan*, 555 U. S. 223, 233, and "is at its weakest when [the Court] interpret[s] the Constitution," *Agostini* v. *Felton*, 521 U. S. 203, 235. Some of the Court's most important constitutional decisions have overruled prior precedents. See, *e.g.*, *Brown* v. *Board of Education*, 347 U. S. 483, 491 (overruling the infamous decision in *Plessy* v. *Ferguson*, 163 U. S. 537, and its progeny).

The Court's cases have identified factors that should be considered in deciding when a precedent should be overruled. *Janus* v. *State, County, and Municipal Employees*, 585 U. S. ___, ___–___.

Five factors discussed below weigh strongly in favor of overruling *Roe* and *Casey*. Pp. 39–66.

The nature of the Court's error. Like the infamous decision in *Plessy* v. *Ferguson*, *Roe* was also egregiously wrong and on a collision course with the Constitution from the day it was decided. *Casey* perpetuated its errors, calling both sides of the national controversy to resolve their debate, but in doing so, *Casey* necessarily declared a winning side. Those on the losing side—those who sought to advance the State's interest in fetal life—could no longer seek to persuade their elected representatives to adopt policies consistent with their views. The Court short-circuited the democratic process by closing it to the large number of Americans who disagreed with *Roe*. Pp. 43–45.

(2) *The quality of the reasoning*. Without any grounding in the constitutional text, history, or precedent, *Roe* imposed on the entire country a detailed set of rules for pregnancy divided into trimesters much like those that one might expect to find in a statute or regulation. See 410 U. S., at 163–164. *Roe*'s failure even to note the overwhelming consensus of state laws in effect in 1868 is striking, and what it said about the common law was simply wrong. Then, after surveying history, the opinion spent many paragraphs conducting the sort of fact-finding that might be undertaken by a legislative committee, and did not explain why the sources on which it relied shed light on the meaning of the Constitution. As to precedent, citing a broad array of cases, the Court found support for a constitutional "right of personal privacy." *Id.,* at 152. But *Roe* conflated the right to shield information from disclosure and the right to make and implement important personal decisions without governmental interference. See *Whalen* v. *Roe*, 429 U. S. 589,

> 599–600. None of these decisions involved what is distinctive about abortion: its effect on what *Roe* termed "potential life." When the Court summarized the basis for the scheme it imposed on the country, it asserted that its rules were "consistent with," among other things, "the relative weights of the respective interests involved "and "the demands of the profound problems of the present day." *Roe*, 410 U. S., at 165. These are precisely the sort of considerations that legislative bodies often take into account when they draw lines that accommodate competing interests. The scheme *Roe* produced *looked* like legislation, and the Court provided the sort of explanation that might be expected from a legislative body. An even more glaring deficiency was *Roe*'s failure to justify the critical distinction it drew between pre- and post-viability abortions. See *id*., at 163. The arbitrary viability line, which *Casey* termed *Roe*'s central rule, has not found much support among philosophers and ethicists who have attempted to justify a right to abortion. The most obvious problem with any such argument is that viability has changed over time and is heavily dependent on factors—such as medical advances and the availability of quality medical care—that have nothing to do with the characteristics of a fetus.

When *Casey* revisited *Roe* almost 20 years later, it reaffirmed *Roe*'s central holding, but pointedly refrained from endorsing most of its reasoning. The Court abandoned any reliance on a privacy right and instead grounded the abortion right entirely on the Fourteenth Amendment's Due Process Clause. 505 U. S., at 846. The controlling opinion criticized and rejected *Roe*'s trimester scheme, 505 U. S., at 872, and substituted a new and obscure "undue burden" test. *Casey*, in short, either refused to reaffirm or rejected important aspects of *Roe*'s analysis, failed to remedy glaring deficiencies in *Roe*'s reasoning, endorsed what it termed *Roe*'s central holding while suggesting that a majority might not have thought it was correct, provided no new support for the abortion right other than *Roe*'s status as precedent, and imposed a new test with no firm grounding in constitutional text, history, or precedent. Pp. 45–56.

(3) *Workability*. Deciding whether a precedent should be overruled depends in part on whether the rule it imposes is workable—that is, whether it can be understood and applied in a consistent and predictable manner. *Casey*'s "undue burden" test has scored poorly on the workability scale. The *Casey* plurality tried to put meaning into the "undue burden" test by setting out three subsidiary rules, but these rules created their own problems. And the difficulty of applying *Casey*'s new rules surfaced in that very case. Compare 505 U. S., at 881–887, with *id.*, at 920–922 (Stevens, J., concurring in part and dissenting in part). The experience of the Courts of Appeals provides further evidence that *Casey*'s "line between" permissible and unconstitutional restrictions "has proved to be impossible to draw with precision." *Janus*, 585 U. S., at ___. *Casey* has generated a long list of Circuit conflicts. Continued adherence to *Casey*'s unworkable "undue burden" test would undermine, not advance, the "evenhanded, predictable, and consistent development of legal principles." *Payne*, 501 U. S., at 827. Pp. 56–62.

(4) *Effect on other areas of law*. *Roe* and *Casey* have led to the distortion of many important but unrelated legal doctrines, and that effect provides further support for overruling those decisions. See *Ramos* v. *Louisiana*, 590 U. S. ___, ___ (KAVANAUGH, J., concurring in part). Pp. 62–63.

(5) *Reliance interests*. Overruling *Roe* and *Casey* will not upend concrete reliance interests like those that develop in "cases involving property and contract rights." *Payne*, 501 U. S., at 828. In *Casey*,

the controlling opinion conceded that traditional reliance interests were not implicated because getting an abortion is generally "unplanned activity," and "reproductive planning could take virtually immediate account of any sudden restoration of state authority to ban abortions." 505 U. S., at 856. Instead, the opinion perceived a more intangible form of reliance, namely, that "people [had] organized intimate relationships and made choices that define their views of themselves and their places in society . . . in reliance on the availability of abortion in the event that contraception should fail" and that "[t]he ability of women to participate equally in the economic and social life of the Nation has been facilitated by their ability to control their reproductive lives." *Ibid.* The contending sides in this case make impassioned and conflicting arguments about the effects of the abortion right on the lives of women as well as the status of the fetus. The *Casey* plurality's speculative attempt to weigh the relative importance of the interests of the fetus and the mother represent a departure from the "original constitutional proposition" that "courts do not substitute their social and economic beliefs for the judgment of legislative bodies." *Ferguson* v. *Skrupa*, 372 U. S. 726, 729–730.

The Solicitor General suggests that overruling *Roe* and *Casey* would threaten the protection of other rights under the Due Process Clause. The Court emphasizes that this decision concerns the constitutional right to abortion and no other right. Nothing in this opinion should be understood to cast doubt on precedents that do not concern abortion. Pp. 63–66.

(c) *Casey* identified another concern, namely, the danger that the public will perceive a decision overruling a controversial "watershed "decision, such as *Roe*, as influenced by political considerations or public opinion. 505 U. S., at 866–867. But the Court cannot allow its decisions to be affected by such extraneous concerns. A precedent of this Court is subject to the usual principles of *stare decisis* under which adherence to precedent is the norm but not an inexorable command. If the rule were otherwise, erroneous decisions like *Plessy* would still be the law. The Court's job is to interpret the law, apply longstanding principles of *stare decisis*, and decide this case accordingly. Pp. 66–69.

(d) Under the Court's precedents, rational-basis review is the appropriate standard to apply when state abortion regulations undergo constitutional challenge. Given that procuring an abortion is not a fundamental constitutional right, it follows that the States may regulate abortion for legitimate reasons, and when such regulations are challenged under the Constitution, courts cannot "substitute their social and economic beliefs for the judgment of legislative bodies." *Ferguson*, 372 U. S., at 729–730. That applies even when the laws at issue concern matters of great social significance and moral substance. A law regulating abortion, like other health and welfare laws, is entitled to a "strong presumption of validity." *Heller* v. *Doe*, 509 U. S. 312, 319. It must be sustained if there is a rational basis on which the legislature could have thought that it would serve legitimate state interests. *Id.*, at 320.

Mississippi's Gestational Age Act is supported by the Mississippi Legislature's specific findings, which include the State's asserted interest in "protecting the life of the unborn." §2(b)(i). These legitimate interests provide a rational basis for the Gestational Age Act, and it follows that respondents' constitutional challenge must fail. Pp. 76–78.

(e) Abortion presents a profound moral question. The Constitution does not prohibit the citizens of each State from regulating or prohibiting abortion. *Roe* and *Casey* arrogated that authority. The Court overrules those decisions and returns that authority to the people and their elected representatives. Pp. 78–79. 945 F. 3d 265, reversed and remanded.

ALITO, J., delivered the opinion of the Court, in which THOMAS, GORSUCH, KAVANAUGH, and BARRETT, J. J., joined. THOMAS, J., and KAVANAUGH, J., filed concurring opinions. ROBERTS, C. J., filed an opinion concurring in the judgment. BREYER, SOTOMAYOR, and KAGAN, J. J., filed a dissenting opinion.

Appendix C

State-by-State Abortion Laws Until January 1, 2024

Prepared by Elizabeth Reichman, J.D., M.A.

Updated as of December 2023

Alabama

Leader in anti-abortion movement.

1800s: allowed therapeutic exception to abortion ban

Pre *Roe:* banned unless mother's physical health in danger

2007: required ultrasound be done before abortion (consent law)

2014: tried to pass so-called Heartbeat Law, making it illegal to have an abortion after the first 21 days. Tried to ban D&E in 2016–

2019: March 24 hour waiting period before abortion (2 appointments required)

May 2019: no abortion for rape or incest

2024: banned unless life of mother at risk. Provider can be prosecuted, including one who helps pregnant woman leave state

Alaska

Legal during any trimester since 1970; criminalized before then

2007: woman required to be told there was a link between third trimester abortion and breast cancer (not true)

2024: legal at any time if performed by a doctor; state will pay for poor women

Arizona

Banned abortion except to save life of mother when became a territory in 1864. Law stayed on the books but unenforceable after *Roe.*

2024: in effect again, but so is a newer 2022 law that allows abortion up to 15 weeks. Providers could be imprisoned, but current (12/2023) Democratic governor and state attorney general not prosecuting

Arkansas

1800s: allowed therapeutic exceptions to abortion ban

Late 1960s to early 1970s: more specific guidance on "therapeutic." Followed Model Penal Code movement

1988: provision in state constitution protecting "life of unborn child" as allowed by federal law

2007: consent law required showing ultrasound to woman.

2013: banned at twelve weeks, but law struck down by federal courts

in 2024 unless life of mother in danger. Doctors may be prosecuted

California

Abortion was illegal from statehood.

In 1850, abortion was a crime under the Crimes and Punishment Act (Stats 1850 ch 99 45). It was revised in 1872.

Banned again in 1900, criminalized in 1950, adopted a version of the Model Penal Code in 1962 that allowed abortion in some circumstances, including physical/mental risk to mother

Allowed with no cause stated in late 1960s.

2015: law to control and balance statements made by pregnancy crisis centers

2019: more of providers can perform abortions legally, abortifacients specifically allowed with abortion allowed up to viability

2022: Californians voted during the mid-term election to make abortion a state constitutional right. Students at public universities may receive mifpristone free of charge

Colorado

Adopted Model Penal Code in 1967

1978: Medicaid would pay

2024: legal at all stages, can be done outpatient until 26 weeks. Legally reaffirmed in Reproductive Health Equity Act in 2022

Connecticut

Allowed early in the state's history

1821: codified ban (to protect mother) that had developed in the common law.

Criminalized abortifacients, too

1965: *Griswold v. Connecticut* (contraception and penumbral rights in U.S. Constitution)

2024: allowed up to viability, beyond to protect mother's physical/mental health.

Delaware

Therapeutic exception to ban by 1900

2024: legal to viability, affirmatively protected by state law

Florida

Abortion ban with therapeutic exception in place by 1900

1980: right to privacy enshrined in state constitution

2017: state court ruled this right protected abortion

2019: tried to pass heartbeat bill and failed

2024: Heartbeat bill passed in 2023 so illegal after six weeks.

Georgia

Fetus is a tax deduction

Tried to ban abortion since 2011

Consent laws since 2007

2000: banned after 22 weeks (fetus can feel pain argument)

2024: 2019 heartbeat law in effect—banned after six weeks

Hawaii

1970: first state to allow abortion (but state residency required)

2019: allowed until viability, but permitted after to save the life of the mother.

Idaho

1950: women who sought abortions criminalized

2000s: banned after 22 weeks (fetus can feel pain)

2024: 2020 trigger law may go into effect, does allow for life of mother, rape, and incest exceptions

Illinois

Laws limiting from early 1800s, criminal penalties 1827, first in nation, ban in 1867

1870: ban abortifacients except when prescribed by well-known physicians

1956: hospital committees controlled therapeutic exceptions

Parental control in 1990s (repealed 2021)

2024: legal, protected by state law

Indiana

1950: illegal for the woman to have it

2000: fetal pain law banned after 22 weeks

2024: trigger law will ban in all cases but life of mother, rape, and incest

Iowa

2022: Iowa Supreme Court ruled no right to abortion in state constitution

Ban at 22 weeks currently, may be greater restrictions (six week ban) after 2022 ruling above

Kansas

Allowed up to 20 weeks, that limitation on the grounds that fetus can feel pain.

2019: Kansas Supreme Court upheld right to abortion under the STATE constitution, striking down a law that would limit D&E

August 2022: referendum to amend the constitution to deny abortion defeated by wide margin

Kentucky

Required abortion clinics to obtain licenses in late 1990s

(Attempts to limit the right for decades, including an early parental notification law)

Abortion illegal from conception, no rape or incest exception (trigger law went into effect) only life of mother exception

During the 2022 mid-term elections, voters rejected a proposed state constitutional amendment to ban abortions

Louisiana

By the end of the 1800s, Louisiana was the only state to not have a therapeutic exception in their legislative bans on abortions.

Civil penalties allowed in late 1990s (before Texas)

May 2022 law may allow prosecution of women and doctors.

May criminalize destruction of IVF fetuses (much uncertainty)

Maine

Legislation since 1821, at first banning abortion to protect the mother

1990s: to limit abortion to pre viability

2024: legal to viability, permitted later in some cases.

Maryland
Allowed until viability, longer if mother's life at stake
Both tightened regulation of clinics and allowed more providers to prescribe abortifacients
Massachusetts
Passed parental consent law in 1980s
Buffer zone around clinics 2007
2017: allowed more non-physicians to prescribe abortifacients
Legal to 24 weeks, longer to protect life of mother, sweeping new reproductive rights law in 2022

Michigan
1932: banned
During mid-term elections in 2022, Michigan voters enshrined the right to abortion in their state constitution.

Minnesota
1950: criminalized
1980s: parental consent law
Today: legal and protected by state law
Mississippi
Exception for rape 1966
Exception for rape and incest 1972
1990: parental consent law
Heartbeat law passed in 2019
Ban on abortions sought for gender, race, or genetic abnormality reasons in 2020
2024: no exceptions but rape and to protect the life of the mother

Missouri
1900: criminalized
1990: parental consent
2024: banned except in case of medical emergency, no rape or incest exception. Burden of proof on provider that the life of the mother is at risk.

Montana
Non-physicians can do some first trimester abortions (not just with drugs)
2019 banned after viability (22–24 weeks)
2024: allowed to viability, state supreme court finds right in state constitution

Nebraska
2007: consent laws
2024: allowed up to 12 weeks have banned abortion

Nevada
1990: voted to affirm a law allowing abortion; this has effect of locking in the law, unless there is a referendum to change it
state funds won't pay
2019: legal to viability.

New Hampshire
1900: criminalized
2024: legal to 24 weeks, no public funds
Parental consent laws passed 2x: 2003, 2011

New Jersey

1900: laws to ban

1940: hospital committees carved out exceptions and controlled right to abortion

2024: no limits on when can be done

New Mexico

1960s and 1970s: more guidance to when therapeutic abortion okay

1969: carve out exceptions for mother's health, rape, and incest

2024: now allowed with no limit

New York

1827: Felony post quickening, misdemeanor pre quickening

Many salacious abortion stories in newspapers

Hospital committees allowed exceptions in 1950s

1970: decriminalized, allowed up to 24 weeks (viability framework predated *Roe*)

2019: legal to 24 weeks, permitted to save the life of the mother or dead fetal abnormalities

North Dakota

1950: criminalized

2024: banned except to save life of the mother

Allowed up to six weeks in cases of rape or incest *if* reported to authorities

North Carolina

1900: ban with therapeutic exception

2024: legal up to 12 weeks, 20 weeks if rape or incest, 24 weeks if life-limiting fetal abnormalities, and always allowed to save the life of the mother.

Ohio
Heartbeat law, so banned after six weeks
Narrow welfare of mother exception
2023: legal to viability after voters approve constitutional amendment.

Oklahoma
1950: criminalized
2007: consent law
2000s: banned after 22 weeks (fetal pain law)
2024: now banned after conception, rape and incest exception if reported to police in timely way, narrow life of mother exception.

Oregon
During 1960s and 1970s, looked to British law and not Model Penal Code
2024: allowed at all stages

Pennsylvania
1982: required 24-hour waiting period, consent of parents and husbands
2024: legal to 24 weeks, no public funds
Rhode Island
Legal to 24 weeks

South Carolina
Heartbeat law allowed for six weeks

South Dakota
Banned except to save life of mother, providers are class 6 felons
Movement to restrict since early 2000s

Tennessee

2007 consent law

2013 regulated clinics (had to be affiliated with hospitals)

Heartbeat law passed, superseded by fertilization law, no exceptions for rape and incest

2024: banned from conception, unclear if there can be therapeutic exceptions

Texas

1854 criminalized, sanction on provider of abortion (mother's life exception)

Beginning in 1990s, incremental limitations on right and access: only doctors could perform abortions, health care providers could refuse on moral grounds, parental consent, waiting period, limited funding for Planned Parenthood, forced ultrasound counseling

2021: Heartbeat law with civil (bounty) enforcement by private actors.

2023: Some counties criminalize use of public roads to travel to obtain abortion. Women challenge law on grounds it prevents medical decision making.

2024: banned no rape/incest exception

Utah

Criminalized 1950

2007 consent law

2013 limiting drug abortions

2024: banned after 18 weeks, but a trigger law (prohibiting abortion after a fetal heartbeat is detected) poised to go into effect

Vermont

2017: allowed non-physicians to do first trimester aspiration abortions and prescribe abortifacients

2022: Vermonters voted to protect abortion and contraception in the state constitution, legal at all stages

Virginia

Banned in 1900, therapeutic exception

Hospital committees assessed and determined need

2007: consent law

2013: tighter clinic rules

2024: legal to 25 weeks

Washington

1959: Illegal

1970: Legal —one of first to allow it (but residency requirement)

2024: legal to viability

West Virginia

Criminalized in 1848-

2002 counseling law passed

2024: illegal except to save life of mother, some fetal abnormalities and rape exception to 11 weeks.

Wisconsin

1849: illegal for providers to perform

1950: women prosecuted

2007: consent laws

2013: Targeted Restriction Abortion Providers law passed. At one time, enlightened birth control education, now abstinence.

2023: abortions prohibited after 21 weeks. If under the age of 18, a parent or legal guardian must give permission

Wyoming

2023: Governor signed into law a bill prohibiting abortion pill.

2024: State attempted to ban medical abortions, but state court overturned, legal to viability.

Bibliography

SOCIAL HISTORY

Baker, Jean H. *Margaret Sanger: A Life of Passion*. New York: Hill & Wang, 2011.

Doyle, Nora. *Maternal Bodies: Redefining Motherhood in Early America*. Chapel Hill: University of North Carolina Press, 2018.

Frank, Gillian. "The Abortionist," *Perspectives on History*, November 29, 2021. https://www.historians.org/publications-and-directories/perspectives-on-history/december-2021/emthe-abortionist/em.

Garner Masarik, Elizabeth. "Anthony Comstock: Sex, Censorship, and the Power of Policing the Subjective" *Dig: A History Podcast*. Podcast audio. March 24, 2019. https://digpodcast.org/2019/03/24/anthony-comstock/.

Hull, N. E. H. and Peter Charles Hoffer. *Roe v. Wade: The Abortion Rights Controversy in American History*. Lawrence: University Press of Kansas, 2021.

Millar, Erica. *Happy Abortions: Our Bodies in the Era of Choice*. London: Zed, 2017.

Schoen, Johanna. *Abortion after Roe*. Chapel Hill: University of North Carolina Press, 2016.

Solinger, Rickie. *Pregnancy and Power: A Short History of Reproductive Politics in America*. New York: New York University Press, 2005.

———, ed. *Abortion Wars: A Half Century of Struggle, 1950–2000*. Berkeley: University of California Press, 1998.

———. *Beggars and Choosers: How the Politics of Choice Shapes*

Adoption, Abortion, and Welfare in the United States. New York: Hill & Wang, 2001.

Swedlund, Alan C. *Shadows in the Valley: A Cultural History of Illness, Death, and Loss in New England, 1840–1916*. Amherst: University of Massachusetts Press, 2010.

Syrett, Nick. *The Trials of Madame Restell: Nineteenth-Century America's Most Infamous Female Physician and the Campaign to Make Abortion a Crime*. New York: New Press, 2023.

Tannenbaum, Rebecca J. *The Healer's Calling: Women and Medicine in Early New England*. Ithaca: Cornell University Press, 2002, 2009.

Thompson, Lauren MacIvor. "Women Have Always Had Abortions." *New York Times Interactive*, December 13, 2019. https://www.nytimes.com/interactive/2019/12/13/opinion/sunday/abortion-history-women.html.

Wilmot Voss, Kimberly. *Women Politicking Politely: Advancing Feminism in the 1960s and 1970s*. Lanham: Lexington, 2017.

COURT CASES

Doe v. Bolton. 410 U.S. 179 (1973).

Doe v. Bolton. Oral arguments, Oyez.

Roe v. Wade. 410 U.S. 113 (1973).

Roe v. Wade. Oral arguments, Oyez.

LEGAL AND POLITICAL HISTORY

Andrews, Becca. *No Choice: The Destruction of Roe v. Wade and the Fight to Protect a Fundamental American Right*. New York: Public Affairs, 2022.

Bazelon, Emily. "America Almost Took a Different Path Toward Abortion Rights," *New York Times Magazine*, May 20, 2022.

Benson Gold, Rachel. "Lessons from Before Roe: Will Past be Prologue?" *Guttmacher Institute*, March 1, 2003.

Butler, Pam. "Microsyllabus: U.S. Abortion Politics in Context." *The Abusable Past* (blog), June 11, 2019. https://www.radicalhistoryreview.org/abusablepast/microsyllabus-u-s-abortion-politics-in-context/

Colgrove, James, and Ronald Bayer. "Manifold Restraints: Liberty, Public Health, and the Legacy of *Jacobson v. Massachusetts*." *American Journal of Public Health* 95, no. 4 (2005): 571–576.

Cooper Davis, Peggy. *Neglected Stories: The Constitution and Family Values*. New York: Hill & Wang, 1998.

Daniel, Clare. "Compromising Justice: Reproductive Rights Advocacy in the Time of Trump," *Frontiers: A Journal of Women Studies* 43, no. 1 (2022): 68–92.

———. *Mediating Morality: The Politics of Teen Pregnancy in the Post-Welfare Era*. Amherst: University of Massachusetts Press, 2017.

Ely, John Hart. "The Wages of Crying Wolf: A Comment on *Roe v. Wade*," *Yale Law Journal* 82, no. 5 (April 1973): 920–949.

Faux, Marian. *Roe v. Wade: The Untold Story of the Landmark Supreme Court Decision that Made Abortion Legal*. New York: Scribner, 1988.

Flavin, Jeanne. *Our Bodies, Our Crimes: The Policing of Women's Reproduction in America*. New York: New York University Press, 2010.

Garrow, David J. *Liberty & Sexuality: The Right to Privacy and the Making of Roe v. Wade*. New York: Lisa Drew, 1994.

Gorney, Cynthia. "Justice Blackmun, Off the Record." *New York Times*, March 7, 1999.

Greenhouse, Linda. "How a Ruling on Abortion Took On a Life of Its Own," *New York Times*, April 10, 1994.

———. "Justice Blackmun, Author of Abortion Right, Dies." *New York Times*, March 5, 1999.

———. "Justice Blackmun's Journey: From Moderate to a Liberal." *New York Times*, April 7, 1994.

———. *Becoming Justice Blackmun: Harry Blackmun's Supreme Court Journey*. New York: Times Books, 2005.

Gutierrez-Romine, Alicia. "Abortion and the Law in California: Lessons for Today," *California History* 99, 1 (2022): 10–29.

———. *From Back Alley to the Border: Criminal Abortion in California, 1920–1969*. Lincoln: University of Nebraska Press, 2020.

Haridasani Gupta, Alisha. "Why Ruth Bader Ginsburg Wasn't All That Fond of *Roe v. Wade*." *New York Times*, September 21, 2020.

Hart, Evan Elizabeth. "Manslaughter or Necessary Operation? Abortion and Murder in Early 20th-Century Missouri." *Nursing Clio*, 2021. https://nursingclio.org/2021/06/15/manslaughter-or-necessary-operation-abortion-and-murder-in-early-20th-century-missouri/

Howard, Grace. "The Pregnancy Police: Surveillance, Regulation, and Control." *Harvard Law and Policy Review* 14 (2020): 347–363.

Jacobs, Julia. "Remembering an Era before Roe, When New York Had the 'Most Liberal' Abortion Law." *New York Times*, July 19, 2018.

Jeffries Jr., John C. *Justice Lewis F. Powell, Jr.* New York: Scribner, 1994.

Kerber, Linda K. "The 40th Anniversary of *Roe v. Wade*: A Teachable Moment." *Perspectives on History*, October 2012.

Kesselman, Amy. "Women's Liberation in Action, 'Women vs. Connecticut.'" *Conference at Boston University*, March 27–29, 2014.

Lithwick, Dahlia. "RBG's Prophetic Warning on *Roe v. Wade* Went Ignored." *Slate*, September 22, 2020.

Mohr, James. *Abortion in America: The Origins and Evolutions of National Policy, 1800–1900*. New York: Oxford University Press, 1979.

Munson, Ziad. *Abortion Politics*. Cambridge: Polity Press, 2018.

Newman, Jon O. *Benched: Abortion, Terrorists, Drones, Crooks, Supreme Court, Kennedy, Nixon, Demi Moore, and Other Tales from the Life of a Federal Judge*. Getzville, N.Y.: Hein, 2017.

Nixon, Laura. "The Right to (Trans)Parent: A Reproductive Justice Approach to Reproductive Rights, Fertility, and Family-Building Issues Facing Transgender People." *William and Mary Journal of Race, Gender, and Social Justice* 20 (2013–14).

Perez-Pena, Richard. "'70 Abortion Law: New York Said Yes, Stunning the Nation." *New York Times*, April 9, 2000.

Prager, Joshua. "Roe v. Wade Made Viability the Key to Abortion Law." *Wall Street Journal*, December 2, 2021.

Reagan, Leslie J. "The First Time Abortion was a Crime." *Slate*, June 1, 2022.

Reagan, Leslie J. *When Abortion Was a Crime: Women, Medicine, and Law in the United States, 1867–1973*. Oakland: University of California Press, 1997.

Robenalt, James D. "The Unknown Supreme Court Clerk Who Single-Handedly Created the *Roe v. Wade* Viability Standard." *Washington Post*, November 29, 2019.

Saxon, Wolfgang, "George Michaels, 80, Legislator Who Changed Abortion Law, Dies." *New York Times*, December 5, 1992.

Seelye, Katharine Q. "Sarah Weddington, Who Successfully Argued *Roe v. Wade*, Dies at 76." *New York Times*, December 27, 2021.

Sheldon, Sally. *Beyond Control: Medical Power and Abortion Law*. London: Pluto, 1997.

Siegel, Reva. "Reasoning from the Body: A Historical Perspective on Abortion Regulation and Questions of Equal Protection." *Stanford Law Review* 44, no. 2 (1992): 261–381.

Silliman, Jael, and Anannya Bhattacharjee, eds. *Policing the National Body: Race, Gender, and Criminalization*. Cambridge: South End Press, 2002.

Thompson, Lauren MacIvor. "Abortion: The Archive Doesn't Lie, but Republicans Do." *Nursing Clio*, 2019. https://nursingclio.org/2019/05/16/abortion-the-archive-doesnt-lie-but-republicans-do/.

Thomsen, Carly. "From Refusing Stigmatization toward Celebration: New Directions for Reproductive Justice Activism." *Feminist Studies*, 39, no. 1 (2013): 149–58.

Weddington, Sarah Ragle. *A Question of Choice: By the Lawyer Who Won Roe v. Wade*. New York: Penguin, 1992, 1993.

Ziegler, Mary. *Abortion and the Law in America: Roe v. Wade to the Present*. Cambridge: Cambridge University Press, 2020.

———. *After Roe—The Lost History of the Abortion Debate*. Cambridge: Harvard University Press, 2015.

———. *Beyond Abortion: Roe v. Wade and the Battle for Privacy.* Cambridge: Harvard University Press, 2018.

———. *Dollars for Life: The Anti-Abortion Movement and the Fall of the Republican Establishment.* New Haven: Yale University Press, 2022.

PUBLIC HEALTH, MEDICINE, AND DISEASE

Anderson, William. "'The Next Great Plague to Go': How the U.S. Surgeon General Used Public Relations to Fight Venereal Disease during the Great Depression." *Journalism History* 44, no. 2 (July 2018): 63–69.

Biskupic, Joan. "The 115-Year-Old Supreme Court Opinion That Could Determine Rights during a Pandemic" *CNN*, April 10, 2020. https://www.cnn.com/2020/04/10/politics/pandemic-coronavirus-jacobson-supreme-court-abortion-rights/index.html

Brandt, Allan. *No Magic Bullet: A Social History of VD in the United States Since 1880*. Oxford: Oxford University Press, 1987.

Brown, Kathleen M. "Part IV: Crusades." in *Foul Bodies: Cleanliness in Early America*. New Haven: Yale University Press, 2009.

Bygdeman, Marc and Kristina Gemzell-Danielsson. "An Historical Overview of Second Trimester Abortion Methods." *Reproductive Health Matters* 16, no. 31, (2008): 196–204.

Carter, Julian. "Birds, Bees, and Venereal Disease: Toward an Intellectual History of Sex Education." *Journal of the History of Sexuality* 10, no. 2 (2001): 213–249.

Clark, Randall Baldwin. "Bleedings, Purges, and Vomits: Dr. Benjamin Rush's Republican Medicine, the Bilious Remitting Yellow-Fever Epidemic of 1793, and the Non-Origin of the Law of Informed Consent." *Journal of Contemporary Health Law and Policy* 24, no. 2 (2008): 209–250.

Owens, Dierdre Cooper. *Medical Bondage: Race, Gender, and the Origins of American Gynecology*. Athens: University of Georgia Press, 2017.

Daniels, Cynthia R., Janna Ferguson, Grace Howard, and Amanda Roberti, "Informed or Misinformed Consent? Abortion Policy in the United States," *Journal of Health Politics, Policy and Law* 41, no. 2 (April 2016): 181–209.

DiCaglio, Sara. "Placental Beginnings: Reconfiguring Placental Development and Pregnancy Loss in Feminist Theory," *Feminist Theory* 20, no. 3 (August 2019): 283–98.

———. "Staging Embryos: Pregnancy, Temporality and the History of the Carnegie Stages of Embryo Development." *Body & Society* 23, no. 2 (June 2017): 3–24.

Dubow, Sara. *Ourselves Unborn: A History of the Fetus in Modern America*. Oxford: Oxford University Press, 2017. First published 2010.

Duffin, Jacalyn. *Lovers and Livers: Disease Concepts in History*. Toronto: University of Toronto Press, 2005.

Farmer, Paul. *Infections and Inequalities: The Modern Plagues, Updated with a New Preface*. Berkeley: University of California Press, 2001.

Fee, Elizabeth. "Sin vs. Science: Venereal Disease in Baltimore in the Twentieth Century." *Journal of the History of Medicine* 43 (1988): 141–164.

Ferber, Sarah, Nicola J. Marks, and Vera Mackie, *IVF and Assisted Reproduction: A Global History*. Singapore: Palgrave Macmillan, 2020.

Fields, Jessica. *Risky Lessons: Sex Education and Social Inequality*. New Brunswick: Rutgers University Press, 2008.

Greene Foster, Diana. "The Court Is Ignoring Science." *Science*, 376, no. 6595 (May 2022): 776. https://www.science.org/doi/10.1126/science.adc9968.

———. *The Turnaway Study: Ten Years, A Thousand Women, and the Consequences of Having–or Being Denied–An Abortion*. New York: Scribner, 2020.

Greenhouse, Linda, and Reva B. Siegel. *Before Roe v. Wade: Voices That Shaped the Abortion Debate Before the Supreme Court's Ruling*. New Haven: Yale Law School, 2012.

Grimes, David A. *Every Third Woman in America: How Legal Abortion Transformed Our Nation*. With Linda G. Brandon. Carolina Beach, N.C.: Daymark, 2014.

Groneman, Carol. *Nymphomania: A History*. New York: Norton, 2000.

Gross, Terry. *Fresh Air*. "Study Examines the Lasting Effects Of Having—Or Being Denied—An Abortion," featuring Diana Greene Foster. June 16, 2020. NPR. https://www.npr.org/2020/06/16/877846258/study-examines-the-lasting-effects-of-having-or-being-denied-an-abortion.

Haugeberg, Karissa. "Nursing and Hospital Abortions in the United States, 1967–1973." *Journal of the History of Medicine and Allied Sciences* 73, no. 4 (2018).

Herzog, Dagmar. *Cold War Freud: Psychoanalysis in an Age of Catastrophes*. Cambridge: Cambridge University Press, 2017.

Imada, Adria L. "Promiscuous Signification: Leprosy Suspects in a Photographic Archive of Skin." *Representations* 138, no. 1 (2017): 1–36. https://doi.org/10.1525/rep.2017.138.1.1.

Lederer, Susan E., and John Parascandola. "Screening Syphilis: Hollywood, the Public Health Service and the Fight against Venereal Disease." In *Major Problems in the History of American Medicine and Public Health*, edited by John Harley Warner and Janet A. Tighe. New York: Houghton Mifflin, 2001, 444–450.

Lunbeck, Elizabeth. *The Psychiatric Persuasion: Knowledge, Gender, and Power in Modern America*. Princeton: Princeton University Press, 1996.

Martin, Emily. *Flexible Bodies: The Role of Immunity in American Culture from the Days of Polio to the Age of AIDS*. Boston: Beacon Press, 1994.

McKiernan-González, John. *Fevered Measures: Public Health and Race at the Texas-Mexico Border, 1848–1942*. Durham, N.C.: Duke University Press, 2012.

Micale, Mike. *Hysterical Men: The Hidden History of Male Nervous Illness*. Cambridge: Harvard University Press, 2016.

Moran, Jeffrey. *Teaching Sex: The Shaping of Adolescence in the 20th Century*. Revised edition, Cambridge: Harvard University Press, 2002.

Nilsson, Lennart. "Drama of Life Before Birth." *Life*, April 30, 1965.

Palmer, Julie. "Seeing and Knowing: Ultrasound Images in the Contemporary Abortion Debate." *Feminist Theory* 10, no. 2 (August 2009): 173–189.

Petrzela, Natalia Mehlman. *Classroom Wars: Language, Sex, and the Making of Modern Political Culture*. New York: Oxford University Press, 2017.

Reznik, Eugene. *From Lemon Rinds to Knitting Needles: a Visual History of Abortion and Birth Control. Hopes and Fears*, 2015. http://www.hopesandfears.com/hopes/now/politics/216773-abortion-contraception-birth-control-visual-history.

Rosenberg, Charles. "The Therapeutic Revolution: Medicine, Meaning, and Social Change in 19th-Century America." In *Sickness and Health in America: Readings in the History of Medicine and Public Health*, edited by Judith Walzer Leavitt and Ronald L. Numbers. Madison: University of Wisconsin Press, 1985.

Rosenberg, Charles E. "Pathologies of Progress: The Idea of Civilization as Risk." *Bulletin of the History of Medicine* 72, no. 4 (Winter 1998): 714–730.

Sanger, Carol. *About Abortion: Terminating Pregnancy in Twenty-First-Century America*. Cambridge: Belknap Press, 2017.

Shah, Courtney Q. *Sex Ed, Segregated: The Quest for Sexual Knowledge in Progressive-Era America*. Rochester: University of Rochester Press, 2015.

Smith-Rosenberg, Carroll and Charles Rosenberg. "The Female Animal: Medical and Biological Views of Woman and Her Role in Nineteenth-Century America." *Journal of American History* 60, no. 2 (1973): 332–356

Stormer, Nathan. *Sign of Pathology: U.S. Medical Rhetoric on Abortion, 1800s–1960s*. University Park: Penn State University Press, 2015.

Thompson, Lauren MacIvor. "'The Presence of a Monstrosity': Eugenics, Female Disability, and Obstetrical-Gynecologic Medicine in Late 19th-Century New York." *Miranda* 15 (2017).

Tindol, Robert. "Getting the Pox off All Their Houses: Cotton Mather and the Rhetoric of Puritan Science." *Early American Literature* 46, no. 1 (2011): 1–23.

Tomes, Nancy. *The Gospel of Germs: Men, Women, and the Microbe in American Life*. Cambridge: Harvard University Press, 1999.

Vilda, Dovile, Maeve E. Wallace, Clare Daniel, Melissa Goldin Evans, Charles Stoecker, and Katherine P. Theall. "State Abortion Policies and Maternal Death in the United States, 2015–2018." *American Journal of Public Health* 111 (2021): 1696–1704.

Wood, Ann Douglas. "'The Fashionable Diseases': Women's Complaints and Their Treatment in Nineteenth-Century America." *Journal of Interdisciplinary History* 4, no. 1 (1973): 25–52.

GENDER AND SEXUALITY

Baird, Barbara, and Erica Millar. "More than Stigma: Interrogating Counter Narratives of Abortion." *Sexualities* 22, nos. 7–8 (October 2019): 1110–1126.

Berlant, Lauren G. *The Queen of America Goes to Washington City: Essays on Sex and Citizenship*. Durham: Duke University Press, 1997.

Canaday, Margot. *The Straight State: Sexuality and Citizenship in Twentieth-Century America*. Princeton: Princeton University Press, 2009. Kunzel, Regina. *Criminal Intimacy: Prison and the Uneven History of Modern American Sexuality*. Chicago: University of Chicago Press, 2008.

BIRTH CONTROL AND CONTRACEPTION

Dine, Ranana. "Scarlet Letters: Getting the History of Abortion and Contraception Right." *Center for American Progress*, August 8, 2013. https://www.americanprogress.org/article/scarlet-letters-getting-the-history-of-abortion-and-contraception-right/.

Eig, Jonathan. *The Birth of the Pill: How Four Crusaders Reinvented Sex and Launched a Revolution*. New York & London: Norton, 2014.

Garner Masarik, Elizabeth. "Abortion and Birth Control in America: Jane Roe & The Pill" *Dig: A History Podcast*. Podcast audio. February 11, 2018. https://digpodcast.org/2018/02/11/jane-roe-the-pill/

———. "Early American Family Limitation." *Dig: A History Podcast*, April 25, 2021. https://digpodcast.org/2021/04/25/early-american-family-limitation-2/.

Gordon, Linda. *The Moral Property of Women: A History of Birth Control Politics in America*. Chicago: University of Illinois Press, 2007.

Gordon, Linda. *Woman's Body, Woman's Right: Birth Control in America*. 2nd ed. New York: Penguin, 1990.

Klepp, Susan E. *Revolutionary Conceptions: Women, Fertility, and Family Limitation in America, 1760–1820*. Chapel Hill: University of North Carolina Press, 2009.

Lahey, Joanna N. "Birthing a Nation: The Effect of Fertility Control Access on the Nineteenth-Century Demographic Transition." *Journal of Economic History* 74, no. 2 (2014): 482–508.

Marcellus, Jane. "My Grandmother's Black-Market Birth Control: 'Subjugated Knowledges' in the History of Contraceptive Discourse." *Journal of Communication Inquiry* 27, no. 9 (January 2003): 9–28.

Matthiesen, Sara. *Reproduction Reconceived: Family Making and the Limits of Choice after Roe v. Wade*. Oakland: University of California Press, 2021.

McCann, Carole R. *Birth Control Politics in the United States, 1916–1945*. Ithaca: Cornell University Press, 1994.

Onion, Rebecca. "19th-Century Classified Ads for Abortifacients and Contraceptives." *Slate*, August 6, 2014. https://slate.com/human-interest/2014/08/history-of-contraception-19th-century-classified-ads-for-abortifacients-and-contraceptives.html.

Tone, Andrea. *Devices & Desires: A History of Contraceptives in America*. New York: Hill & Wang, 2001.

Tyler May, Elaine. *America and the Pill: A History of Promise, Peril and Liberation*. New York: Basic, 2010.

Watkins, Elizabeth Siegel. *On the Pill: A Social History of Contraceptives, 1950–1970*. Baltimore: Johns Hopkins University Press, 1998.

LIFE BEFORE *ROE*

Delay, Cara, Cora Webb, Regina Day, and Madeleine Ware, "'No-Tell Motels': Abortion in Pre-Roe South Carolina." *Nursing Clio*, 2018. https://nursingclio.org/2018/04/11/no-tell-motels-abortion-in-pre-roe-south-carolina/.

Dudley-Shotwell, Hannah. *Revolutionizing Women's Healthcare: The Feminist Self-help Movement in America*. New Brunswick: Rutgers University Press, 2020.

Farrell Brodie, Janet. *Contraception and Abortion in Nineteenth-Century America*. Ithaca: Cornell University Press, 1994.

Fessler, Ann. *The Girls Who Went Away: The Hidden History of Women Who Surrendered Children for Adoption in the Decades Before Roe v. Wade*. New York: Penguin, 2006.

Frank, Gillian. "Life Before Roe: The Story of a Back Alley Abortionist." *Jezebel*, September 4, 2018. https://jezebel.com/life-before-roe-the-story-of-a-back-alley-abortionist-1827863376.

———. "People Helping Women Get Abortions Pre-Roe Were Heroes. It Wasn't Enough." *Slate*, June 21, 2022. https://slate.com/news-and-politics/2022/06/clergy-consultation-service-pre-roe-abortion-access-history.html.

Frank, Gillian, and Ronit Y. Stahl. "The Miseries and Heartbreak of Backstreet Abortions: Before and After Roe." *Nursing Clio*, 2017. https://nursingclio.org/2017/03/28/the-miseries-and-heartbreak-of-backstreet-abortions-before-and-after-roe/.

Hajo, Cathy Moran. *Birth Control on Main Street: Organizing Clinics in the United States, 1916-1939*. Urbana: University of Illinois Press, 2010.

Joffe, Carole E. *Doctors of Conscience: The Struggle to Provide Abortions Before and After Roe v. Wade*. Boston: Beacon, 1996.

Kaplan, Laura. *The Story of Jane: The Legendary Underground Feminist Abortion Service*. Chicago: University of Chicago Press, 1995, 2016.

Moravec, Michelle. "What Feminists Did Last Time Abortion Was Illegal." *Nursing Clio*, 2021. https://nursingclio.org/2021/12/14/what-feminists-did-the-last-time-abortion-was-illegal/.

Nadle, Marlene. "The Abortionist on the Circuit of Fear." *Village Voice*, August 18, 1966.

Pripas, Sarah. "Coat Hangers and Knitting Needles: A Brief History of Self-Induced Abortion." *Nursing Clio*, 2016. https://nursingclio.org/2016/03/10/coat-hangers-and-knitting-needles-a-brief-history-of-self-induced-abortion/.

Robenalt, James. *January 1973: Watergate, Roe v. Wade, Vietnam, and the Month That Changed America Forever*. Chicago: Chicago Review, 2015.

Solinger, Rickie. *Wake Up Little Susie: Single Pregnancy and Race before Roe v. Wade*. New York: Routledge, 2016. First published 1992.

Tuohy, Lynne. "*Roe vs. Wade*: Before and After." *Hartford Courant*, January 18, 1998.

LIFE AFTER *DOBBS*

Benton-Cohen, Katherine. "women's historian here for new #historicalcontext for #SCOTUS #abortion ruling. One word: #coverture. #Alito rails on in re: illegality of #abortion in past, but most of that time pd was under #coverture, the #commonlaw doctrine of yore." @guprofbc, June 24, 2022. https://twitter.com/guprofbc/status/1540409928157986816.

Biden, Joe. "Remarks by President Biden on Protecting Access to Reproductive Health Care Services." *White House Briefing Room*, July 8, 2022. https://www.whitehouse.gov/briefing-room/speeches-remarks/2022/07/08/remarks-by-president-biden-on-protecting-access-to-reproductive-health-care-services/.

———. "The Constitution protects the right to privacy for all Americans—the right to make private decisions about parenthood, marriage, and family. And despite what those Justices in the majority said, reversing *Roe* was not a decision driven by history." @POTUS, July 9, 2022. https://twitter.com/POTUS/status/1545869363655360514.

Fulton, R. E. "Mail-Order Abortion: A History (and a Future?)." *Nursing Clio*, 2016. https://nursingclio.org/2017/05/23/mail-order-abortion-a-history-and-a-future/.

Goodwin, Michele. "No, Justice Alito, Reproductive Justice Is in the Constitution." *New York Times*, June 26, 2022. https://www.nytimes.com/2022/06/26/opinion/justice-alito-reproductive-justice-constitution-abortion.html.

Hasday, Jill Elaine. "On Roe, Alito Cites a Judge Who Treated Women as Witches and Property." *Washington Post*, May 9, 2022. https://www.washingtonpost.com/opinions/2022/05/09/alito-roe-sir-matthew-hale-misogynist/.

"Inside Four Abortion Clinics on the Day Roe Ended." *New York Times: The Daily*. Podcast Audio, June 27, 2022. https://www.nytimes.com/2022/06/27/podcasts/the-daily/roe-v-wade-abortion-clinics.html.

Klibanoff, Eleanor. "Inside a Texas Abortion Clinic after the Fall of Roe." *Texas Tribune*, June 25, 2022.

Kluchin, Rebecca. "If Courts Recognize Fetal Personhood, Women's Rights are Curtailed." *Made by History, Washington Post*, May 12, 2022.

McKenna, Britney. "Amanda Shires Demands More Artists Stand Up for Abortion Rights." *Rolling Stone*, June 3, 2022.

McMillan Cottom, Tressie. "Citizens No More." *New York Times*, June 28, 2022.

Morgan, Jennifer L. "Reproductive Rights, Slavery, and 'Dobbs v. Jackson.'" *Black Perspectives*, August 2, 2022. https://www.aaihs.org/reproductive-rights-slavery-and-dobbs-v-jackson/.

Papenfuss, Mary. "Harvard Constitutional Law Expert Says Justice 'Misleadingly' Quoted Him In Roe Ruling." *HuffPost*, June 25, 2022. https://www.huffpost.com/entry%20laurence-tribe-samuel-alito-supreme-court-roe_n_62b79da2e4b04a61736b4b14.

Thompson, Lauren MacIvor. "Justice Alito argues . . ." @lmacthompson1, May 3, 2022. https://mobile.twitter.com/lmacthompson1/status/1521583034897739779.

Tolentino, Jia. "We're Not Going Back to the Time Before Roe. We're Going Somewhere Worse." *New Yorker*, June 24, 2022.

Traister, Rebecca. "The Necessity of Hope in a Post-Roe America." *The Cut*, June 24, 2022. https://www.thecut.com/2022/06/rebecca-traister-on-the-necessity-of-hope.html.

Tribe, Lawrence. "Even after a real historian ripped to shreds the armchair pseudo-history in Alito's leaked opinion, he didn't bother to fix his shoddy work product but regurgitated it verbatim. And why not? He and those joining him feel untouchable and answer to no one." @tribelaw, June 24, 2022. https://mobile.twitter.com/tribelaw/status/1540527665605656576.

Walker, Rachel. "#twitterstorians: I'm angry and feeling helpless, so I'm designing a course on #reproductiverights for Spring 2023. We have some limited funds to hire guest lecturers. So, let me know if you study pregnancy, Abortion, birth control, repro justice & want to chat with my students?" @rachel_e_walker, June 24, 2022. https://twitter.com/rachel_e_walker/status/1540421460396843008

Weingarten, Karen. "Making Sense of Dobbs v. Jackson Women's Health Organization." *Nursing Clio*, 2021. https://nursingclio.org/2021/12/08/making-sense-of-dobbs-v-jackson-womens-health-organization/.

Ziegler, Mary. "If the Supreme Court Can Reverse *Roe*, It Can Reverse Anything." *Atlantic*, June 24, 2022. https://www.theatlantic.com/ideas/archive/2022/06/roe-overturned-dobbs-abortion-supreme-court/661363/.

CULTURAL COMPARISONS

Belfrage, Madeleine, Eva Didier, and Lucía Vázquez-Quesada. "Voicing Abortion Experiences to Reduce Stigma: Lessons from an Online Storytelling Platform in Mexico." *Women's Reproductive Health* 9, no. 3 (2021): 203–217.

Bloomer, Fiona, Claire Pierson, and Sylvia Estrada Claudio. *Reimagining Global Abortion Politics: A Social Justice Perspective*. Bristol, U.K.: Policy, 2018.

Christopoulos, John. *Abortion in Early Modern Italy*. Cambridge: Harvard University Press, 2021.

Elvins, Sara. "A Guide from the Past on Traveling to Get an Abortion." "Made by History," *Washington Post*, June 27, 2022.

Fitzsimons, Camilla. "The Fight for Repeal: An Activist's Story." *Pluto Press* (blog). https://www.plutobooks.com/blog/the-fight-for-repeal/.

Fitzsimons, Camilla, and Sinead Kennedy. *Repealed: Ireland's Unfinished Fight for Reproductive Rights*. London: Pluto, 2021.

Gammeltoft, Tine. *Haunting Images: A Cultural Account of Selective Abortion in Vietnam*. Oakland: University of California Press, 2014.

Greenhalgh, Susan. *Just One Child: Science and Policy in Deng's China*. Berkeley: University of California Press, 2008.

———. "Planned Births, Unplanned Persons: 'Population' in the Making of Chinese Modernity." *American Ethnologist* 30, no. 2 (May 2003): 196–215.

Hartmann, Betsy. *Reproductive Rights and Wrongs: The Global Politics of Population Control*. Chicago: Haymarket, 2016.

Jáuregui, G., E. Derbez, C. Freeman, and S. Rodríguez. *Será Deseada: A Graphic Novel about Abortion Access in Mexico*. Balance, 2021.

Ma, Ling. "Repositioning the Family and the Household in a Global History of Abortion: The Case of Early-Twentieth-Century China." *Nursing Clio*, August 30, 2018. https://nursingclio.org/2018/08/30/family-and-the-household-and-abortion-in-early-twentieth-century-china/.

Mackie, Vera. "Google Babies and Google Earth: Nation, Transnation and the Australian Reproscape." In *Transnational Spaces of India and Australia*, edited by Paul Sharrad and Deb Narayan Bandyopadhay. Cham, Switzerland: Palgrave Macmillan, 2022.

Mackie, Vera, Nicola J. Marks, and Sarah Ferber, eds. *The Reproductive Industry: Intimate Experiences and Global Processes*. Lanham: Lexington, 2019.

Mackie, Vera, Nicola J. Marks, and Sarah Ferber. "Where the Domestic Meets the Global: Writing the History of Assisted Reproduction," *Vida*, February 2020.

Mackie, Vera, Sarah Ferber, and Nicola J. Marks, "IVF and Assisted Reproduction: Why a Global History?" *History Workshop Online*, April 2021.

Moore, Francesca. "'Go and see Nell; She'll Put You Right': The Wisewoman and Working-Class Health Care in Early Twentieth-century Lancashire." *Social History of Medicine* 26, no. 4 (November 2013): 695–714.

Mullally, Una, ed. *Repeal the 8th: A Collection of Stories, Essays, Poetry and Photography Around the Movement for Reproductive Rights in Ireland*. London: Unbound, 2018.

Palmer, Beth. "'Lonely, tragic, but legally necessary pilgrimages': Transnational Abortion Travel in the 1970s." *Canadian Historical Review* 92, 4 (2011): 637–64.

Rhodes, Marissa. "Communism & Uteruses: How the Soviet Union & the People's Republic of China Sought to Control Women's Reproduction." *Dig: A History Podcast*. Podcast audio. August 20, 2017. https://digpodcast.org/2017/08/20/communists-and-uteruses/.

———. "Mizuko: The History Behind Vengeful Aborted Fetus Hauntings in 1980s Japan" *Dig: A History Podcast*. Podcast audio. October 10, 2021. https://digpodcast.org/2021/10/10/mizuko-the-history-behind-vengeful-aborted-fetus-hauntings-in-1980s-japan/.

———. "Family Limitation in the Pre-Modern World" *Dig: A History Podcast*. Podcast audio. January 29, 2017. https://digpodcast.org/2017/01/29/family-limitation-in-the-pre-modern-world/.

Roth, Cassia. *A Miscarriage of Justice: Women's Reproductive Lives and the Law in Early Twentieth Century Brazil*. Stanford: Stanford University Press, 2020.

———. "ES LEY: Argentina Legalizes Abortion," *Nursing Clio*, January 12, 2021. https://nursingclio.org/2021/01/12/es-ley-argentina-legalizes-abortion/.

———. "A Quiet Inquisition." *Nursing Clio*, July 13, 2017. https://nursingclio.org/2017/07/13/a-quiet-inquisition/.

———. "The New Rubella: Zika and What it Means for Abortion Rights," *Nursing Clio*, February 11, 2016. https://nursingclio.org/2016/02/11/the-new-rubella-zika-and-what-it-means-for-abortion-rights/.

Sethna, Christabelle and Gayle Davis, eds. *Abortion across Borders: Transnational Travel and Access to Abortion Services*. Baltimore: Johns Hopkins University Press, 2019.

Sreenivas, Mytheli. *Reproductive Politics and the Making of Modern India*. Seattle: University of Washington Press, 2021.

Stettner, Shannon, Katrina Ackerman, and Kristin Burnett, eds., *Transcending Borders: Abortion in the Past and Present*. Cham, Switzerland: Palgrave Macmillan, 2017.

Suh, Siri. *Dying to Count: Post Abortion Care and Global Reproductive Health Politics in Senegal*. New Brunswick: Rutgers University Press, 2021.

Takeuchi-Demirci, Aiko. *Contraceptive Diplomacy: Reproductive Politics and Imperial Ambitions in the United States and Japan*. Stanford: Stanford University Press, 2017.

White, Tyrene. *China's Longest Campaign: Birth Planning in the People's Republic, 1949–2005*. Ithaca: Cornell University Press, 2006.

PERSONAL ACCOUNTS AND BIOGRAPHIES

"ACT UP Oral History Project." ACT UP. https://actuporalhistory.org/

Adkins, Carrie. "An Imperfect Abortion Story," *Nursing Clio*, 2020. https://nursingclio.org/2020/03/18/an-imperfect-abortion-story/.

Agg, Jennie. "My Four Miscarriages: Why Is Losing a Pregnancy So Shrouded in Mystery?" *Guardian*, May 5, 2020.

"Alice Lake" *History of America Women* (blog), January 2008. https://www.womenhistoryblog.com/2008/01/alice-lake.html.

Black, Linda. "My Great-Grandpa Killed My Great-Grandma Giving Her an Abortion on the Kitchen Table." *Huffington Post*, May 6, 2022.

Daloz, Kate. "My Grandmother's Desperate Choice." *New Yorker*, May 14, 2017.

Engholm, Ginny. "The Pain of Choice: Late-Term Abortion and Catastrophic Fetal Diagnoses." *Nursing Clio*, 2014. https://nursingclio.org/2014/03/18/the-pain-of-choice-late-term-abortion-and-catastrophic-fetal-diagnoses/.

Evens, Elizabeth. "Plainclothes Policewomen on the Trail: NYPD Undercover Investigations of Abortionists and Queer Women, 1913–1926." *Modern American History*, 4, no. 1 (2021): 49–66.

Frank, Gillian. "The Death of Jacqueline Smith" *Slate*, December 22, 2015. https://slate.com/human-interest/2015/12/jacqueline-smiths-1955-death-and-the-lessons-we-havent-yet-learned-from-it.html

Garner Masarik, Elizabeth. "The Suitcase Murder: Abortion, Mystery, and Murder in 20th-Century America." *Dig: A History Podcast*. Podcast audio. February 4, 2018. https://digpodcast.org/2018/02/04/suitcase-murder-mystery/.

Goldberg, Whoopi. "I passed this big dude walkin' round in circles with a picket sign talkin' about 'Stop Abortion.' I said 'Mothafucka, when was the last time you were pregnant?' And he looks at me. He said 'I don't have to discuss that with you.' I said, 'Well you should because I have the answer to abortion." He said 'What is it?' I said 'shoot your dick!' Hey man. I did. I told him. I said, 'take that tired piece of meat down to the ASPCA and they'll put it to sleep.' And hey, you know I feel better because you know he put his money where his mouth is." Thomas Schlamme, dir. *Direct From Broadway*. 1985. HBO.

Johns, Fran Moreland. *Perilous Times: An Inside Look at Abortion Before and After Roe v. Wade*. New York: YBK, 2013.

Miller, Patricia G. *The Worst of Times: Illegal Abortion—Survivors, Practitioners, Coroners, Cops and Children of Women Who Died Talk About Its Horrors*. New York: HarperPerennial, 1994.

Morantz-Sanchez, Regina. *Conduct Unbecoming a Woman: Medicine on Trial in Turn-of-the-Century Brooklyn*. New York: Oxford University Press, 1999.

O'Donnell, Kelly. "Reproducing Jane: Abortion Stories and Women's Political Histories." *Signs: Journal of Women in Culture and Society* 43, no. 1 (Autumn 2017): 77–96.

Oulton, Emma. "Steinem's Book Dedication is Insanely Powerful." *Bustle*, October 29, 2015. https://www.bustle.com/articles/120437-gloria-steinems-my-life-on-the-road-dedication-adds-beautifully-to-the-conversation-on-abortion.

Parker, Willie. *Life's Work: A Moral Argument for Choice*. New York: 37 Ink/Atria, 2017.

Wicklund, Susan. *This Common Secret: My Journey as an Abortion Doctor*. New York: Public Affairs, 2007.

Prager, Joshua. *The Family Roe: An American Story*. New York: Norton, 2021.

Srebnick, Amy Gilman. *The Mysterious Death of Mary Rogers: Sex and Culture in Nineteenth-Century New York*. New York: Oxford University Press, 1997.

Starobinets, Anna. *Look at Him*, translated by Katherine E. Young. Indiana: Three String/Slavica, 2020.

Steinem, Gloria. "Dedication" in *My Life on the Road.* New York: Random
Stern, Scott W. *The Trials of Nina McCall: Sex, Surveillance, and the Decades-Long Government Plan to Imprison "Promiscuous" Women.* Boston: Beacon, 2018.
"Alice Lake." *History of America Women* (blog), January 2008. https://www.womenhistoryblog.com/2008/01/alice-lake.html.
The Abortion Diary Podcast. Podcast Audio. https://www.theabortiondiary.com.
Tierce, Merritt. "The Abortion I Didn't Have." *New York Times Magazine*, December 2, 2021.
Tolentino, Jia. "Interview with a Woman Who Recently Had an Abortion at 32 Weeks." *Jezebel*, 2016. https://jezebel.com/interview-with-a-woman-who-recently-had-an-abortion-at-1781972395.
Weingarten, Karen. "The Collective Power of Our Abortion Stories." *Nursing Clio*, 2020. https://nursingclio.org/2020/08/27/the-collective-power-of-our-abortion-stories/.
Withycombe, Shannon. "My Story of 20 Weeks." *Nursing Clio*, 2017. https://nursingclio.org/2017/10/09/my-story-of-20-weeks/.

ABORTION AND RELIGION

Balik, Shelby M. "Delivery and Deliverance: Religious Experiences of Childbirth in Eighteenth-Century America." *Church History* 91 (March 2022): 62–82.
Frank, Gillian. "A Theology of Choice." *Brown Alumni Magazine*, April 18, 2022. https://www.brownalumnimagazine.com/articles/2022-04-18/a-theology-of-choice.
Frank, Gillian. "The Deep Ties Between the Catholic Anti-Abortion Movement and Racial Segregation." *Jezebel*, January 22, 2019. https://jezebel.com/the-deep-ties-between-the-catholic-anti-abortion-moveme-1831950706.
———. "The Surprising Role of Clergy in the Abortion Fight Before *Roe v. Wade.*" *Time*, May 2, 2017. https://time.com/4758285/clergy-consultation-abortion/.

Griffith, R. Marie. *Moral Combat: How Sex Divided American Christians and Fractured American Politics*. New York: Basic Books, 2017.

Pogin, Kathryn. "The 'Original Sin' of the Religious Right." *Slate*, May 5, 2022.

Rosenberg, Charles E. "Religion, Science, and Progress." In *The Cholera Years: The United States in 1832, 1849, and 1866*. Chicago: University of Chicago Press, 1987.

Ware, Madeleine. "'Defining "Problem Pregnancies': Religion, Medicine, and Pre-Roe Politics of Abortion in the South Carolina Clergy Consultation Service." *Journal of the Southern Association for the History of Medicine and Science* 3, no. 1 (2021): 23–40.

———. "'Our Moral Obligation:' The Pastors that Counseled in Pre-Roe South Carolina." *Nursing Clio*, 2019. https://nursingclio.org/2019/05/09/our-moral-obligation-the-pastors-that-counseled-in-pre-roe-south-carolina/.

MOTHERHOOD, MISCARRIAGE, AND CHILDBEARING

Freidenfelds, Lara. *The Myth of the Perfect Pregnancy: A History of Miscarriage in America*. New York: Oxford University Press, 2020.

Garner Masarik, Elizabeth. "Miscarriage in Nineteenth Century America" *Dig: A History Podcast*. Podcast audio. February 10, 2019. https://digpodcast.org/2019/02/10/miscarriage-nineteenth-century-america/.

Handley-Cousins, Sarah. "A History of Childbirth in America" *Dig: A History Podcast*. Podcast audio. August 15, 2021. https://digpodcast.org/2021/08/15/a-history-of-childbirth-in-america/.

Hopwood, Nick, Rebecca Flemming, and Lauren Kassell, eds., *Reproduction: Antiquity to the Present Day*. Cambridge: Cambridge University Press, 2018.

Kastor, Peter, and Conevery Bolton Valencius. "Sacagawea's "Cold": Pregnancy and the Written Record in the Lewis and Clark

Expedition." *Bulletin of the History of Medicine* 82, no. 2 (Summer 2008): 276–309.

Leavitt, Judith Walzer. *Brought to Bed: Childbearing in America, 1750–1950*. New York: Oxford University Press, 1986, 2016.

Millar Fisher, Michelle, and Amber Winick. *Designing Motherhood*. Cambridge: MIT Press, 2021.

Parsons, Kate. "Feminist Reflections on Miscarriage, in Light of Abortion." *International Journal of Feminist Approaches to Bioethics* 3, no. 1 (Spring 2010): 1–22.

Rapp, Rayna. *Testing Women, Testing the Fetus: The Social Impact of Amniocentesis in America*. New York: Routledge, 1999.

Riggs, Damien Ruth Pearce, Carla A. Pfeffer, Sally Hines, Francis Ray White, and Elisabetta Ruspini. "Men, Trans/Masculine, and Non-binary People's Experiences of Pregnancy Loss: An International Qualitative Study." *BMC Pregnancy and Childbirth* 20, no. 482 (August 2020).

Scarry, Elaine. *The Body in Pain: The Making and Unmaking of the World*. Oxford: Oxford University Press, 1987.

Withycombe, Shannon. *Lost: Miscarriage in Nineteenth-Century America*. New Brunswick: Rutgers University Press, 2018.

LIFE BEFORE *ROE*: CONTEMPORANEOUS ACCOUNTS AND REPORTS

"Abortion Bill Hearing Opens." *Bridgeport Post*, March 26, 1971.

"Abortion Can Jail Her For 20 Years." *Associated Press*, September 23, 1971.

"Abortion Case Puzzling." *Florida Today*, October 5, 1971.

"Abortion Laws Challenged by Women." *Naugatuck Daily News*, January 26, 1971.

"Abortion One of Ballot's Hot Items." *United Press International*, October 27, 1972.

"Abortion Recipient Angry." *Associated Press*, October 16, 1971.

Abramson, Martin. "One Case Gains National Attention." *Lowell Sun*, September 5, 1972.

Austin, Dottie. "Heavy Support Predicted for Wheeler Appeal." *Daytona Beach Morning Journal*, October 16, 1971.

Baird, Willard. "Proposal B Gives Voters a Voice on Abortion." *Lansing State Journal*, October 26, 1972.

Bishop, Bernie. "Abortion Appeal Promised," *Orlando Sentinel*, July 15, 1971.

———. "Manslaughter Verdict Ruled In Abortion." *Orlando Sentinel*, July 14, 1971.

———. "Mrs. Wheeler First Convicted of Abortion in Florida, Placed on Two Years' Probation." *Orlando Sentinel*, October 16, 1971.

Branzburg, Paul M. "Liberalized Abortion Loses by 3–2 Margin." *Detroit Free Press*, November 8, 1972.

"Capitol Demonstration: They Enjoy Being Just Girls." *Hartford Courant*, April 5, 1972.

Carlson, Barbara. "Abortion Law Suit Hits Meskill's Role." *Hartford Courant*, May 27, 1972.

"Casts Abortion Vote for His Family." *New York Daily News*, April 10, 1970.

"Confused, Bitter, Going Back Home; Woman Lashes Conviction on Abortion." *United Press International*, October 21, 1971.

"Court Fight Looms on Abortion Law." *Associated Press*, April 28, 1972.

"Court Sets Aside Verdict in Abortion." *Orlando Sentinel*, October 7, 1972.

"Daytonan Guilty of Abortion." *Daytona Beach Morning Journal*, July 14, 1971.

Finney, Bill. "Convicted of Manslauter For Having An Abortion: Gets Probation in Abortion Case." *Daytona Beach Morning Journal*, October 15, 1971.

———. "Volusia County's 1st Abortion Trial Enters Second Day." *Daytona Beach Morning Journal*, July 13, 1971.

"Florida High Court Voids 103-Year-Old Abortion Law." *United Press International*, February 15, 1972.

Frankfort, Ellen. "From Hester Prynne to Shirley Wheeler." *Village Voice*, November 4, 1971.

Gallup, George. "Abortions Seen Up to Woman, Doctor." *Washington Post*, August 25, 1972.

Goltz, Gene. "Abortion Reform Vote Is Sought." *Detroit Free Press*, April 11, 1971.

Graham, Fred P. "The Court: Not Made to Be a Political Football." *New York Times*, April 12, 1970.

Greenhouse, Linda J. "Constitutional Question: Is There a Right to Abortion?" *New York Times Magazine*, January 25, 1970.

Heimlich, Barbara. "1,200 Women Involved in Suit Asking Court to End State's Abortion Laws." *Bridgeport Post*, June 13, 1971.

Jedrusiak, Marian. "Court Says Leave State Or Wed." *Florida Alligator*, October 18, 1971.

Kandell, Jonathan. "Meskill Accused on Abortion Role." *New York Times*, May 27, 1972.

———. "Tough Abortion Law in Connecticut Is Attributed to Meskill and Catholics." *New York Times*, May 5, 1972.

Kantrowitz, Barbara. "20 Catholic Women Favoring Abortion Ready to Speak Out." *Hartford Courant*, May 19, 1972.

———. "Changing Abortion Laws Woman's Full-Time Job." *Hartford Courant*, December 18, 1971.

———. "Women Tell About Their Abortions." *Hartford Courant*, November 5, 1971.

McFadden, Robert D. "President Supports Repeal of State Law on Abortion." *New York Times*, May 7, 1972.

"Meskill Pledges Abortion Fight." *Associated Press*, October 21, 1972.

Morrissey, Elaine. "Fear Stalks Florida Girl Convicted of Abortion." *Dayton Daily News*, October 10, 1971.

Morse, Charles F. J. "Committee Backs Stiff Abortion Bill; Debate to Open in House." *Hartford Courant*, May 20, 1972.

———. "State's Abortion Law Plea Turned Down; Meskill to Call Special Session." *Hartford Courant*, May 13, 1972.

"New Abortion Law Faces Court Test by State Foes; 'Tough' Bill Is Signed by Meskill." *Associated Press*, May 24, 1972.

Nordheimer, Jon. "She's Fighting Conviction For Aborting Her Child." *New York Times*, December 4, 1971.

"Old Abortion Law Is Back in Effect." *Associated Press*, May 10, 1972.

"Pathologist Testifies In Abortion Case." *Daytona Beach News Journal*, July 13, 1971.

"Record Majority Endorse Liberal Abortion Law." *Gallup Poll*, August 25, 1972.

Richards, Carol R. "Termination of My Career." *Gannett News Service*, April 10, 1970.

"Shirley Ann Wheeler: 'I Don't Belong Here.'" *Associated Press*, October 29, 1971.

"Shirley Switches; Off To the Folks." *Daytona Beach Morning Journal*, October 23, 1971.

Shoenhaus, Alan E. "Abortion Law Backers and Foes Press Fight Over New Legislation at Capitol," *Bridgeport Post*, May 19, 1972.

Sinclair, Molly. "Daytona Woman in Hurricane Eye Over Abortion," *Miami Herald*, October 11, 1971.

Smith, Sherry. "Shirley Wheeler: First U.S. Woman Convicted For Having an Abortion," *Militant*, October 29 1971.

"State to Appeal Ruling on Anti-Abortion Laws," *Hartford Courant*, April 22, 1972.

"The Nation: Nixon's Court: Its Making and Its Meaning," *Time*, November 1, 1971.

Tolchin, Susan and Martin Tolchin. *Clout: Womanpower and Politics*. New York: Coward, McCann, & Geoghegan, 1973.

"Top Court Lets Abort Ban Stand," *Associated Press*, October 17, 1972.

Truxaw, Patsy. "Women Fight Abortion, Contraceptive laws in Florida," *Guardian*, October 27, 1971.

"U.S. High Court Getting State's Anti-Abortion Law," *Associated Press*, September 21, 1972.

Weaver Jr., Warren. "Blackmun Approved, 94-0; Nixon Hails Vote by Senate," *New York Times*, May 13, 1970.

"White House Sees No Delay on Court," *New York Times*, October 20, 1971.

Williams, Thomas D. "Decision on Abortion Reversed," *Hartford Courant*, July 1, 1972.

———. "Court Strikes Down State Abortion Law," *Hartford Courant*, April 19, 1972.

Winters, Stephen J. "Committee Favors New Abortion Law Backed by Meskill," *Bridgeport Telegram*, May 20, 1972.

Willis, Ellen. "Hearing," *New Yorker*, February 14, 1969.

"Woman Fighting 'Go North' Order," *United Press International*, October 21, 1971.

"Women Challenge Abortion Laws Today," *Naugatuck Daily News*, February 19, 1971.

"Women Jam Conn. Abortion Law Hearing," *Associated Press*, May 19, 1972.

Zimmerman, Matilde and Calvin Goddard. "'It's all a case of hypocrisy' Shirley Wheeler Condemns Abortion Laws," *Militant*, November 26, 1971.

ARCHIVAL SOURCES

Harry A. Blackmun Papers, 1913–2001. Library of Congress.

In Their Own Words: NIH Researchers Recall the Early Years of AIDS. NIH Document Archive. https://history.nih.gov/display/history/Document+Archive.

Women's National Abortion Action Coalition records, 1969–1973. Wisconsin Historical Society, u786a2_2.

Women's National Abortion Action Coalition records, 1969–1973, Wisconsin Historical Society, u786a18_4.

HISTORICAL VIEWS OF PUBLIC HEALTH, MEDICINE, AND HYGIENE

Affleck, Thomas. "On the Hygiene of Cotton Plantations and the Management of Negro Slaves." *Southern Medical Reports* 2 (1850): 434.

Beecher, Catherine E. *Letters to the People on Health and Happiness.* New York: Harper, 1855. https://collections.nlm.nih.gov/catalog/nlm:nlmuid-61360570R-bk

Bieberback, Walter D. "Venereal Disease and Prostitution." *Boston Medical and Surgical Journal* 172, no. 6 (1915): 201–208.

Cartwright, Samuel A. "Diseases and Peculiarities of the Negro Race." *DeBow's Review* 11, no. 1 (July 1851): 64–74.

Collins, Dr. *Practical Rules for the Management and Medical Treatment of Negro Slaves, in the Sugar Colonies.* London: King's College London, 1803, 51–85.

DuBois, W. E. B., and Isabel Eaton. *The Philadelphia Negro: A Social Study.* Philadelphia: University of Pennsylvania Press, 1996.

"'Ethically Impossible': STD Research in Guatemala from 1946 to 1948." *Presidential Commission for the Study of Bioethical Issues,* September 13, 2011. https://papers.ssrn.com/sol3/papers.cfm?abstract_id=2456798.

Gilman, Charlotte Perkins. "The Yellow Wallpaper" *New England Magazine,* January 1892.

———. "Why I Wrote 'The Yellow Wall-Paper.'" *The Forerunner,* October 1913.

Holemon, R. Eugene, and George Winokur. "Effeminate Homosexuality: A Disease of Childhood." *American Journal of Orthopsychiatry* 35, no. 1 (1965): 48.

Hollick, Frederick. *The Diseases of Woman: Their Causes and Cure Familiarly Explained; With Practical hints for Their Prevention and for the Preservation of Female Health.* New York: American News, 1853. https://collections.nlm.nih.gov/catalog/nlm:nlmuid-67040690R-bk.

Hunter, Robert. *Tenement Conditions in Chicago.* United States: City Homes Association, 1901.

King, A. F. A. *Hysteria*. New York: Wood, 1891. https://collections.nlm.nih.gov/catalog/nlm:nlmuid-101282532-bk

Lowry, E. B. *False Modesty That Protects Vice by Ignorance*. Chicago: Forbes, 1914. https://babel.hathitrust.org/cgi/pt?id=mdp.39015076744302.

Madsen, William. *Society and Health in the Lower Rio Grande Valley*. Austin: University of Texas Printing Division, 1961.

Mills, Charles K. "A Case of Nymphomania." *Philadelphia Medical Times* 15 (April 18, 1885): 534–540.

Mullan, E. H. "Mental Examination of Immigrants: Administration and Line Inspection at Ellis Island." *Public Health Reports (1896–1970)* 32, no. 20 (May 18, 1917): 733–746. https://www.jstor.org/stable/4574515.

Ray, Isaac. *Mental Hygiene*. Boston: Ticknor & Fields, 1863. https://collections.nlm.nih.gov/catalog/nlm:nlmuid-66550110R-bk.

Riis, Jacob. *How the Other Half Lives: Studies among the Tenements of New York*. New York: Scribner, 1890. https://www.historyonthenet.com/authentichistory/1898-1913/2-progressivism/2-riis/index.html.

Rubel, Arthur J. "Illness, Behavior, and Attitudes." In *Across the Tracks: Mexican Americans in a Texas City*, chapter 7. Austin: University of Texas Press, 1966.

Savage, Henry. "Dr. James Marion Sims and Nurse Repairing a Vesico-Vaginal Fistula Patient." In *The Surgery, Surgical Pathology, and Surgical Anatomy of the Female Pelvic Organs, in a Series of Coloured Plates Taken from Nature*. London: Churchill, 1862. Image available in Cooper Owens, Dierdre. *Medical Bondage: Race, Gender, and the Origins of American Gynecology*. Athens: University of Georgia Press, 2017, 113.

Sims, J. Marion. *On the Treatment of Vesico-Vaginal Fistula*. Philadelphia: Blanchard & Lea, 1853. https://collections.nlm.nih.gov/catalog/nlm:nlmuid-67130240R-bk.

Snow, William F., and Wilbur A. Sawyer. "Venereal Disease Control in the Army." *Journal of the American Medical Association* (August 10, 1919).

Social Diseases in Men. Short film, c. 1920s. San Francisco: Prelinger Archives. https://archive.org/details/social_diseases_in_men

Solomon, Harry C., and Maida Herman Solomon. *Syphilis of the innocent; A Study of the Social Effects of Syphilis on the Family and the Community*. Washington, D.C.: United States Interdepartmental Social Hygiene Board, 1922. https://archive.org/details/syphilisofinnoce00solo/page/n5/mode/2up.

Stallard, J. H. *Female Health and Hygiene on the Pacific Coast*. San Francisco: Bonnard & Daly, 1876.

"The Fight against the Communicable Diseases." *Communicable Disease Control*. Short film. United States Public Health Service, 1950. https://www.c-span.org/video/?471750-1/the-fight-communicable-diseases.

Tipton, F. "The Negro Problem from a Medical Standpoint." *New York Medical Journal* (May 22, 1886). https://collections.nlm.nih.gov/catalog/nlm:nlmuid-101710951-bk.

Ulrich, Laurel Thatcher. *A Midwife's Tale: The Life of Martha Ballard, Based on Her Diary, 1785–1812*. New York: Vintage, 1991.

ANTI-ABORTION MOVEMENT

Allain, Jacqueline Mercier. "The Anti-Abortion Politics of White Women." *Nursing Clio*, 2019. https://nursingclio.org/2019/06/25/the-anti-abortion-politics-of-white-women/.

Baird-Windle, Patricia, and Eleanor J. Bader. *Targets of Hatred: Anti-Abortion Terrorism*. New York: Palgrave for St. Martin's Press, 2001.

Flowers, Prudence. "'Voodoo Biology': The Right-To-Life Campaign Against Family Planning Programs in the United States in the 1980s." *Women's History Review* 29, no. 2 (2020): 331–56.

Frank, Gillian. "The Colour of the Unborn: Anti-Abortion and Anti-Bussing Politics in Michigan, United States, 1967–1973." *Gender & History* 26, no. 2 (August 2014): 351–78.

Gorney, Cynthia. "The Dispassion of John C. Willke." *Washington Post*, April 22, 1990.

———. *Articles of Faith: A Frontline History of the Abortion Wars*. New York: Simon & Schuster, 1998.

Haugeberg, Karissa. *Women against Abortion: Inside the Largest Moral Reform Movement of the Twentieth Century*. Urbana: University of Illinois Press, 2017.

Holland, Jennifer L. *Tiny You: A Western History of the Anti-Abortion Movement*. Oakland: University of California Press, 2020.

———. "Abolishing Abortion: The History of the Pro-Life Movement in America." *American Historian*, November 2016.

Horn, Dan. "The Willke Way: How a Cincinnati Couple Put *Roe v. Wade* on the Ropes." *Cincinnati Enquirer*, November 24, 2018.

Karrer, Robert. "The Formation of Michigan's Anti-Abortion Movement 1967–1974." *Michigan Historical Review* 22, no. 1, (Spring 1996): 67–107.

"Pro Life Pioneer Barbara Willke Dead at 90." *Catholic Telegraph*, April 16, 2013.

Puckett-Pope, Lauren. "The True Story of Phyllis Schlafly, the Ironic Anti-Feminist." *Harper's Bazaar*, April 14, 2020.

"Right to Life: The Voice of the Unborn." Right to Life/John C. Willke and Barbara Willke Collection (Unprocessed). Cincinnati History Library and Archives, Cincinnati Museum Center, c. 1970, MI-98-121.

Risen, James, and Judy L. Thomas. *Wrath of Angels: The American Abortion War*. New York: Basic, 1999.

Rosen, Kenneth R. "John C. Willke, Doctor Who Led Fight Against Abortion, Dies at 89." *New York Times*, February 22, 2015.

Someone Knows Something: The Abortion Wars. CBC Podcasts. Podcast audio. 2016–2022. https://open.spotify.com/show/4Hjo10gwMdbNojBeGgj8e4.

Williams, Daniel K. *Defenders of the Unborn: The Pro-Life Movement before Roe v. Wade*. Oxford University Press, 2016.

Willke, Dr. & Mrs. John C. *Handbook on Abortion*. Cincinnati: Hayes/Hiltz, 1971, 1973.

———. *Abortion and the Pro-life Movement: An Inside View*. With Marie Willke Meyers, M.D.. West Conshohocken, Penn.: Infinity, 2014.

RACE, ETHNICITY, AND EUGENICS

Baynton, Douglas. *Defectives in the Land: Disability and Immigration in the Age of Eugenics*. University of Chicago Press, 2016.

Brennan, Amanda. "Abortion Rights and the Racist Origins of Having It All." *Nursing Clio*, 2022. https://nursingclio.org/2022/05/10/abortion-rights-and-the-eugenic-and-racist-origins-of-having-it-all/.

Bridges, Khiara M. *Reproducing Race: An Ethnography of Pregnancy as a Site of Racialization*. Berkeley: University of California Press, 2011.

Briggs, Laura. *Taking Children: A History of American Terror.* Oakland: University of California Press, 2020.

Brandt, Allan. "Racism and Research: the Case of the Tuskegee Syphilis Study." In *Sickness and Health in America: Readings in the History of Medicine and Public Health*, edited by Judith Walzer Leavitt and Ronald L. Numbers. Madison: University of Wisconsin Press, 1985, 331–343.

Butler, Anthea. *White Evangelical Racism: The Politics of Morality in America*. Chapel Hill: University of North Carolina Press, 2021. http://antheabutler.com.

Castles, Katherine. "Quiet Eugenics: Sterilization in North Carolina's Institutions for the Mentally Retarded, 1945–1965." *Journal of Southern History* 68, no. 4 (November 2002): 849–878.

Chavez-Garcia, Miroslava. "Youth of Color and California's Carceral State: The Fred C. Nelles Correctional Facility." *Journal of American History* 102, no. 1 (June 2015): 47–60.

Dunbar-Ortiz, Roxanne., and Dina Gilio-Whitaker. *"All the Real Indians Died Off": And 20 Other Myths About Native Americans*. Boston: Beacon Press, 2016.

Earls, Averill. "Marie Stopes: Married Sexual Pleasure, Birth Control and Eugenics." *Dig: A History Podcast*. Podcast audio. September 3, 2017. https://digpodcast.org/2017/09/03/marie-stopes/.

Fett, Sharla M. "Doctoring Women." Chap. 5 in *Working Cures: Healing, Health, and Power on Southern Slave Plantations*. Chapel Hill: University of North Carolina Press, 2002.

Frank, Gillian, and Lauren Gutterman. "Abortion on Trial" *Sexing History*. Season 1, Episode 2. Podcast audio. https://www.sexinghistory.com/episode2.

———. "Sherri" *Sexing History*. Season 2, Episode 3. Podcast audio. https://www.sexinghistory.com/sexinghistory/2019/2/24/season-2-episode-3-sherri.

Garner Masarik, Elizabeth. "Choice, Sterilization, and Eugenics in 20th Century Puerto Rico." *Dig: A History Podcast*. Podcast audio. May 12, 2019. https://digpodcast.org/2019/05/12/choice-sterilization-and-eugenics-in-twentieth-century-puerto-rico/.

Gibney, Shannon, and Kao Kalia Yang. *What God Is Honored Here? Writings on Miscarriage and Infant Loss by and for Native Women and Women of Color*. Minneapolis: University of Minnesota Press, 2019.

Guerrero, Perla M. *Nuevo South: Latinas/os, Asians, and the Remaking of Place*. Austin: University of Texas Press, 2017.

Gurr, Barbara. *Reproductive Justice: The Politics of Healthcare for Native American Women*. New Brunswick: Rutgers University Press, 2014.

Herzog, Dagmar. *Unlearning Eugenics: Sexuality, Reproduction, and Disability in Post-Nazi Europe*. Madison: University of Wisconsin Press, 2018.

Kline, Wendy. *Building a Better Race: Gender, Sexuality, and Eugenics from the Turn of the Century to the Baby Boom*. Berkeley: University of California Press, 2005.

Kluchin, Rebecca. *Fit to Be Tied: Sterilization and Reproductive Rights in America, 1950–1980*. New Brunswick: Rutgers University Press, 2009.

Kraut, Alan. *Silent Travelers: Germs, Genes and the "Immigrant Menace."* Baltimore: Johns Hopkins Press, 1995.

Kudlick, Catherine. "Comment: On the Borderland of Medical and Disability History." *Bulletin of the History of Medicine Bulletin of the History of Medicine* 87, no. 4 (2013): 540–559.

Kunzel, Regina. "The Rise of Gay Rights and the Disavowal of Disability in the United States." In *The Oxford Handbook of Disability History*, edited by Michael Rembis, Catherine Kudlick, and Kim E. Nielson. New York: Oxford University Press, 2018.

Lawrence, Jane. "The Indian Health Service and the Sterilization of Native American Women." *American Indian Quarterly* 24, no. 3 (2000): 400–419.

Luna, Zakiya. *Reproductive Rights as Human Rights: Women of Color and the Fight for Reproductive Justice.* New York: New York University Press, 2020.

Mercredi, Morningstar, and Fire Keepers. *Sacred Bundles Unborn.* Altona, Manitoba: FriesenPress, 2021.

Molina, Natalia. *Fit To Be Citizens: Public Health and Race in Los Angeles, 1879–1939.* Berkeley: University of California Press, 2006.

Morgan, Edmund S. *American Slavery, American Freedom: The Ordeal of Colonial Virginia.* New York: Norton, 1975, reprint, 2003.

Morgan, Jennifer L. *Laboring Women: Reproduction and Gender in New World Slavery.* Philadelphia: University of Pennsylvania Press, 2004.

Nelson, Jennifer. *Women of Color and the Reproductive Rights Movement.* New York: New York University Press, 2003.

Niles, P. Mimi and Michelle Drew. "Constructing the Modern American Midwife: White Supremacy and White Feminism Collide." *Nursing Clio*, 2020. https://nursingclio.org/2020/10/22/constructing-the-modern-american-midwife-white-supremacy-and-white-feminism-collide/.

Peoples, Whitney, Loretta J. Ross, Erika Derkas, and Pamela Bridgewater. *Radical Reproductive Justice: Foundation, Theory, Practice, Critique.* New York: Feminist Press at CUNY, 2017.

Pernick, Martin S. *The Black Stork: Eugenics and the Death of "Defective" Babies in American Medicine and Motion Pictures Since 1915*. New York: Oxford University Press, 1995.

Reagan, Leslie J. *Dangerous Pregnancies: Mothers, Disabilities and Abortion in Modern America*. Berkeley: University of California Press, 2012.

Roberts, Dorothy. *Killing the Black Body: Race, Reproduction, and the Meaning of Liberty*. New York: Vintage & Penguin Random House, 1997, 2017.

Rodriguez, Michael A., and Robert García. "First, Do No Harm: The U.S. Sexually Transmitted Disease Experiments in Guatemala." *American Journal of Public Health* 103, no. 12 (December 2013): 2122–2126.

Ross, Loretta J. "Reproductive Justice as Intersectional Feminist Activism," *Souls: A Critical Journal of Black Politics, Society, and Culture* 19, no. 3 (2017): 286–314.

Ross, Loretta J., and Rickie Solinger. *Reproductive Justice: An Introduction*. Oakland: University of California Press, 2017.

Schiebinger, Londa. *Plants and Empire: Colonial Bioprospecting in the Atlantic World*. Cambridge: Harvard University Press, 2004.

Schoen, Johanna. *Choice and Coercion: Birth Control, Sterilization, and Abortion in Public Health and Welfare*. Chapel Hill: University of North Carolina Press, 2005.

Schwartz, Marie Jenkins. *Birthing a Slave: Motherhood and Medicine in the Antebellum South*. Cambridge: Harvard University Press, 2006.

Shah, Nayan. "Cleansing Motherhood: Hygiene and the Culture of Domesticity in San Francisco's Chinatown, 1875–1900." In *Gender, Sexuality, and Colonial Modernities*, edited by Antoinette Burton. London: Routledge, 1999.

Sharma, Alankaar. "Diseased Race, Racialized Disease: The Story of the Negro Project of American Social Hygiene Association Against the Backdrop of the Tuskegee Syphilis Experiment." *Journal of African American Studies* 14, no. 2 (July 2009): 247.

Silliman, Jael, Marlene Gerber Fried, Loretta Ross, and Elena R. Gutiérrez. *Undivided Rights: Women of Color Organize for Reproductive Justice*. Chicago: Haymarket, 2016.

Simmons, Christina. "African Americans and Sexual Victorianism in the Social Hygiene Movement, 1910–40." *Journal of the History of Sexuality* 4, no. 1 (July 1993), 51–75.

Social Sciences and Humanities Research Council of Canada. *The Eugenics Archive*. https://eugenicsarchive.ca

Stern, Alexandra Minna. "Buildings, Boundaries, and Blood: Medicalization and Nation-building on the U.S.-Mexico Border, 1910–1930." *Hispanic American Historical Review* 79, no. 1 (Feb 1999): 41–81.

———. *Eugenic Nation: Faults and Frontiers of Better Breeding in Modern America*. Berkeley: University of California Press, 2016.

Stern, Alexandra Minna, and Natalie Lira. "Mexican Americans and Eugenic Sterilization: Resisting Reproductive Injustice in California, 1920–1950," *Aztlán: A Journal of Chicano Studies* 39, no. 2 (2014): 9–34.

Tajima-Peña, Renee, dir. *No Más Bebés: The Fight for Reproductive Rights after the Sterilization of Mexican Immigrant Mothers in Los Angeles in the 1960s and 1970s*. 2015, PBS.

Theobald, Brianna. *Reproduction on the Reservation: Pregnancy, Childbirth and Colonialism in the Long Twentieth Century*. Chapel Hill: University of North Carolina Press, 2019.

Turner, Sasha. *Contested Bodies: Pregnancy, Childrearing, and Slavery in Jamaica*. Philadelphia: University of Pennsylvania Press, 2017.

Ware, Madeleine, Cara Delay, and Beth Sundstrom. "Abortion and Black Women's Reproductive Health Networks in South Carolina, 1940–1970." *Gender & History* 32, no. 3 (October 2020): 637–656.

Webster, Crystal. "Enslaved Women's Sexual Health: Reproductive Rights as Resistance." *Black Perspectives*, December 1, 2021.

Weinbaum, Alys Eve. *The Afterlife of Reproductive Slavery: Biocapitalism and Black Feminism's Philosophy of History*. Durham: Duke University Press, 2019.

Zavella, Patricia. *The Movement for Reproductive Justice: Empowering Women of Color through Social Activism*. New York: New York University Press, 2020.

———. "Intersectional Praxis in the Movement for Reproductive Justice: The Respect ABQ Women Campaign." *Signs: Journal of Women in Culture and Society* 42, no. 2 (Winter 2017): 509–33.

ABORTION, PREGNANCY, AND POPULAR CULTURE

Ben Folds Five. "Brick." Track 3 on *Whatever and Ever Amen*. Epic Records, 1997, CD.

Blachor, Devorah. "Abortion is Immoral, Except When It Comes to My Mistresses." *McSweeney's Internet Tendency*, July 11, 2018. https://www.mcsweeneys.net/articles/abortion-is-immoral-except-when-it-comes-to-my-mistresses.

Crawford, Marisa. "The Back Alley Abortion that Almost Didn't Make It Into 'Dirty Dancing.'" *VICE*, August 21, 2017.

Day, Carolyn. *Consumptive Chic: A History of Beauty, Fashion, and Disease*. London: Bloomsbury, 2017.

"Dirty Dancing to Knocked Up: Abortion in the Movies." *Washington Post*. Podcast audio. June 3, 2022. https://www.washingtonpost.com/podcasts/post-reports/dirty-dancing-to-knocked-up-abortion-in-the-movies/.

Freeman, Cordelia. "Feeling Better: Representing Abortion in 'Feminist' Television." *Culture, Health & Sexuality* 24, no. 5 (2022): 597–611.

Hall, Lesley A. *Literary Abortion* (blog). http://www.lesleyahall.net/abortion.htm#US.

Hayes, Leah. *Not Funny Ha-Ha: A Handbook for Something Hard*. Seattle: Fantagraphics, 2015.

Hearn, Karen. *Portraying Pregnancy: From Holbein to Social Media*. London: Holberton, 2020.

Herndl, Diane Price. *Invalid Women: Figuring Feminine Illness in American Fiction and Culture, 1840–1940*. Chapel Hill: University of North Carolina Press, 1993.

Horgan, Meghan. "Crime Skyrockets as Government Invents New Crimes." *Reductress*, June 30, 2022. https://reductress.com/post/crime-skyrockets-as-government-invents-new-crimes/.

Jansen, Charlotte. "Foetus 18 Weeks: The Greatest Photograph of the 20th Century?" *The Guardian*, November 18, 2019.

Johnson, Jenell. *Graphic Reproduction: A Comics Anthology*. University Park: Pennsylvania State University Press, 2018.

"Kavanaugh, Thomas Champion Creating Better Future For Next Generation Of Rapists." *The Onion*, June 24, 2022. https://www.theonion.com/kavanaugh-thomas-champion-creating-better-future-for-n-1849106105

Schwedel, Heather. "Movies that Depict Abortion Shouldn't Leave Out the Money Part." *Slate*, May 31, 2022.

Spangler, Todd. "The Onion Savagely Mocks Supreme Court *Roe v. Wade* Ruling With Homepage Takeover." *Variety*, June 25, 2022. https://variety.com/2022/digital/news/onion-supreme-court-roe-v-wade-homepage-takeover-1235303268/.

Weber-Smith, Chelsea. "Teenage Sex." *American Hysteria*. Podcast audio. February 2019. https://open.spotify.com/episode/1fYyxjbSptveBoyXrVQbAf?si=a6fb8131009d44bd&nd=1.

"Woman's Preventable Death during Childbirth Upheld in 6–3 Supreme Court Vote." *The Onion*, June 24, 2022. https://www.theonion.com/womans-preventable-death-during-childbirth-upheld-in-6-1849105455.

Zieger, Susan Marjorie. *Inventing the Addict: Drugs, Race, and Sexuality in Nineteenth-century British and American Literature*. Amherst: University of Massachusetts Press, 2008.

MISCELLANEOUS

Albers, Jo-Ann. "Willkes' Instruct the Parents." *Cincinnati Enquirer*, January 21, 1966.

Abortion Clinic. PBS documentary, 1983. https://www.pbs.org/wgbh/pages/frontline/twenty/watch/abortion.html

The Abortion Divide. PBS documentary, 2019.
https://www.pbs.org/wgbh/frontline/documentary/the-abortion-divide/
Abortion Is a Human Right. Spotify playlist. https://open.spotify.com/playlist/2D9XKBlT67PdbSrcP4kcy9?si=.
"Antiviral Drug Tested by NCI and Other Scientists 'Revives' Immune System of Some AIDS Patients." *NIH Record,* March 25, 1986.
Cohen, Sascha. "The Day Women Went on Strike." *Time,* August 26, 2016.
Earls, Averill. "Fascism & Uteruses." *Dig: A History Podcast.* Podcast audio. February 26, 2017.
https://digpodcast.org/2017/02/26/fascism-and-uteruses/.
Las Comadres. *Abortos en Plural.* Zine. Quito, 2020.
Lessen, Tia, and Emma Pildes, dirs. *The Janes.* HBO Films, 2022.
Lewis, Finlay. "Terms of Estrangement." *Washington Post,* July 9, 1995.
Lynn, Denise. "Anti-Nazism and the Fear of Pronatalism in the American Popular Front." *Radical Americas* 1, no. 1 (2016).
Murder on Abortion Row. PBS documentary, 1996.
Nagy, Phyllis, dir. *Call Jane.* Redline Entertainment Production, 2022.
Prager, Joshua. "The Accidental Activist." *Vanity Fair,* February 2013.
"*Roe v. Wade*: Get Married or Go Home." *Slow Burn: Slate.* Season 7, Episode 1. Podcast audio. June 1, 2022. https://slate.com/podcasts/slow-burn/s7/roe-v-wade/e1/shirley-wheeler-illegal-abortion-roe-v-wade.
"*Roe v. Wade*: Life or Death." *Slow Burn: Slate.* Season 7, Episode 2. Podcast audio. June 8, 2022. https://slate.com/podcasts/slow-burn/s7/roe-v-wade/e2/jack-barbara-willke-anti-abortion-activism-pro-life-movement.
"*Roe v. Wade*: Roe Against Wade." *Slow Burn: Slate.* Season 7, Episode 4. Podcast audio. June 22, 2022. https://slate.com/podcasts/slow-burn/s7/roe-v-wade/e4/harry-blackmun-roe-v-wade-abortion-supreme-court.
"*Roe v. Wade*: Women vs. Connecticut." *Slow Burn: Slate.* Season 7, Episode 3. Podcast audio. June 15, 2022. https://slate.com/podcasts/slow-burn/s7/roe-v-wade/e3/women-vs-connecticut-abortion-lawsuit-roe-v-wade-abele-v-markle.

Shilts, Randy. *And the Band Played On: Politics, People, and the AIDS Epidemic*. New York: St. Martin's Press, 1987.

Shires, Amanda. "Why Abortion Rights Matter." *Rolling Stone*, October 30, 2020.

"Shirley Stroupe." *News Herald*, February 20, 2013.

Simpson, Monica. "To Be Pro-Choice, You Must Have the Privilege of Having Choices." *New York Times*, April 11, 2022.

Sue, Kimberly. *Getting Wrecked: Women, Incarceration, and the American Opioid Crisis*. Berkeley: University of California Press, 2019.

"The Procedure." *Criminal*. Episode 70. Podcast Audio. July 7, 2017. https://thisiscriminal.com/episode-70-the-procedure-7-7-2017/.

Permission Credits

"How the Right to Legal Abortion Changed the Arc of All Women's Lives," by Katha Pollitt, from *The New Yorker*, May 24, 2019, is reprinted by permission of Katha Pollitt and *The New Yorker*.

"Reproductive Justice, Not Just Rights," by Dorothy Roberts, from *Dissent*, Fall 2015, is reprinted by permission of Dorothy Roberts and *Dissent*.

"Reproductive Rights, Slavery, and 'Dobbs v. Jackson,'" by Jennifer Morgan, from *Black Perspectives*, August 2, 2022, is reprinted by permission of Jennifer Morgan and *Black Perspectives* (African American Intellectual History Society).

"'Caught in the Net': Interrogated, Examined, Blackmailed: How Law Enforcement Treated Abortion-Seeking Women Before *Roe*," by Leslie Reagan, from *Slate*, September 10, 2021, is reprinted by permission of Leslie Reagan and *Slate*.

"The Abortion Fight Has Never Been About Just *Roe v. Wade*," by Mary Zeigler, from *The Atlantic*, August 14, 2022, reprinted by permission of Mary Zeigler and *The Atlantic*.

"The Reconstruction Amendments Matter When Considering Abortion Rights," by Peggy Cooper Davis, from *The Washington Post*, May 3, 2022, reprinted by permission of Peggy Cooper Davis and *The Washington Post*.

"The Racist History of Abortion and Midwifery Bans," by Michele Goodwin, from *ACLU Online Journal*, July 1, 2020, reprinted by permission of Michele Goodwin.

Supreme Court's Selective Reading of U.S. History Ignored

19th-Century Women's Support for 'Voluntary Motherhood,' by Lauren Thompson, from , *The Conversation*, September 6, 2022, reprinted by permission of Lauren Thompson.

"Letters From an American," by Heather Cox Richardson, January 21, 2023, reprinted by permission of Heather Cox Richardson.

"A Major Problem for Minors: Post-Roe Access to Abortion" by Tracey Wilkinson, Julie Maslowsky, and Laura Lindberg, from *STAT*, June 26, 2023, reprinted by permission of Tracey Wilkinson, Julie Maslowsky, and Laura Lindberg.

www.ingramcontent.com/pod-product-compliance
Lightning Source LLC
LaVergne TN
LVHW091518200926
848483LV00002B/247
* 9 7 8 0 8 2 0 3 6 5 6 8 8 *